THE NEXT GENERATION

The publication of this book has been supported by generous grants from Southwestern Bell Telephone Company, The Kerr Foundation, Inc., Boatmen's First National Bank of Oklahoma, and The University of Oklahoma Foundation, which are gratefully acknowledged.

The Full Circle Bookstore in Oklahoma City has generously donated a copy to each of the ninety-five municipal libraries in Oklahoma.

THE NEXT GENERATION

*Dialogues Between
Leaders and Students*

Written and Edited by
Ronald M. Peters, Jr.

UNIVERSITY OF OKLAHOMA PRESS : NORMAN AND LONDON

By Ronald M. Peters, Jr.

The Massachusetts Constitution of 1780: A Social Compact (Amherst, 1978)
The American Speakership: The Office in Historical Perspective (Baltimore, 1990)
(co-editior, with Allen D. Hertzke) *The Atomistic Congress: An Interpretation of Congressional Change* (Armonk, N.Y., 1991)
The Next Generation: Dialogues Between Leaders and Students (Norman, 1992)

Library of Congress Cataloging-in-Publication Data

Peters, Ronald M.
    The next generation : dialogues between leaders and students /
written and edited by Ronald M. Peters, Jr.—1st ed.
        p.   cm.
    Includes bibliographical references.
    ISBN 0-8061-2426-1 (alk. paper).—ISBN 0-8061-2430-X (pbk. :
alk. paper)
    1. University of Oklahoma—Congresses.   2. University of
Oklahoma—Students—Attitudes—Congresses.   3. Education—
United States—Aims and objectives—Congresses.   4. United States—
Social conditions—1980—Congresses.   5. Social prediction—United
States— Congresses.   6. Community leadership—United States—
Congresses.   I. Title.
LD4326.P48   1992
370.11'0973—dc20   92-54133
                                                                          CIP

1   2   3   4   5   6   7   8   9   10   11   12   13   14   15   16   17   18   19

This book is dedicated to the
students of the University of Oklahoma—
past, present, and future.

CONTENTS

PREFACE

IN 1990 THE UNIVERSITY OF OKLAHOMA celebrated its centennial. Celebratory events included academic conferences, ceremonial dinners, exhibits, reunions, dramatic presentations, and fund-raising campaigns. Among all of them, one more than the rest reflected the character and culture of the university on its one hundredth birthday. The university's Centennial Leadership Symposia aimed at academic enrichment for the next generation of Oklahoma leaders. Sponsored by the university's Office of Student Affairs, the Leadership Symposia brought national and state leaders in government, business, the arts and humanities, and education together with student leaders from every nook and cranny of the university's broad curriculum. These students, and the leaders with whom they conversed, shared one quality that cut across the gulfs of age, experience, and outlook that might have otherwise divided them. The generation gap was bridged, at least for a short time, by a common commitment to affect the character of American public life, to lead the country into the next century.

The synergy of the events generated a dialogue that was like no other that the university had witnessed in its one-hundred-year history. United States senators and representatives, the White House chief of staff, the former chairman of the Joint Chiefs of Staff, corporate chief executive officers, state leaders, university administrators and faculty, civic leaders, and student leaders came face-to-face (and sometimes nose-to-nose) in a series of conversations about their, and the nation's, future. This was no sterile academic exercise and demonstrated none of the esotery that sometimes marks academic discourse. Instead, there occurred extensive and sometimes searching exchanges about America, Oklahoma, these students, generations past, and generations to come. It is the task of this volume, and my privilege, to capture the essence of these dialogues in the pages that follow.

There were four Leadership Symposia. The Symposia in Government and in the Arts and Humanities were conducted together during spring semester 1990. The Symposia in Business and Technology and in Education were conducted together during fall semester 1990. Over two hundred student leaders participated in each set of symposia, and many participated in both. Most of the students enrolled in the credit option and were asked to do extensive readings and write a paper based on the experience. This requirement gave rise to over four hundred student papers, excerpts from which make an essential contribution to this book. When combined with transcripts of keynote addresses, panel discussions, and question and answer sessions, the volume of available material exceeded five thousand pages.

In seeking to distill from this enormous amount of material the main themes that emerged during the symposia, I have had to exercise considerable judgment. It is certain that my perceptions of what was most important have had an impact on the manner in which this book frames the symposia dialogues. No doubt, another person coming to the same task might have chosen different points of emphasis and developed different contexts in which to set the dialogues. Still, reality is not simply what we choose to make it, and the main themes and issues that this book presents were, in fact, those that emerged most clearly from the symposia themselves. In developing this volume I have viewed it as my responsibility to present to the reader that which was most central to the meaning of the events as they occurred. This required fidelity to the statements of the participants, reflected here in the transcripts of major speeches and other statements, and excerpts from student papers and published sources. Because the symposia ranged so widely in topic and focus, however, it has also been necessary to supply the connecting tissue that binds the various elements into a coherent whole. A brief overview of the book's organization and main themes will, perhaps, be useful in guiding the reader through it.

Although the four symposia addressed discrete topics, there was considerable overlap in issues and themes. Still, it seemed best to present the events as they occurred, and so the book is organized into chapters on each symposium. The first chapter introduces the symposia and explores the main concerns of the student participants. Chapters two through five address the symposia in government, arts and humanities, business and technology, and education, in that order. Each chapter presents revised versions of the main addresses and synthesizes the responses of students, the comments of panelists, and of the main speakers themselves. In drawing the material together, I thought it best to permit each chapter to focus on a few main themes. In some instances the themes are tied fairly closely to the immediate topic of the symposium, and in other cases they carried through all four symposia. Among the latter, four issues dominated the rest and can be traced through the entire volume: the nature and requirements of leadership; the relationship of public commitment and private aims in shaping the lives of these student leaders; America's stature in the world in the next generation; and, above all else, the American system of education and its capacity to prepare the next generation for the challenges it will face.

These four main issues arose repeatedly during the symposia and do so again in this book. They reflect the concerns of today's leaders and the aspirations of tomorrow's. The emphasis placed upon these questions suggests a degree of uncertainty about the future that is a reflection of the uncertainty that Americans in fact face. There have been periods in modern American history when the country was robust in confidence: when Teddy Roosevelt sent the Great White Fleet around the world; during the Roaring Twenties; in the euphoric aftermath of World War II; at the time of John F. Kennedy's call for a New Frontier of American leadership; in Lyndon Johnson's Great Society. This is not such a time, and the triumph of the Persian Gulf War is not comparable to the defeat of fascism. Even the collapse of communism, surely an occurrence of world-historic proportions, is not sufficient to sustain America's confidence about its future.

Students today do not suffer the malaise of which President Carter allegedly spoke, but neither are they infused with the confidence that Ronald Reagan sought to inspire. They have come of age during one of the most prosperous periods in American history, yet they have witnessed the greedy underbelly of capitalism. They live by and large in comfortable circumstances, yet most are worried about the spiraling costs of their education. They believe that America is and should be the world's dominant economic power, yet they are told that we are rapidly losing ground to Japan and Germany. Surrounding the fertile valley of American prosperity are mountains of private and public debt. The students know that it could all come crashing down in the next generation.

There is reflected in their attitudes, then, an odd combination of hope, determination, and doubt. Because they have hope, they believe that the world can be better than it is. Because they have determination, they believe that they can do something about it. But because they realize how intractable many of the problems are, they are skeptical about what the future may bring. This set of attitudes is directly tied to the issues that the leadership symposia most frequently addressed. If these new leaders are to lead, how should it be done? If they want to enjoy satisfying private lives, how will they balance their lives with a sense of public purpose? Is

America a society that is coming together or one that is coming apart? Can America compete with other nations in the global marketplace, or is it destined to decline as all other great nations have in the past? And if education is the key to the future (as virtually every speaker emphasized), what will it take to ensure that America's systems of common and higher education will be up to the challenge? These are the themes that are woven through the fabric of this book.

In assembling this volume I have had a lot of help. Matt Peacock and Cindy Simon Rosenthal researched sources. Cindy Rosenthal also did extensive editing of the quotations from speeches, panel discussions, and student papers. Maryanne Maletz provided statistics on Oklahoma's higher education system. Carma Nuss transcribed excerpts from student papers, tracked down identifications of students, and prepared the list of participants. LaDonna Sullivan helped organize the project from beginning to end and prepared the final version of the manuscript. Ellen Jonsson provided useful feedback on the manuscript, and some of her suggestions have been incorporated into the text. Kimberly Wiar of the University of Oklahoma Press facilitated the Press's consideration of the manuscript and Barbara Siegemund-Broka did the final copy editing. Alexa Selph prepared the index. Glenda, John, and Julie Peters provided moral support throughout.

In addition to these persons who have contributed directly to the book, I also gratefully acknowledge the efforts of those who were most responsible for planning and running the Centennial Leadership Symposia. Anona Adair, then vice-president for Student Affairs at the University of Oklahoma, had general responsibility for the project. John Lancaster served as the faculty member of the Steering Committee. Chris Purcell and Rich Coberg gave endless hours to the symposia and are largely responsible for a flawless program.

The Board of Regents and President Richard Van Horn

are to be commended for lending the Leadership Symposia their full support. Above all other persons, however, credit for the Centennial Leadership Symposia is due to University Regent Sarah Hogan. Regent Hogan conceived the idea and provided the motive force to see it realized. Her contributions to the university, its centennial, and the symposia are a model of leadership.

RONALD M. PETERS, JR.

Norman, Oklahoma

DRAMATIS PERSONAE

The Advisory Committee

M. Craig Adkins
Hon. Henry Bellmon
William J. Crowe, Jr.
William R. Howell
John Randall McDaniel

Robert Purgason
Baird W. Trice
Richard L. Van Horn
Judy and Ron Yordi

The Broadcast and Television Committee

Elizabeth ("Liz") Burdette
Barbara Buzin
Connie Dillon
Bruce H. Hinson
Sue Ann Hyde

John E. McGuinness
James P. Pappas
David W. Smeal
Carol Wilkinson

The Steering Committee

Anona Adair
Richard L. Coberg
Sarah C. Hogan

John H. Lancaster
Chris Purcell

The Symposia Committee

(The panelists and discussion leaders also served
on this committee.)

David Dary
E. Murray Gullatt
Frank A. McPherson
Samuel R. Noble
Charles F. Sarratt

Arthur B. Van Gundy
Cy Wagner, Jr.
Wanda E. Ward
J. Cooper West
Ronald H. White

The Speakers

Ernest Boyer
William J. Crowe, Jr.
John S. Foster, Jr.

Vartan Gregorian
John Naisbitt

The Panelists

Michael D. Anderson
Virginia Austin
Hon. David Boren
Hans Brisch
Edwin G. Corr
Mary Johnston Evans
Mary Y. Frates
Sandy Garrett
Frederick Jones Hall
Robert H. Henry
William R. Howell
Jenkin Lloyd Jones
George B. Kaiser
Timothy D. Leonard

Anita Rasi May
Hon. David McCurdy
J. W. McLean
Hon. Don J. Nickles
Rodger A. Randle
George Jeffrey Records
Paul F. Sharp
C. J. ("Pete") Silas
George A. Singer
Jeanne Hoffman Smith
John H. Sununu
Carolyn Thompson
James R. Tolbert III
Joseph H. Williams

The Discussion Leaders

David Ernest Albert
Hannah Diggs Atkins

G. T. Blankenship
Edward N. Brandt, Jr.

Peggy Chambers
Terry L. Childers
B. L. Crynes
T. J. ("Ted") D'Andriole
Nancy J. Davies
Leonard J. Eaton, Jr.
Patty Eaton
Nat Eek
J. Rufus Fears
J. Clayton Feaver
Edward L. Glotzbach
John Kennedy, Jr.
James F. ("Jeff") Kimpel
Alex J. Kondonassis
David W. Levy
Sylvia A. Lewis
Dan Little

Robert F. Lusch
Patrick A. McKee
Nancy L. Mergler
H. Wayne Morgan
J. R. Morris
Ronald M. Peters, Jr.
Betty Pfefferbaum
H. E. ("Gene") Rainbolt
Allan Ross
Paul F. Sharp
George A. Singer
David Swank
William G. Thurman
Joan K. Wadlow
Joe W. Walkoviak
Frederick H. Wood
Ronald N. Yordi

The Students

Kevin Abbey
Eugene B. Adelson
Craig Adkins
Scott D. Adzigian
John M. Alagood
Victoria Allred
Braddon Altshuler
Thomas E. Anderson III
Kevin D. Anderson
Jennifer R. Annis
Annette Orr Arthur
Katherine Bailey
Kimberly E. Baker
Melissa ("Paige") Barby
James Barnett
Billy L. Barto

John J. Barto
John A. Basinger
Michael A. Bell
Stacie L. Bell
Nancy Belshe
Lea M. Bengels
Fredericka A. Benken
Brenton T. Benson
Shannon K. Bird
Jamie Birdsong
Sara D. Blackburn
David W. Bobb
Maximilian T. Boone
Alicia Jill Boscarelli
Erik V. Bowen
Kristi G. Bowline

Olen E. Boydstun, Jr.
Pamela Brandes
Darin K. Brannan
Jonathan K. Brewer
Katherine L. Brookman
Carrie P. Brown
Michael L. Brown
Veronica L. Bruehl
Mary E. Buendia
Rebecca G. Bunch
Thomas L. Burghart
Nicole Burgin
Bryan M. Burke
Richard M. Burke
Ryan P. Burke
Christine R. Burkhart
Melanie A. Burris
Ronna Burton
Jill D. Bykofsky
Regan Calhoun
Elizabeth A. Calvey
Suanne Carlson
Linzett M. Carter
Constancio B. ("Bobby")
  Cater
Terry B. Cater
James F. Caylor
Samantha L. Cestari
Kevin L. Chappell
Charles C. Chavalitandnda
Edwin Chen
Precia Chesnutt
Mini Chhabra
Angie Christopher
Kristi Christopher
Sarah Clarke

D. Brian Claypool
Kimberly Clinton
Truman E. Coe
Kellie A. Coffey
David L. Cogburn
Lanette R. Cole
Grover L. Compton
George F. Coppedge
Jana L. Gilbreath Cornelius
John G. Coulter
Clarence C. Courtnay
Jennifer A. Coyle
James K. Crawford
David S. Crow
Chris D. Cuzalina
Robert Lee Daniel, Jr.
Angie L. Daniels
Ami D. Davis
Darin S. Davis
C. Kristen Dearing
Marcy M. Dense
Christi J. Dining
John D. Doshier
Mark E. Doshier
Sharon W. Doty
Ingrid C. Dowdy
Andrew P. Dugan
Daniel Dunlap
Marianne Dunlap
Anne E. Dutcher
Mona E. Easley
Karin C. Eccellente
Edna C. Edmondson
Alice L. Ellenberger
Mike Enriquez
Jimmy L. Etti-Williams

Deborah Kay Evans
Lisa C. Evans
Ann M. Fagan
Thad C. Farmer
Kris Farnsworth
Kathleen A. Feighny
Tomme Jeanne Fent
Tiffany Laine Feuerborn
Martin W. Fielder
Jodi R. Walker Fite
Darby J. Fitzpatrick
Erik Flexner
Richard E. Flood
Lisa S. Floyd
Jackie Follis
Amy K. Ford
Timothy R. Ford
Joe B. Fowler
Amy Fradd
John C. Francis
Brett D. Frantz
Derek L. Freeman
Susan E. Freese
James E. Frieda
Cynthia Gates
Bradley R. Gerow
Candace Noel Gethoefer
Timothy J. Gifford
David Gillespie
Eden B. Gillespie
Kim R. Gillmore
David V. Gillum
Dustin A. Gish
Morris R. Goff
Charles B. Goodwin
Blake Gordon

Marty A. Gore
David P. Gorgas
Marla Gornetski
Belinda J. Goss
Larry R. Greene
Shelley Gregory
Erin A. Griffith
Carl A. Guthrie
Mikon A. Haaksman
Laura J. Hailey
Joseph C. Haines, Jr.
Shane A. Hainzinger
Garrick L. Hall
Jeffrey B. Hall
Laura J. Halley
Larry M. Harbour
Gabriel K. Harman
Rebecca LeAnn Harmon
Robbin Harrison
Tracy L. Harrison
Julie R. Harvey
Brandon Heiberger
Sarah Helin
Samantha K. Hendrix
Johnny W. Higdon
Nia T. Hill
Kristi Hintergardt
Briana Holman
Anilee D. Holmes
Stephen M. Holmes
Angela D. Honigsberg
Cori M. Hook
Kevin M. Hook
Don Howerton
Lynn R. Huff
William D. Huff

Lance Humphreys
Cortney Hunt
John R. Ingram
Lisa A. Ingram
Daphne Jenkins
Deborah L. Jernigen
Daryle L. Johnson, Jr.
David L. Johnson
Rebecca Johnson
Frances W. Johnston
James R. Jones
Marvin L. Jones
Janet M. Kassen
Carolyn Kaye
Joy Kelly
Jenessa A. Kendall
David C. Kendrick
Brian G. Kennedy
Tracy E. Kersey
Kelli Kinder
Steven M. Kobos
Karen K. Kubicek
Ashley R. Kunzman
Sunday Kurtz
Rachel E. Kyle
Lara K. Lambert
Steve Latham
Richard K. Ledbetter II
Kris T. Ledford
Jimmy Liddell
Ashley E. Linn
Shawn P. Linn
Corey W. Lipps
Anthony C. Littrell
Brad S. Lomenick
Michael J. Loomis

Marla Luna
Carla R. Lynch
Melanie Madsen
Kelly B. Mangum
John A. Manley
Mark H. Mann
Holly D. Marsh
Matt O. Martin
Jeff Mason
Bart M. Massey
John M. Mathena
Wynde Mathis
Cindy L. Matthiesen
Patrick J. Maupin
Wendi L. McConathy
Leigh A. McCreary
Sean M. McCurdy
John R. McDaniel
Mark B. McDaniel
Robert W. McEver
Jason P. McGinn
Scott C. McGowan
Jill McKenzie
John C. McKinney
Dennis McLaughlin
Shari L. McLaughlin
Melissa D. McLawhorn
Clint E. McPherson
Ed McSweeney
Tony Medina, Jr.
W. Bradford Mello
Paula Meyer
Matthew J. Miller
Sondra J. Miller
Cindy L. Mills
Teresa R. Montgomery

Michael R. Morrison
Krista K. Morton
Lori Moses
Michael R. Moses
Laura M. Moxley
Melissa L. Moxley
Christin V. Mugg
Don C. Murray
Todd R. Neaves
Paul D. Nelson
Michael R. Newman
Carrie Newton
Trang T. Nguyen
Kelly Northcott
David L. Nunnally
Dirk P. O'Hara
Kristin Ockershauser
Michael Opitz
Andrew R. Osborn
Wally R. Owens
Stephanie C. Parker
Johnny E. Pate
Steven L. Patterson
Jennifer J. Paul
Michael D. Peay
Deborah D. Perkins
Jana M. Perkins
Marcy L. Phillips
Son Hda Phu
Rob Piester
Jerry M. Ponder
Katherin E. Powell
Mike J. Powers
Paul F. Prather
Joseph D. Price
Kevin M. Price

Ken Primrose
Stephen B. Pringle
Gail M. Puckett
Betty K. Quinn
Vicki L. Randall
Nancy Rapp
Cindy J. Reichert
Nancy C. Reitz
Martin M. Rene
Lenny Rice
Shannon K. Richison
Camille Richter
Randall L. Ridenour
Mike D. Riley
Kerri L. Robinett
James M. Robinson IV
Mark A. Rodgers
Michelle L. Rodgers
James R. Rogers
Cynthia A. Rucker
Peter J. Rueth
John N. Ryerson
John R. Sacra
Kerry R. Salter
Vicki Sanders
Janet H. Sandlin
Lee-Ann F. Sanger
Lillie-Beth Sanger
Victoria L. Sarinopoulos
Ron A. Schaeffer
Ruth E. Schafer
Eric C. Schultz
Margaret N. Scott
Trudy A. Seay
Jennifer Selling
Erik L. Sells

Roger L. Sharp
Michael B. Shults
Daniel P. Silvey
Amy Skurcenski
Janna C. Slamans
Cassandra D. Smith
Cristy K. Smith
Terry L. Smith
Melinda A. Sossamon
Grant C. Sparks
Scott R. Spence
Chris L. Spencer
Jeffrey T. Spielmann
Jason L. Sprowls
Steven P. Stacy
Tina L. Steeves
Misty R. Steiner
Amy D. Stewart
Gayle D. Stewart
Virginia C. Storm
Casey T. Stowe
Clair H. Stubblefield
Jamie V. Summers
Derric Sutton
Ami Swank
Traci A. Tarwater
Beth Taylor
Jerry M. Taylor
Eric J. Thomas
Elaine B. Thompson
Maria L. Thompson
Dung Tran
Melissa J. Treadwell
Kristin L. Tullis
John S. Tyner
Melisa Lyn VanMeter
Steven R. VanWinkle

William J. Veitenheimer
Eldon T. Vernon
Chad A. Vesper
Jill D. Vierling
James M. Waites
April L. Waldroop
Kelly L. Waldrop
Luke N. Walker
Kristi C. Wallen
Frank L. Wanker
Thomas J. Ward Jr.
Warren D. Waters
Heather Weaver
John M. Weaver
Beth L. Westhafer
James M. Wheeler
Randal J. White, Jr.
Melissa L. White
Keith Wiles
Jeffrey R. Wilkie
Brian J. Willemssen
Mikel B. Willey
Christopher Williams
Greg S. Willis
Amy S. Wilson
Tyson V.T. Wilson
Regina C. Windsor
Amy R. Wise
David Wise
Robert J. Witte
Stefanie J. Wolf-Trott
Rodney B. Wolfard III
Laura E. Woodall
Tamara B. Worthen
Lori J. Wylie
Bincy Yohannan
John A. Zenker

THE NEXT GENERATION

CHAPTER 1

THE NEXT GENERATION

THE YEAR 1989 MARKED a turning point in the history of human civilization. To historians of a later day will be left the task of deciding whether the events of 1989 were more significant in shaping history than, say, those of 1789 (the adoption of the U.S. Constitution and the French Revolution), 1517 (the Reformation), 1453 (the fall of Constantinople), 1215 (the Magna Carta), 4 B.C. (the birth of Christ), or 221 B.C. (the unification of China.) But there can be no doubt that the demise of the communist regimes in the Soviet Union and Eastern Europe, symbolized by the destruction of the Berlin Wall, opened a new era in world history. What will be the defining characteristics of that new era, and what will be the role of the United States of America in it? This question raises several others. Who are we Americans as a people? What do we want for ourselves and for our country? What role are we prepared to play in the unfolding drama of history, and what sacrifices are we prepared to make in order to do it?

To the generation of Americans born after World War I, and to their children, these questions had ready reference points for answers. The defining experiences of the former generation were the Great Depression and World War II. The members of this generation of Americans had known economic deprivation and international threat. In combating the depression at home and fascism abroad, they were fighting for a way of life in which they believed. Their children were born into a world that became divided between good and evil, East and West, Russia and China versus Western Europe and America. During the coldest period of the cold war, they lived under the "protective umbrella" of nuclear holocaust while enjoying decades of unchecked economic prosperity.

Unlike their parents, this generation of Americans was broadly educated. In 1940 only one American in twenty had earned a college degree. After the war, the G.I. Bill sent millions of returning soldiers back to school. They would become the foundation of a new system of higher education in America through which the nation sought to extend the availability of higher education to every American who wanted to attend college. The plinth upon which this system rested was the great public universities. In 1947 total college enrollment was 2,338,226, with 1,185,849 students attending private universities and 1,152,377 attending public institutions. By 1961, total enrollment had grown to 4,145,065, with 2,561,447 attending public colleges and universities and 1,583,618 in private schools. This dramatic shift toward public higher education was only a foretaste of what was to come. In 1988 total enrollment was 13,043,118 of which 10,156,375 was in public institutions and only 2,886,743 was in private institutions.[1] By 1985 one in five Americans had college degrees.[2] In 1989–90, 52.3 percent of students at public institutions of higher education and 86.4 percent of students attending private institutions received some form of financial aid, funded in good part by the federal government.[3]

The first generation of Americans to benefit from this system of higher education was the "baby boom" cohort born in the decade following the war. Unlike their grandparents and parents, these Americans have not experienced global economic or political catastrophe. Instead, they have enjoyed a period of steady economic growth interrupted only occasionally by recession or military conflict. Not all Americans have been able to share in this abundance. The urban ghettos and rural backwaters are infested with poverty, and black Americans especially have been denied the abundance that white citizens enjoyed. But millions of Americans did take advantage of the opportunity to attain the college degree at public institutions financed in major part by public subsidies.

Like their parents and grandparents, these Americans too had defining experiences. Amidst the plenty that the world-dominant American economy produced, they witnessed upheaval in the nation's political consciousness, as the pestilence of poverty, racism, and war attacked the widespread assumption that everything was all right. The civil rights movement, the Watergate affair, and the Vietnam War shaped the political outlook of the baby boom generation. From the idealism of the 1960s, this "new generation" of Americans of and to whom John F. Kennedy had spoken turned introspective. The "Now Generation" of the 1960s ventured into the "Me Decade" of the 1970s.[4] By the 1980s, all sense of idealism seemed to have been lost. In middle age, the generation called by John Kennedy turned to the leadership of Ronald Reagan and his call for a rebirth of confidence in America. Reagan's rhetoric had as its positive face a renewal of national spirit; but at the same time, its darker side was manifested in the pursuit of material reward, sometimes at the expense of the public good. Main participants in the scams that rocked the economies of the energy-producing states in the early 1980s, the Wall Street insider stock scandals of mid-decade, and the savings and loan fiasco that marked the decade's end were men and women who had been born in the decade following World War II. As in all social transformations, however, the main impact of these defining "cultural" events of the 1980s would be felt not by the boomers themselves, but instead by their children.

Consider the life experience of Americans born around 1970. They will not be able to remember either the Vietnam War or the Watergate crisis, but the cynicism that pervaded the national psyche as a result of these two events have affected the perceptions of every young American nurtured in their shadows. The presidency that they will first remember is that of Jimmy Carter, its defining episode the Iran hostage crisis. The president they will best know is Ronald Reagan, whose final years in office were marred by the Iran/Contra scandal. Many people of this generation have been raised in broken homes, and many of those who haven't have been raised in homes where both the mother and the father are employed outside the home in the perpetual American quest for material comfort.

For these Americans the main effect of the Reagan presidency was not a call to public service but instead a message that the pursuit of private gain was the best path to the public good. It was okay to want to get rich. The self-conscious self-absorption of the "Me Decade" gave way to the unabashed love of gain of the Reagan era. As Ivan Boesky put it, "Greed is all right." As this most recent generation of Americans reached college age, their perceptions of the future were reflected in the choices that they made about where to go to college and what to study once they arrived there. Preprofessional and vocationally oriented programs thrived, while interest in the liberal arts declined. Ironically, this trend, which had begun in the 1970s, led to calls for a renewal of the arts and humanities by some high-level officials in the cultural corners of the Reagan administration itself.

While America witnessed these generational changes, its institutions of higher education were also undergoing change. In the decades following World War II America's public colleges proliferated in number and its public universities exploded in size and scope. Access to public two- and four-year colleges made it possible for most Americans to attend a public institution within commuting distance from their home. The dramatic growth of major state universities provided opportunities for advanced, specialized, and professional education and training. As a result, 85 percent of all new college students today attend institutions in their home state.

The state of Oklahoma reflected this national trend and in some respects stood in the vanguard. Oklahoma's political culture was shaped by a prairie populism that valued education and believed that it should be made universally accessible. The state's three major universities were founded in the 1890s. The University of Oklahoma was founded on December 19, 1890, and six days later the Oklahoma Agricultural and Mechanical College at Stillwater (later to be called Oklahoma State University) and the Oklahoma Normal School for Teachers (later to be called Central State University, and in 1991, the University of Central Oklahoma) were founded.[5] Four other public institutions were founded prior to 1907, when Oklahoma became a state. By 1939 the state had created thirty-eight institutions of higher education with a total enrollment of less than 27,000 students. In 1941 the state organized all of its institutions into a comprehensive system of public higher education under the direction of an independent board of regents. In the years after World War II the system was pruned in number to twenty-five institutions, but enrollment had burgeoned to almost 221,000 students comprising just under 117,000 full-time equivalent (FTE) enrollments by 1990–91.[6]

At the apex of the Oklahoma system of higher education are its three universities, which together enroll 40 percent of the 117,000 FTE enrollments. The two comprehensive institutions, the University of Oklahoma and Oklahoma State University, are roughly comparable in size (typically enrolling around 20,000 students each year), and each is reasonably diverse in academic programs, demographic profile, and mission. The two universities differ somewhat in character, however. As a land-grant institution, Oklahoma State University has drawn students from the many small rural towns that dot the state. Its many vocational programs in fields such as agricultural economics, agronomy, and veterinary science are flagships to which its general education programs have become attached. The University of Oklahoma, by contrast, is historically the state's main venue for higher education broadly defined. Like most state universities, it has broadened its curriculum to include diverse programs in fields such as business, education, engineering, law, and medicine, but its flagship remains the college of arts and sciences. As its curriculum has become more diversified, the profile of its student body has significantly changed. Due in part to its proximity to the Oklahoma City metropolitan area, a large percentage of the OU student body today are commuter students. These students are, on average, older than the typical student of the past, in many instances raising families and pursuing careers while attending college.

As the University of Oklahoma greeted its centennial in 1990, then, it stood as a very different kind of institution than it had been during most of its history, serving the needs of a very different kind of state. Rocked by the collapse in oil prices of the early 1980s, Oklahoma sought to diversify its economy, strengthen its educational institutions, and modernize its governmental establishment in order to meet the challenges of a new and more competitive world. Oklahoma students of the centennial period face an uncertain future and know it. They aspire to a materially comfortable life. They want good things for their state and for their country. They are typically quite patriotic, wanting their country to be powerful and respected around the world. At the same time, they are preoccupied with their own life plans, their studies, and the amusements that college life still affords. It is at this interface of public and private consciousness that the university's Centennial Leadership Symposia occurred.

The conflicting claims of public and private life on these students was reflected in one of the main dialogues of the symposia, with futurist John Naisbitt. Naisbitt, one of two principal speakers at the Business and Technology Symposium, first came to national attention in the early 1980s with the publication of his widely read book *Megatrends*.[7] In *Megatrends*, Naisbitt argued that America was in the midst of a "restructuring," a transition from an old to a new form of social, economic, and political existence (xxii). To grasp the character of this social transformation was, in Naisbitt's view, essential in order for the country to take best advantage of the opportunities that the new order would offer. Such an understanding could only be had, he contended, by a "bottom up" analysis of the local events and behavior that serve as harbingers of the future. "The most reliable way to anticipate the future," he wrote, "is by understanding the present" (xxiii). Based on a canvas of thousands of local newspapers and other periodic sources, Naisbitt traced out ten "mega-trends" that would shape the new world. These included trends toward an information economy, high technology, a world economy, decentralization in business and govern-ment, participation in politics, networking in management, and an era in which the range of human choice would be greatly increased. Calling the 1980s a "time of the parenthesis" (297), Naisbitt stressed the transitional character of the times and the optimistic prospects for the future. The book was purchased by over nine million people around the globe.

By the time he was called to the podium of the Centennial Leadership Symposium, Naisbitt, with his wife Patricia Abur-dene, had published a sequel that was similar in design but somewhat different in purpose. *Megatrends 2000*, published in 1990, sought to look at the world of the millennium from the perspective of the 1990s.[8] While affirming the continuation of the patterns identified in *Megatrends*, Naisbitt and Aburdene chose in *Megatrends 2000* to address the style and quality of life that the new century would greet. In a book that the authors themselves describe as millenarian (16), Naisbitt and Aburdene offer a glimpse of a twenty-first-century world in which "an expanding concept of what it means to be human" (16) will lead to the "triumph of the individual" (chap. 10). Their focus is on the kind of culture that the megatrends of the 1990s will produce, and they like what they see.

Ten broad theses define Naisbitt and Aburdene's vision of the twenty-first century. They anticipate a rapidly growing global economy, a renaissance in the arts, the emergence of what they call free-market socialism, the development of global life-styles in the midst of cultural nationalism, the privatization of the welfare state, the rise of the countries of the Pacific Rim to world leadership, the ascension of women to positions of leadership, a new age of biology, a revival of religion, and the triumph of individualism (13). The authors devote a chapter to each of these trends. Running through the book is a spirit of optimism about the future. The world's economy will grow, the arts will flourish, women will stand equal to men in the global marketplace, there will be a renewal of faith and a return to principles of market-driven free enterprise that will maximize material prosperity while providing for an expanding range of human choice.

There is, in this vision, little mention of poverty, disease, crime, drugs, war, and the anomie of life in mass society. As the authors frankly declare:

We are often asked why our books seem so "positive" and why we do not describe more of the problems facing humankind.

Headlines about crime, drugs, the Brazilian rain forest, AIDS, chemical warfare, corruption, and double-digit deficits assault us daily, causing us to wonder whether any good can exist side by side with so much of the bad? If the evil, ignorance, and negativity we all read about are true, how can any positive trends be valid?

The people reporting the bad news are doing their job. We respect them for it. And we admire the activists whose life's work is to right the world's wrongs. Our mission is a different one. Because the problems of the world get so much attention, we, for the most part, point out information and circumstances that describe the world trends leading to opportunities. (Naisbitt, 15)

This self-conscious exercise in what Herbert Marcuse called "happy consciousness" raised two fundamental questions for the University of Oklahoma students to whom it was addressed. On the one hand, would they accept the one-sided character of the argument as adequately defining the choices facing them in their lives, and especially in their aspirations to leadership? On the other hand, would they believe in the vision of the future that Naisbitt's writings and symposium presentation offer? In assessing the students' responses to Naisbitt and *Megatrends 2000*, their existential dilemma comes squarely into view. They want to have faith and hope in their future, but they are skeptical that the future will offer them the range of good choices that Naisbitt foretells. They want to be leaders in shaping a better American society in the twenty-first century, but they are still drawn to the enrichment of their private lives that Naisbitt emphasizes.

To some students, such as sophomore architecture major John R. Ingram, the *Megatrends 2000* vision of the future was enthralling, reinforcing a natural predisposition.

I think it is one of the most thought-provoking books I could read at this juncture in my life. . . . I hope to work internationally, and so therefore love to hear about the increased need and prevalence of this activity. In his talk he mentioned the town in Colorado where he lives. He said it is made up almost entirely of highly educated people and the ratio of people who own PCs is probably the highest in the world. The town is nestled into a valley between some of the highest mountains in the Rockies. . . . my favorite book, *Atlas Shrugged* by Ayn Rand, ends in an almost mystical town, hidden in a valley within the Rocky Mountains. The description of the people he gave was also similar to the kind of people who were drawn to live in that town.

The hero of *Atlas Shrugged*, John Galt, was presaged by the character Howard Roark in Rand's earlier book, *The Fountainhead*. Roark is an architect who stands for the purity of his creative vision amidst a society that is determined to diminish its worth. As an architecture major, Ingram is naturally drawn to a world in which a Howard Roark would be esteemed and rewarded for his creative vision. But the Naisbitt vision of the future was also attractive to business majors. A world in which free market forces drive a global economy toward new levels of economic prosperity, spiritual commitment is renewed, and a commitment to individual freedom is reborn is naturally attractive to a generation of students reared in the optimism of Ronald Reagan's America.[9] Representative of these students is Lance Humphreys, a senior marketing major:

> For me, the "triumph of the individual" means that now more than ever I am not bound by any constraints. Increased technology and social change are allowing me the opportunity to use my creativity and intelligence to accomplish the things that I would like to accomplish. I believe that the United States has been a worldwide leader to this point in realizing the importance and power of the individual. Our nation is based on the individual and it excites me to see other nations following our lead in realizing that a successful society and economy hinge on the success of its individual members. Our "free enterprise" system is based on the fact that an individual can succeed by meeting needs through hard work and creativity. I am proud to be a part of the country which is setting the standard for all the world to follow.

Yet not every student found the Naisbitt vision so comforting. Some students found something missing in it. Eden B. Gillespie, a junior journalism major who wrote a regular column in the student newspaper, expressed her reservations metaphorically:

> The gypsy squinted into the murky red remains in the bottom of the teacup. With all the confidence of one sure she has the knowledge to predict the future, she told the man across the table of his responsibilities—the musts and mustn'ts on which the next generation would depend. Then she cheerily threw all these aside and informed her confused client that his future would be as rosy as the tea leaves. Never mind that there are war, poverty, pestilence, and apathy now . . .

John Naisbitt would get along well with our friend the gypsy. He too sees a rosy picture of the coming decade, featuring exponentially increasing freedom, free trade, communication, humanity, and peace. EC '92 won't hurt us at all. President Bush won't declare war on Saddam. In fact, "it has been unthinkable, but the stage is set for no more war," Naisbitt said.

But let's back up from the roses. What will our leaders *really* have to face in the coming decade, and beyond? What kind of people will they need to be to face these things successfully? At the base of the rosebush, where can we find such leaders, and how can we motivate them to serve?

This skepticism was shared by many students who searched Naisbitt's vision and found too much missing. Shelley Gregory, a junior letters major, expressed her concern about the lacunae in Naisbitt's future. "I am concerned about what is not included in Mr. Naisbitt's book. What I believe is missing are the poor, uneducated population, and social ills such as AIDS." Craig Adkins, a senior economics major, found Naisbitt's predictions "to be heartwarming and hopeful. If we choose to believe him, and who wouldn't want to, we will live in a world free of war and driven by freedom of exchange; ideas, information and products. Yet all these visions appear just too good to be true." Paula Meyer, a senior philosophy major, rejected the world of Ayn Rand's John Galt:

My skepticism of John Naisbitt's *Megatrends 2000* was only solidified and reinforced by his presentation at the Business and Technology Symposium. The predictions made in the book seemed so incredulous and exaggerated I thought that surely I was reading too critically and at the lecture he would explain and legitimize himself and his claims. Unfortunately, no such redemption occurred, and I left the seminar even more critical of his philosophy and teachings.

Perhaps the first objection to his claims is that of a booming global economy. Mr. Naisbitt seems to be under the assumption that all is well for everyone and that the future shall only bring unbridled prosperity. Perhaps, secluded in the mountains of Colorado, he has managed to become out of touch with the realities of the majority of the population and mistakenly projects his own situation onto those of others.

Meyer sees in Naisbitt's optimism an implicit endorsement of some values over others. His book purports to describe and predict, but it also endorses and recommends.

What we should be well aware of by now is that our society's saving power lies not in trying to finally get what we do (i.e., technology) "right" but in the reevaluation of what we are doing in the first place. Naisbitt, like so many others in our world, seems to be driven by this goal of efficiency and productivity to such a degree that it clouds the ability to see other categorically different concerns. It seemed as though every reason or justification for accepting his suggestions rested upon its superior effectiveness or improved efficiency in the competitive market. I for one scream caution at such dangerous planning.

Competitive market economies, in Meyer's view, may provide for more economic efficiency but fail to produce social justice. The opportunities afforded to the fortunate do not compensate, in her view, for the burdens of the unfortunate.

Obviously, Mr. Naisbitt has been more often than not on the profitable end of the market situation and forgets that people everyday are abused and forgotten by such policy. He presents the dangerous possibility of destroying the only avenue of advancement that many underprivileged people have. Education is the only way up, and by privatization of the school systems we shall bear witness to the rich having access to better schooling and training and the development of a perhaps then unbreakable cycle of the rich begetting the rich and the poor continually staying poor.

Paula Meyer's protests hinge on the assumption that Naisbitt's projections may prove all too accurate. Other students questioned this. Interestingly, economics majors were well represented among those who doubted that a free market world would produce the kind of economic growth that Naisbitt anticipates. While agreeing with Naisbitt's belief that trends are best observed on the ground level, Christopher Williams, a junior economics and business major, questioned the reliability of the data upon which the analysis rests.

Overall, John Naisbitt's "trend analysis" seems to present a somewhat skewed and overly optimistic view of the decade of the 1990s. He never did answer the question of how his analysis was developed, which casts a shadow of doubt over the validity of his assertions. Mr. Naisbitt has sent his views down from his mountaintop perch in Colorado with his FAX machine humming and his television tuned to CNN. He needs to get out more in the day-to-day grind or the "real world" as some people like to call it. Meeting with Mikhail Gorbachev or a powerful Tokyo businessman may present an idea of how they would envision the world trends for the next decade, but it is the person on the street in Seattle who will ultimately determine if that trend will ever take permanent hold. It is that type of person that Mr. Naisbitt needs to focus more on when determining his predictions.

Williams's challenge to Naisbitt's data was matched by a corresponding skepticism about the theoretical foundations of Naisbitt's analysis on the part of senior finance major Steve Latham.

One of Naisbitt's major reliances is his prediction of a global economic boom in the 1990s. He predicts strong economic growth around the world. A timely example is the process of lifting the trade barriers in Europe in 1992. He says that despite the tremendous growth, we will somehow be able to contain inflation and interest rates. I wonder exactly what he means when he says we can contain inflation and interest rates. With growth comes inflation and with that comes higher interest rates. According to many economic theories, the interest rate and economic growth are positively related. According to the "loanable funds theory," the interest rate is determined by the demand for money. As the demand for it goes up, so does the rate at which loanable funds can be obtained. Additionally, according to the "liquidity preference" theory, the interest rate is determined solely by the increase in gross national product. As it increases, so does the interest rate. Both theories point out that if there is economic growth, there will be an increase in inflation and the interest rate. I subscribe to these beliefs and that the economy moves in a cycle. It starts out flat and as it grows, there is an increase in inflation until the growth is stopped; this is followed by a recession which then levels off and starts to grow again. When he says we will be able to contain inflation, I wonder if he means immediately, which is improbable, or in the long run, which I believe is more realistic.

Latham is convinced that Naisbitt's future cannot repeal the law of business cycles. To one schooled in economics and finance, unbridled optimism about the future is the currency of the stock market, not "the dismal science." If the business cycle that has been characteristic of mature capitalism persists, then there will be consequences for those who are the victims of economic downturns. Even in a growing economy, there will be losers, as junior philosophy major Anne E. Dutcher emphasized.

Naisbitt also concludes that the poor are not getting poorer. Although the incomes of the poorest one-fifth of the population have not decreased, they have not increased either (Naisbitt, 46). It is important to note that the statistics only describe the monetary aspect of poverty. But there is more to being poor than not having a current income. There is also a lack of the education and skills necessary to escape poverty permanently. Naisbitt recognizes that the challenge is to absorb the poor into mainstream society. But it will be more and more difficult to do so as the mainstream society moves further ahead in education and skills.

Naisbitt argues that "the information economy is a high wage economy" (Naisbitt, 48). He repudiates the myth that the information economy produces only low-paying jobs. In fact, he says, "From March 1988 to March 1989 alone, 53.4 percent of the new jobs created fell under the category termed 'professional and managerial.' Certainly not low-wage jobs" (Naisbitt, 41). However, these jobs require education and skills. Those who do not have these qualifications will not be able to take advantage of the well-paying, challenging jobs the information economy has to offer.

But what will happen to the unskilled, uneducated workers whose jobs are being eliminated?

Even if the growth economy of the 1990s provides expanding opportunities for those at the bottom as well as for those at the top, material prosperity may be purchased at the cost of the quality of life more broadly defined. This is both a physical and a metaphysical problem. From a material point of view, the pursuit of wealth through unfettered free enterprise sacrifices public goods to private gain. Alicia Jill Boscarelli, a junior letters major, was taken aback by Naisbitt's apparent lack of concern with the environment. In *Megatrends 2000*, Naisbitt and Aburdene take note of the persistence of environmental issues and take solace in what they perceive to be an increasing global awareness of them (30). Yet Boscarelli contends that "our current economic practices have grave ecological consequences. When viewed from an ecological perspective, the trend for a global economic boom of the 1990s with 'virtually no limits to growth' (24) becomes impossible, even dangerous." Boscarelli is convinced that there are limits to growth, limits that are not captured by traditional measures such as gross national product.

However, while the environment and the economy are tightly interwoven in reality, "they are almost completely divorced from one another in economic structures and institutions." [10] This separation is evident in the accounting system used to calculate the ever popular GNP. In simple terms, this totals the value of all goods and services produced and subtracts depreciation of capital assets. The depreciation of natural capital . . . is not considered. Naisbitt and Aburdene do mention natural resources in reference to a global economy. They state that "there will be an abundance of natural resources through the 1990s" (Naisbitt, 24). I would question this assessment, but even if it were true, I would maintain that it is better to conserve these resources because many more generations will depend on them. Their trend for an economic boom is looking at the short-term monetary gains only, not at the long-term ecological losses.

Boscarelli's analysis cuts straight to the heart of Naisbitt's position. An increasing global awareness of environmental problems offers no remedy to them in a world that is hell-bent on economic growth, if economic growth must eventually be purchased at the cost of environmental quality. Boscarelli contends that this is so, while Naisbitt does not address the question.

Even were it possible to resolve problems such as those relating to the environment in a world shaped according to Naisbitt's vision, the quality of life in that world would remain an issue. We measure our existence not merely according to standards of material prosperity but also by the condition of our soul. Recognizing this, Naisbitt predicts a rebirth of religious commitment in the 1990s, not so much among the established religious denominations to which most Americans claim allegiance, but instead within the New Age movement that, according to Naisbitt, now numbers between 5 and 10 percent of the population, concentrated on the coasts and in the Southwest (280). In a millenarian book, this is the most millenarian prophecy. New Age believers have "sewn up the market in channel mediums—individuals who say they permit their bodies and voices to be used as vehicles for teachers and messages from the great beyond." The main goal of the New Age movement, according to Naisbitt, is to foster spiritual development by "cultivating one's own inner guidance. A responsible channel might encourage you to seek guidance but would also urge you to measure it against your own inner voice" (281).

In the meantime, mainline denominations are challenged by fundamentalists who use a different kind of channeling, television, to extend their reach to more and more people. In response to the rise of the New Age movement and the growing popularity of evangelicals, the mainline churches have become more aggressive in using mass communication media and other business techniques to maintain their market share. The whole thing has economic implications. From books, music, and videotape to new church buildings, the religious revival feeds the capitalist system (291–92).

Many students found reassurance in religious renewal of any sort, typically imputing their own religious values into the trend Naisbitt projects. About the New Age movement, however, there was considerable skepticism. Bincy Yohannan, a sophomore political science major, found herself drawn to the main theme but uncomfortable with the subplot.

Another issue that Naisbitt touched on and that I considered to be extremely important is the religious revival of the 1990s. He divided this revival into two major sections: (1) fundamentalism and (2) individual spirituality. Because of my strong faith in Christianity, I am glad to see that Christian fundamentalism, as well as the charismatic movement, is growing rather than withering away due to modernity. However, I must say that I am apprehensive about the growth of what is known as the New Age movement that Naisbitt mentioned. Although man may be made in God's image, he is *not* God, and working with such things as channels and mediums can certainly be satanic (Nasibitt, 281). Yes, I do agree that we need a spiritual revival and a belief in God, but it is often easy to also be misled.

Ken Primrose, a junior marketing major, took a more cynical view of Naisbitt's prognostication. "My theory after considering his book was that Mr. Naisbitt was, in some regard, in the selling game as much as the analysis game. He seems to be selling not only books but a philosophy, a religion. John Naisbitt seems to be selling his views of the New Age movement." The New Age movement and the outlook that it promotes is ideally suited, in Primrose's view, to the aspirations of a society committed to the individual pursuit of material prosperity, as America is. "The average American reader wants to know what will happen in the future of the United States and how that will affect his life. Given a choice, would they prefer a book emphasizing our moral decline and the economic trouble of the United States or a book such as *Megatrends 2000*, offering a rosy answer to most trouble spots?"

Primrose traces the subtext of Naisbitt's book to its final vision, the "triumph of the individual." He sees the entire argument as tending—tendentiously—toward a particular conception of individualism that is, in the end, not individualistic at all.

In Mr. Naisbitt's final chapter, "Triumph of the Individual," he cautiously reveals his underlying views. He states, "Recognition of the individual is the thread connecting every trend described in this book." Naisbitt has slowly prepared the reader to understand and accept the New Age philosophy without truly understanding where New Age itself is headed. He also softens the reader to the thought of the reality of the New Age as a religion and directly mentions the New Age practice of "channeling" and "psychic healing," two keywords in the New Age religious movement. The very philosophy of New Age can be seen in his idealistic view of America and its future. "Today's workplace democracy is guided by enlightened entrepreneurs willing to share ownership," he says. Notice the New Age phrasing with the use of "enlightened" (meaning to discover one's own divineness) and the New Age view of "community." I don't imagine these words coming out of the mouth of the average workplace worker, as Naisbitt suggests.

Naisbitt's predictions and visions of the future and the world also fit the description of the New Age philosophy. As I think of Naisbitt's global society with an increasing standard of life for all through the greater knowledge and "self-realization" of the individual, I would like to contrast those views with the New Age ultimate goal of "transformation." New Age advocates promote both personal and planetary transformation. Personal transformation involves the changes wrought in one's life by increasing self-realization. As more and more people are personally transformed, the planet too will be transformed into a global brotherhood. Possibly I am mistaken in Mr. Naisbitt's assumptions and views, but I see these as very congruent whether Mr. Naisbitt consciously meant it as such or not.

Whether or not one agrees with Primrose's analysis, Naisbitt's world poses a dilemma. What, after all, would it be like to inhabit such a world? Would it be as edifying as he suggests, even assuming it materializes as he predicts? While based on "facts" of a particular sort, in the end any exercise in forecasting the future such as Naisbitt undertakes is more art than science. It is, then, through art that it can best be interpreted and understood. Naisbitt predicts a resurgence of the arts, including, we may hope, the art of fiction. Many students found Naisbitt's vision of fictional quality, "fantastic" in either the positive or negative sense. One student wrote fiction about it. In this short story by David C. Kendrick, the metaphysical dimension of Naisbitt's future world is explored. Kendrick is a freshman chemical engineering major.

A Day in the Life of John Naisbitt's 2000 A.D.

David C. Kendrick

She was running for her life. Behind her roared two hundred and fifty pounds of mechanical fury. She dove behind the counter, and sat panting for a moment, as she struggled to fight back a wave of panic. The machine continued to shudder and scream a terrifying cadence.

What the hell am I gonna do now? What did that old man say to do when this happens?!! I've got to think . . .

But there was no time for thinking. Before she knew what had happened, the machine was upon her. She opened her mouth to scream, but nothing came out, save a long, low buzzing sound. The sound continued long after her silent scream had ended. Gradually, it began to sound like . . .

. . . to sound like . . .

. . . her alarm clock.

Lisa groaned as she rolled over and mumbled something about getting "that damned washing machine fixed." Meanwhile, the alarm continued to buzz. Suddenly, from under the 100 percent synthetic sheets, a hand appeared. With the speed and skill of a hawk making a kill, the hand silenced the alarm clock.

Gradually, Lisa awakened, and, as she lay there, she began mentally planning the day's schedule.

Let's see, she thought. *First, I should go by and see Daddy. I wonder if he's still trying to talk his nurse into letting him launch his model rockets from the roof? And then, hmmmm, let's see. I need to be on the Hill by 12:30 for the afternoon session. Oh yeah, that washer needs something soon. I'd better check my account to make sure that I can afford to have the repairman come. How many times this year have I had to call him?*

Oh, I can't forget. We vote on some big bill. Hmmm . . . I can't remember. Oh well, I'll just check my mail at the office.

The E.C. conferences start tonight in Berlin at 9:00, so I need to leave here by 6:00. I wonder if I can get tickets to the opera on such short notice? That reminds me. I need to set the video disk player to record Monday Night Theater tonight. Well, I'm glad I've already packed, or this may have turned out to be a busy day.

With a chuckle, she crawled out of bed and hurried through the shower and a quick breakfast. She flipped on the morning news for a few minutes while she ate, just to see if any surprises had come up.

". . . Good morning. It's 6:30 A.M. on April 23, 2002, and I'm

William Atherton. Today in world news, Tibet became the last country to make English its official language. The bill passed unanimously in the Tibetan National Senate, after some rumored persuading by the United Nations Communication Committee. It has been three years since the last country to adopt English, the Fiji Islands, officially passed the measure. More on that at eight o'clock.

"Next, there were more terrorist attacks on major religious centers worldwide last night, including the Vatican, Mecca, Salt Lake City, and Jerusalem. U.N. officials once again attribute these attacks to various radical religious groups that have sprung up during the past decade. Mary Sullivan will follow up on this story during Inside Track at 7:30."

With that, Lisa switched off the big screen and donned a light jacket over her favorite outfit, a traditional African sundress. She had actually purchased the dress at Niemann Marcus, but it still made her feel as if she were surrounded by the freedom of the African plains.

"Hello, is this Esher & Mikelsi Appliance Repair? This is Senator Welkins, and I was calling to see if I could make an appointment with Dr. Esher or Dr. Mikelsi to have my washer fixed. Okay, I'll hold.

"What?! He can't get to it until when? Well, I guess that will have to do."

She gave the secretary her name and address and hung up. Grabbing her purse and briefcase, she hopped into her 1989 Cutlass (*attracts voter sympathy*, she thought and giggled as she remembered the excuse she usually gave for keeping such an antique. Actually, she had paid many times the car's worth just to have it converted each year to meet increasingly stringent vehicle emissions laws.) and began the short drive from her Washington, D.C., apartment to the "peaceful hills" of Whispering Willows Resort and Center for the Treatment of Mental Aberrations where her father had lived for the past three years. As she drove, she began thinking about the hassle that it was going to be to have her washing machine fixed. Suddenly, a sensation of déjà vu washed over her as she recalled a fleeting fragment of the nightmare that she'd had that morning. As she remembered the gaping maw of the washing machine, spewing forth suds and dirty laundry, she felt a sort of terror that turned first into amusement at her subconscious imagination, and then into anger at herself. She was angry with herself because she realized that she had a genuine fear of that broken washing machine. Granted, she probably wasn't worried about it actually chasing her, but somehow, she abhorred the very thought of it, sitting there, daring her to fix it. Boy, wouldn't her father get a kick out of that. She had watched her father fix every appliance in their house at one time or another. She remembered sitting there beside him as he worked and handing him tools as he requested them. Most people had dads like that back then. But now it seemed like no one bothered to learn how to do it themselves, instead they just hired a professional.

That would explain, she mused, *the fact that plumbers and repairmen are higher paid than doctors and lawyers now.*

Finally, she arrived at Whispering Willows and was allowed in to see her father. Entering his room always reminded her of going into the Air and Space Museum in D.C. There were rockets and spaceships and airplanes of all types everywhere: on the dresser, on the bed, in the bathroom, even hanging from the ceiling. Daniel Welkins was sitting at a small worktable with his back to her. He appeared to be scrutinizing a set of "blueprints" scrawled into the remains of a Big Chief Tablet, and building a model rocket.

Lisa's father had once been the top aerospace engineer at NASA. Anything designed or built, by or for NASA, first had to be approved by Dan "Welk." His expertise in the field went unquestioned. It was the field itself that was questioned. As the 1990s matured, science appeared to take a back seat to the arts. Scientific research budgets, particularly in the areas of engineering and physics, were cut drastically, while museums and theaters sprang up like weeds. Monday Night Football was officially replaced by Monday Night Theater in 1995. In the middle of this shift, many companies and organizations struggled to make it. Most of them didn't. With the first major round of privatization by the government, which included the welfare system, education, and what was left of the military, NASA was totally dismantled and liquidated, and Dan lost his job in the shuffle.

For Daniel Welkins, the end of NASA was almost the end of him. He had invested his entire career in the Space Program, and to watch it being sold in small chunks to private companies was more than he could handle. Dan spent several months struggling with severe depression, finally suffering a nervous breakdown. However, with support from his wife and his daughter, he was able to recuperate almost completely. It was then that he began gradually to accept the new system. In 1994, the social security system was broken down and sold to private companies. Everyone that had been paying social security received a compensation check from the government proportional to what he had invested. Dan took the credit that he and his wife had received from the government and invested it in a private company. He had everything transferred to that company, from their social security programs to their life insurance policies. For awhile, things had gone smoothly, except, of course for the fact that Dan remained unemployed because he absolutely refused to work for anyone but NASA.

In January of '97, disaster struck. Lisa's mother was killed in a random terrorist bombing in a Middle Eastern airport. Dan was devastated, but somehow he managed to handle it, if not for himself, for the sake of his grieving daughter. Dan continued to be a major support for Lisa, as he took up the role of both parents. However, as survival for two on one income (Lisa's mom worked as a CPA) was difficult, survival for one on no income was going to be damned near impossible. Dan was planning to rely heavily on the life insurance claim, which, added to his unemployment, would carry him for a few years, at least until he qualified for social security. However, when the claim check arrived, it was not a claim check at all, but an apology note. The company had "recently suffered major financial difficulties," and was forced to absorb all of his accounts. Dan would "be receiving quarterly payments of 1000 goods until you have received all that you are owed. Doing some quick multiplication, Dan figured it would be at least one hundred and fifty years before he could see all of his money again. Something snapped, and the short, quiet balding man became a raving madman. As much as it killed her, thirty-year-old Lisa, now an upwardly mobile politician, was forced to put her own father into an asylum.

Since that time, he had almost wholly recuperated, except for an occasional fit of anger. After six months, he was well enough to move to Whispering Willows, where he had since made his home. He complained about it, but Lisa knew that he really liked it, because the nurses there paid special attention to him. He did exactly what he wanted to do, which was usually building and designing air and spacecraft. Lisa knew that there were probably ten miniatures of spacecraft that could carry a human out of the solar system that would most likely never even be seen by anyone who would realize their elegance and efficiency. However, Dan was perfectly content to "play with his rockets" as most people put it, and to leave the rest of the world, except Lisa, of course, on the other side of the Whispering Willows gate.

Lisa and her father chatted for a bit and then went for a short walk along the creek. She told him all about what was going on in her life ("No, Daddy, no men yet.") and, as always, he asked if there were any plans to restart the national space program. They parted with a hug, and Lisa was on her way back to Washington for the afternoon session at the Capitol.

Crowded lunchtitme traffic slowed her almost to a crawl, and Lisa called her office on the car phone to find out exactly what the agenda for the day's session was.

"Hello, Julie? . . . Hi, what's going on? . . . Oh, fine, fine. I'm just returning from Daddy's place and I was wondering if you could fax me today's agenda. Oh, he's doing fine, too. All right, I'll have it set. Thanks, Jules. Goodbye."

Within twenty seconds, Lisa was holding a fresh copy of the agenda. As traffic crawled along, she studied it.

Ah, finally, she thought. *It's out of committee. Now we can see what this bill is made of. I just don't see how we can build a fund to bail out every single school in financial difficulty.*

This bill particularly interested her. In 1994, the public education program had been scrapped to privatize it. Schools were sold to private investors and they were allowed to run the school as they saw fit, providing they followed a few set guidelines. First, they must have met a minimum curriculum requirement, and have taught certain core classes. Next, there was a ceiling placed on the amount that could be charged for tuition, which varied by the average income of the school district. There were many other stipulations that caused a mess of legislative work for the next five years. By 2002, the educational system of the United States was based on such an intertwined and intertangled mess of legislation, that almost any case could be proven or disproven, depending on what bill was referenced. Recently, another problem had arisen: schools were going bankrupt. In business terms, this was really not a problem. Another corporation would just move in and take over the school. However, this case did not deal only with a business, but with education, a necessarily ongoing process. Opening and closing schools was nothing like opening and closing businesses. In some cases, a school had gone for months without a buyer. Meanwhile, kids were either uprooted and sent "temporarily" to another school, or they just did not attend school. This new bill promised to change all of that, but Lisa was skeptical.

Finally, she arrived at the Capitol and went inside. Five hours later, she emerged, tired and bedraggled. The debate on the bill was heated, to say the least. It had gone on for over three hours, with no end in sight. She finally just left so that she could catch her plane. She ran by her apartment and grabbed her luggage. On the way to the airport, she called the opera house in Berlin and arranged to have four tickets for that evening.

Upon arrival at the airport, Lisa checked in her bags and had a quick bite to eat.

Mmmm. McDonald's is sure getting good at doing sushi right, she thought, her mouth full of McSushi.

Customs as usual was just a formality. With one hundred percent open trade agreements established worldwide, the only items really to be checked for were weapons, such as guns and terrorist bombs. As she boarded her plane, she felt a twinge of fear. It always scared her to fly by space plane. Granted, she could get overseas in a couple of hours, but the thought of being in an infinite vacuum always troubled her. The plane would take off and jet almost vertically out of the atmosphere. There it would begin its descent into Europe.

Lisa managed to sleep a little bit, and then turned down the provided meal. She forced herself to stay awake for the evening news and the Arts Report. The plane arrived in Berlin at 7:30 P.M. Her customs experience there was very similar to the one in the States. There was a limousine waiting to take her to her hotel, where she spent the next hour preparing for the conference.

The conferences were being held to evaluate the present condition of the new European Community. The past decade had been very kind to Europe, primarily because of the 1992 Unification. Once again, Europe had become one of the most powerful economic forces on the globe. As an official ambassador, Lisa was assigned to remind the Europeans of their commitment to the 1999 Environmental Restoration Pact, which provided for the actual restoration of the environment. Preservation of the environment was accomplished several years earlier, as the penalties for violating environmental protection laws became harsh enough to include the death penalty.

After the conference, Lisa and several others went to the opera and had dinner afterward. Lisa arrived back at the hotel early in the morning. She went up to her room and got ready for bed. As she drifted off to sleep, she began to wonder whether the washing machine was fixed yet.

What should we make of Kendrick's heroine, Lisa Welkins? On one view, she appears as a new American woman. Elected to the United States Senate at age thirty, she lives life in the fast track, attending hearings and mark-ups by day, flying the space plane to Europe for important meetings at night. A creature of the global culture, she affects African styles while lunching on "McSushi" in the global village of fast-food restaurants. Lisa is the offspring of a prosperous and powerful NASA scientist whose career is lost when NASA is privatized. He loses mental competency when his wife is killed by terrorists and bankruptcy sets in. He is reduced to building model airplanes. A caring daughter has him put away while she pursues her political ambitions. Senator Welkins, the new American politician, brings to her public life the same sense of caring that guides her private affairs. The privatized educational system is in chaos, and schools are failing right and left. Do-gooders in government want to do something about it, but Senator Welkins is hard-nosed. We can't afford to bail out all of these failing private schools, she thinks. She carries these firm convictions into a tough Senate debate, of which she tires after a few hours when it becomes apparent that the Senate is irresolute. More fun to fly off to Europe. Throughout her trying day, Lisa Welkins presents herself as a thoughtful and introspective person. As we learn her innermost thoughts, we find her searching for inner guidance. The most pressing problem is the washing machine. It never works and costs an arm and a leg to fix. America has lost its capacity to produce durable goods and the service people who thrive on repairing washing machines are paid more than doctors and lawyers. Whatever . . . her day begins and ends with the same existential problem—a washing machine that won't work.

Lisa Welkins is a triumphant individual or a parody of one, and we shall never know which. The world Naisbitt envisions may be as fulfilling as he predicts, or empty; the future is in the end unknowable. We are able to know, however, that Kendrick's character faces a life that poses dilemmas, just as do the college students of today. Their existential plight differs from hers only in the context within which it is set. These students may or may not have accepted John Naisbitt's dream, but they surely must have their own.

Oklahoma has, since territorial days, been a place that valued individualism. The settlers who participated in the Land Run of 1889, and those who migrated to Oklahoma thereafter, were individuals and families seeking opportunity for a more materially prosperous life. The American Indians of the Five Civilized Tribes who were driven to Oklahoma down the Trail of Tears had, in many ways, a more stable set of cultural traditions than did the white settlers who came afterward.

When, in the early part of the twentieth century, Oklahoma crude was found in abundance, the state's economy became rooted in the aspirations of independent oilmen as well as small farmers and ranchers. This setting was conducive to a belief in the capacity of individuals to shape their own destinies, even when those destinies were aided by the hidden hand of government. The editorial philosophies of the state's leading newspapers, especially that of the *Daily Oklahoman* in Oklahoma City, have reinforced the belief that individualism is a positive good. It is not surprising that Oklahoma City is the home of Enterprise Square, a free enterprise hall of fame.

But a second strand of Oklahoma culture is equally strong. It is a populist belief in the public good, the kind of belief that led the Oklahoma founding fathers to establish a system of public education from the very first territorial days. It is this strain of populism that makes Oklahoma's constitution one of the most democratic in the nation. It was in the populist cultural roots of the state that socialism found friendly soil in the 1920s and 1930s, and it was here that the labor organizer Oscar Ameringer found his life's work.[11] Populism, in whatever form it takes, is inherently egalitarian. From the state's early days, there was perceived to be no fundamental conflict between a commitment to individualism and the acceptance of populist beliefs. A person could believe in the values associated with free enterprise and be suspicious of an intrusive state and, at the same time, welcome the creation of a far-flung system that made education accessible to most citizens.

These two cultural strains, individualism and populism, shape the perspective of the Oklahoma students who participated in the symposia. It is easy enough simply to assume that they are mirror reflections of a national youth culture grounded in acquisitiveness and popular forms of art and leisure. But however much they may participate in modern mass culture they represent a peculiar Oklahoma version of it. On the one hand, these students want a high quality education so that they can attain life goals typically involving material comfort, service, and leadership; on the other hand, they believe that the state owes to them an education that they can afford. They are strongly committed to carving a better future for Oklahoma; yet in response to a question, only a few thought that they would be living in Oklahoma in 1995. They believe in the research mission of the university, since it brings prestige to the state and enhances the value of their degrees; yet their most often reiterated complaint was that members of the faculty sacrifice their teaching responsibility to their research. They want the state's two comprehensive universities to offer them individualized attention, yet they believe that higher education should remain accessible to all Oklahomans.

How representative were the views of the symposia participants? One measure of the concerns of the student body is the conversation that they have among themselves in the pages of their campus newspaper, the *Oklahoma Daily*. This student-run publication is distributed at no cost to the university community. It emphasizes campus news and student commentary and includes a robust letters-to-the-editor section. Its pages present a sample of the issues that held center stage during the university's centennial year. An inventory of those issues includes the education reform bill that was under consideration by the legislature, the environment, censorship of the arts, the role of Greek-letter social organizations on campus, abortion, the 1990 elections, and the Gulf War. As might be expected, there were numerous references to various aspects of the quality of campus life. There was, in 1990, an ongoing campus debate over questions of racial, ethnic, and sexual harassment, leading to the adoption and/or revision of campus codes of conduct in these matters. In the spring of the year the university sponsored an "OU Together" week during which a variety of campus activities were conducted to bring together members of the university community from various racial and ethnic backgrounds.

Closely related to these concerns was an ongoing campus

dialogue about "multiculturalism," involving issues of social interaction and curricular matters. The national debate over the nature of general education curricula was to some extent reflected in a campus discussion of the need to incorporate into the curriculum at the university more emphasis upon minority and feminist concerns. In the same way, heated controversy arose over the university's attempt to eliminate its women's basketball program in favor of a new one in women's soccer. The proposal led to the threat of lawsuits alleging discrimination, and was quickly rescinded. Questions were also raised about segregated conditions in the Greek-letter social organizations and the campus dormitories. Standing at the periphery of the debate was the local community of gay activists who, in the fall of 1990, formed their own alumni association. These persons sought from the university a commitment to equality of treatment based on sexual orientation similar to that which the university was willing to accord to persons based on gender and race.

The dialogue on race, sex, and sexual orientation was hardly atypical. In 1990 the Carnegie Foundation issued a report, *Campus Life: In Search of Community*, which analyzed the character and quality of life on the nation's college campuses.[12] This report (discussed by Carnegie Foundation Chairman Ernest Boyer in chapter 5) identifies these issues as of serious concern at many institutions of higher education. In the report, college presidents representing 24 percent of all institutions surveyed reported racial tension as a moderate or major problem on their campuses. Interestingly, racial tension was perceived as a problem by 68 percent of presidents at research and doctorate granting institutions, in contrast to only 20 percent of presidents at comprehensive institutions, 28 percent at liberal arts colleges, and 15 percent at two-year institutions.[13] The report provides anecdotal information about racist incidents at some institutions, but provides no account of the generic causes at play across the spectrum surveyed or explanation of why the problem is more commonly perceived by presidents of large research institutions. Nevertheless, it concludes that racism is a significant problem on most college campuses. In placing racism, sexism, and homophobia in context, a table in the report's appendices suggests that interracial/ intercultural relations are identified as a problem by 13 percent of all college presidents surveyed; AIDS education and issues of human sexuality by 9 percent; and sexual harassment by only 2 percent. These figures contrast with substance abuse (45 percent), student apathy (30 percent), and campus crime (25 percent) on the list of issues of greatest concern to college presidents. Whether the perceptions of these college presidents are consistent with those of their students is not ascertained in the report.

Given the attention focused on these concerns throughout the year by students and administration alike, it is not surprising that they emerged during the four Leadership Symposia. What is perhaps surprising is that they were not discussed more than they were. Questions related to race were occasionally raised, but did not become the focus of extended discussion, as did the gender issue of women in leadership. In one small group discussion, the unrepresentative character of the group participating in the symposia was considered. According to social work major Nancy Belshe,

The point was made that there was a noticeable lack of representation of the various nationalities that make up the student body. The person making the observation felt there was a lack of respect shown for other nationalities and their cultures if they had not been invited to be a part of the symposia.

A young man immediately took objection, saying that everyone had an equal opportunity to be in attendance. He continued on in a defensive manner making reference to a bottle-throwing incident as just being some guys having a good time, drinking, and having a little fun. He seemed indignant that anyone should be offended by the behavior. What I was hearing was that the rights of one group of people were of paramount importance and took precedence over the rights and feelings of others. There seemed to be no respect for the feelings of those who felt discriminated against. I don't believe there was any thought of making use of "the golden rule" Mr. Foster had spoken of the previous evening.

The issue of the university's policy on matters of equal opportunity and harassment was put to OU President Richard Van Horn by one discussion group leader.

Question: Our question was, what role should the President's Office play in (1) protecting the rights of OU's various ethnic groups against harassment, and (2) providing a policy for equal opportunities?

Van Horn: I think the President's Office should do all that it can, and let me just suggest two things. Racial harassment policies are very difficult because of First Amendment protection. Most universities that have tried to put together racial harassment policies have had them overturned by the courts. So the first thing we have is a very difficult job. Can we put together a racial harassment policy that will pass the constitutionality test for freedom of speech? I think we can, but you have to understand that we have to balance those issues. A second thing the President's Office should and, I think, has to do if we are going to make progress, is try to set a tone and say what kind of a university we think we should be, and what the characteristics of that university should be with respect to our ability to deal with diversity, to show respect for other cultures, and to really welcome other cultures, other ideas, and all races. That is an important issue. When you get down to the final analysis, it is not the President's Office yelling comments out the third floor window of the fraternity house at two o'clock in the morning, and so it is really something that only works if we all do it. One of the things I hope we can do, one of the things we will be asking each of you to do in the coming year, is to try hard to provide an environment at the University of Oklahoma where we really do value the multicultural experience, and where we value people from other cultures and other races. I think we all have to try a little bit harder. That goes for me, but it also goes for you. If we are going to make this thing work, it is something every one of us has to do. Even if it is little things. Even if it is saying hello to people while you are walking across the campus, and asking them if everything is going OK. Just some sign of friendship, some sign of recognition, some indication that we do value everybody. By the way, you don't have to restrict it to minorities, you can say hello to each other, and say hello to faculty members. We all like it. We have to create an environment. We don't want an environment where people are tolerated. We want an environment where they are really welcome. It is, I think, one of the jobs of the President's Office is to try to encourage that kind of environment, and take any steps that we can.

President Van Horn's suggestion that the university address problems of racial tension by "saying hello" was greeted with some skepticism among members of the university community who felt the need for a formal institutional policy on racial harassment, one that was soon forthcoming. Their insistence on a code of law to serve in lieu of a code of honor says a lot about the nature of the university today. President Van Horn's emphasis on friendliness relies ultimately on a belief in the outward forms of civility. Modern culture seems to regard the outward expression of civility as merely that, a superficial (and perhaps insincere) adherence to form at the expense of substance. That the French Court of the ancien régime made a mockery of its own manners should not conceal from view the underlying basis upon which free civilizations rest: civility.

If the Carnegie report is accurate, then there is a crisis of civility in American universities today. In this volume, one of the main emphases is upon the search for community in a society that stresses individualism. The search for community for these University of Oklahoma students begins on the campus they share. The participants in the Leadership Symposia reflected that broader community in some ways but not in

others. As Belshe noted, the symposia participants were not
a microcosm of the university. Among the speakers, panelists,
and discussion leaders were women and members of minority
groups, but not many. While there were many women participants, only a few minority students attended the symposia.

In fact, the demographic profile of the student participants
differed in discernible ways from that of the student body as
a whole. The symposia participants were disproportionately
young, white, and male. The largest disparity was in age. The
average student at the University of Oklahoma in 1990 was
about twenty-five years old; the average age of the symposia
participants was about twenty-two. There were, proportionately, far more eighteen-, nineteen-, and twenty-year-old students at the symposia than there were in classes at the time.
This disproportion reflects the more active involvement of the
younger, more traditional student in campus activities than
their older counterparts, who are more likely to have job or
family commitments. It also suggests that the participants
might have brought to the symposia an outlook unencum-
bered by the responsibilities of job, home, and family, although surely this was not universally the case. Often, symposia speakers and panelists referred to the "young" people to
whom they were speaking, and they were generally correct.
The symposia spoke primarily, but not exclusively, to one
cohort of a large and complex institution.

Women compose almost 55 percent of the student body at
the University of Oklahoma, and constituted just over half
of the symposia participants. African Americans number 5
percent of the student body but claimed only 2.5 percent of
the symposia seats. American Indians and Hispanic Americans were also somewhat underrepresented. When viewed
across other categories, the group was representative of the
student body. There were, for example, representative numbers of majors from each of the university's colleges, and while
the grade point averages (GPAs) of the students participating
were higher than the campus average (around a 3.2 GPA

compared to a 2.8 GPA), the range of GPAs extended down to a 2.5.

These statistics are significant in a way, but the significance can easily be overstated. They do suggest a tendency for women and minority students to be less involved in events such as this—after all, they might have turned out in disproportionately great numbers. Still, the difference between exact proportional representation for black students and the percentage that in fact occurred would have involved fewer than a dozen students. The data imply more about the preferences of students than about the substance of the symposia, except insofar as the students' perceptions about the symposia might have affected their desire to participate. Still, it is hard to avoid the inference that the extreme interest among the students in the subject of women in leadership in comparison to the lesser emphasis on the subject of minorities in leadership was due mostly to the composition of the group.

The relative paucity of minority students among the symposia participants may have reflected their perception that the symposia did not address issues of relevance to them, sponsored as it was by an institution in which some believe racism to exist. Unsurprisingly, when events such as those marking OU Together week are held, minority students often participate in numbers disproportionate to their ratio in the student body. White students, by contrast, are proportionately less likely to participate in such events. When students choose to participate in only those university-sponsored events that address their particular interests, it makes it more difficult for the university to bring together the cultures of which it is composed. The numerous calls to leadership in the arts, humanities, government, business, and education spheres that were made during the symposia were intended to call the students to a common future, one that both sexes and all races will share. As freshman chemical engineering major Corey W. Lipps saw it,

A big problem of racism has erupted this year on the campus at OU. This problem obviously must be resolved to sustain a good educational program. President Van Horn has proposed that students greet each other by saying "Hi." This plan . . . has been called insulting to the minority students. A written policy of the university will not help solve the problem either. Policies can be written on paper but cannot be placed in the students' minds. A policy must be enforced or it is meaningless. To ease the racial tension between students, a broader plan must help students get to know others who are racially different. People have prejudices that cause them to judge and expect bad characteristics in others even before they meet. If students of different races are able to get to know each other and become friends, the prejudices inside the students will become smaller and the racial tensions will be lessened.

Erik L. Sells, a junior computer science major, gave this thoughtful response to the issue:

Recently the issue of racism and separation of ethnic groups has come to the forefront at the University of Oklahoma. In his speech Dr. Boyer stressed that such separation of races and ethnic groups only increases the amount of fragmentation, violence, and misunderstanding in a community. Until now I paid very little attention to the problem of bigotry and separation of races and cultures at OU. As a student I felt my powers were limited and that other people, especially the college administration, would solve the problem. And so far the administration seems to be making steps in the right direction. President Van Horn, in his statement regarding racial harassment, felt as did Dr. Boyer, that a "great university does more than tolerate diversity; a great university respects, cultivates, and welcomes diversity." He encouraged students to make minority students feel welcome on campus by greeting them between classes, in the cafeteria, and in the dorms. Two student minority leaders complained that this part of the president's statement was awkward, because it seemed to treat students like children by forcing them to say hello to others. I believe that the president is doing his best to promote respect and community among all races and cultures at the University of Oklahoma. There is no doubt that more needs to be done. Students in the majority should not feel that racial and cultural policy is something for "higher-ups" to handle. They should not feel that such policy isn't their business.

If the students participating in the Leadership Symposia are different from their peers in any other way, it is perhaps in their aspirations to leadership. Involvement in leadership roles in campus organizations and activities was one of the explicit criteria used in recruiting symposia participants. In their comments and in their writing there are frequent allusions to the role that they want to play in shaping the future of their state and their country. The aspiration to lead by itself moves them out of the sphere of their private lives and into the arena of public concern. There, they encounter conflict between their sense of mission, their private aims, and the formidable problems facing the society in which they live. Many student participants were active in campus affairs and most saw themselves playing leadership roles in later life. Their self-conceptions sometimes run up against the harsh realities of bureaucratic life, as human relations graduate student Marla Gornetski noted:

Another topic of discussion pertained to the role of student leaders within the bureaucracy of a university. Dr. Ernest Boyer stated in his evening address that, "Bureaucracy causes confusion of purpose." I feel the student leaders of the University of Oklahoma are faced with this dilemma today. It was truly amazing to see over a hundred of the most intelligent and active students at the University of Oklahoma gathered within the OCCE Forum Building. As the symposia progressed and ideas began to flow freely among the participants, I began to wonder what impact this event could wield upon our educational hierarchy. As a member of the student government system on campus, I know

firsthand of the stifling effect of a dysfunctional administration.
The general consensus of my discussion group was that the bar-
rage of ideas garnered by us students would be kept on the
backburner until our generation becomes the decision makers.
This is an unfortunate and unproductive attitude. This attitude is
primarily fostered by the actions and values of the administration.

Students can make a difference. As a member of the University
of Oklahoma Student Association Student Lobbying Force, I
found many legislators supportive and open to the needs of
students. Unfortunately, more than a few leaders are needed for
governmental reform. It also became obvious that our ideas were
either not being heard or understood by President Van Horn.
During the afternoon panel discussion on education, President
Van Horn was asked what ideas he would take with him from
the symposia. Van Horn's response reiterated ideas put forth by
John Naisbitt that were not of primary or secondary interest to
the student leaders in attendance. It is my opinion that the student voice must be heard and granted the attention which it
merits. The University of Oklahoma must foster a proper atmosphere for student leadership. In addition, the university must
then utilize to its fullest capacity the human leadership potential
which it has helped to develop.

The university administration to which Gornetski refers,
like most college administration's today, makes extensive efforts to communicate with faculty, staff, and students. President Van Horn, whose background is in management science,
frequently stresses the need for the university to be "user
friendly" to all of its constituents. The student lobbying effort
to which Gornetski refers was in opposition to a tuition
increase that the university sorely needed. Nevertheless,
President Van Horn publicly supported the student leaders'
position. Gornetski's impatience with the university administration may simply express frustration, but it was shared by a
number of the symposium participants. Sophomore letters
major Timothy R. Ford has a lot of good ideas about how to

improve Oklahoma's educational system, but feels that no one will listen until he has earned his credentials.

My paradox is that I must bow to the gods of education a while longer before I can stand up, demand their attention, and inquire as to what they think they are doing. I need the credentials that I might argue from a platform of strength. My writing and thinking need to be focused that I may speak with clarity. This focusing must be accompanied by a simultaneous broadening of my thinking. My vision must be made concrete, practical, and desirable. I do not intend on a career in education; yet my career is dependent upon education. For that reason, my voice will always champion its reformation. The institution of education must evolve even as the idea of what an education is evolves.

Junior accounting major Melissa L. Moxley sees no necessity in waiting to get credentials. In response to former Oklahoma Attorney General Robert H. Henry's characterization of a crisis caused by a lack of enlightened leadership, she concluded that current leaders are doing little to cultivate a new generation of leaders.

I have a very good friend who is probably much more qualified than most of the fifty people who were chosen to participate in Leadership Oklahoma. He has already run for the State Legislature and received 40 percent of the vote. But he has been told over and over that he doesn't have a chance of getting into Leadership Oklahoma because he is 22 years old instead of the usual 35–55. It seems to me they are wasting their time on the same group of people who Mr. Henry describes as "unenlightened."

In the panel discussion, it was very evident to me that these middle-aged people were totally opposed to listening to any ideas that we, as young people, came up with. Obviously, their ideas are not working, so I don't understand why they don't give us a chance to have a voice, and to make a difference. I sometimes wonder how old you have to be before all of a sudden people will listen to you and look at your ideas for what they are worth, instead of according to how old you are.

Although I may sound bitter, I am really not. Out of all the speakers and panelists, only Virginia Austin called us what we are. "You are not the leaders of tomorrow, you are the leaders of today." At the very least, the symposium was inspiring to each individual who let his/her thoughts flow freely. At the most, there is probably no way to ever measure the effects of these two days on the future of our state, our country, and our world.

In the remarks of these three students we see frustration, calculation, and ambition; but above all else, we see a desire to affect the world. Most of the students who participated in the Centennial Symposia were at the beginning of lives that they hope will be productive and satisfying. Whether they are called to government service, to the world of business, the field of education, or to a life dedicated to the arts and humanities, they want to have an impact. They want their lives to be good ones and they want the world to be better because they are in it.

In the pages that follow, we find these students engaged in a dialogue with their elders. Much of what seems to concern them is tied to the immediate circumstances of their lives as students, but much of it is not. They realize that the role they now play at the University of Oklahoma is merely preparatory to the larger role they will play in society when their university days are over. They are aware of the many problems and issues that face their generation, both now and in the future. They are concerned about what life holds in store for them but also recognize their obligation to repay society's investment in them. Conceiving of themselves as leaders, they were drawn to the Centennial Symposia to learn about leadership. In these dialogues, they demonstrate a considerable capacity for it.

CHAPTER 2

THE CALL TO PUBLIC SERVICE

IN DEMOCRACIES, the public's attitude toward public service is typically schizophrenic. In primary-school civics books, the rhetoric of politicians, and America's guiding myths, public service is noble. America's greatest leaders, those whom history will long remember, are public figures such as Abraham Lincoln and not the anonymous soldiers of whom he spoke at Gettysburg. In democracies, the love of honor and the desire for power call the ambitious to public service. Lincoln often spoke of the burning ambition that drove him. Ambition is, however, undiscriminating among the well and poorly motivated, among those who pursue self-interest and those who pursue the public good. In democracies, it is left to the voters to discern who, among the ambitious, will best serve the public interest. In America, voters have been or have become cynical about the task. The other side of the democratic political persona regards politicians as of marginal ability, always self-interested, too often corrupt, the residue of capitalism. From the Crédit Mobilier to Watergate and Abscam, America has witnessed enough political scandal to reinforce the biases of the cynical and to give the naively optimistic grounds for hesitation.

Not all public servants are elected officials. Governmental service in the United States involves millions of federal, state, and local officials in career service to the government, both civilian and military. Like their elected counterparts, these careerists experience both sides of the democratic attitude toward government. They are "public servants" when in favor, "bureaucrats" when out of favor. They are heroes in time of war (at least wars that the public supports), a part of the "military-industrial complex" when the country is at peace. One thing is certain: the country could no more do without its career service than without its legislative institutions. And today, public policy depends as much upon the decisions of nonelected as of elected public officials. "Bureaucrat-bashing" has been a popular leisure-time activity in America for a long time, and some elected politicians, including several recent presidents, have made it a regular part of their campaign platforms, as if somehow elected officials are more pristine than careerists.

In fact, the public welfare at the end of the twentieth century depends upon the quality and commitment of both elected and nonelected public officials; and if a health report on the government were to have been issued in 1990, it would not have been a good one. In the late 1980s, the public was disenchanted with the government, period. Popular magazines such as *Time* ran front-page stories on the public's skepticism about members of Congress who have succeeded in building sinecures as unassailable as those of the most-entrenched career bureaucrat. The federal bureaucracy was jarred by scandals in the Department of Housing and Urban Development, and bore scars from the public's outrage over the scandals in the insufficiently regulated savings and loan industry. In only one area of federal service was there a clear rebound in public esteem—the military, which in the 1980s was permitted to engage in a number of winning skirmishes culminating with the Persian Gulf War (toward which the country moved during the fall Leadership Symposia, casting doubt among participants on John Naisbitt's prediction that war would become obsolete). The National Commission on the Public Service, headed by former Federal Reserve Board chairman Paul Volcker, announced a crisis within the career civil service, with low salaries, low morale, and regular attrition to the private sector. The Congress, enjoying 90 percent reelection rates, sought to ameliorate some of the problems plaguing the bureaucracy by raising salaries for federal civil servants; in the process, they handed themselves a 25 percent salary hike. It somehow seems unsurprising that, in 1990, the state of Oklahoma along with California and Colorado imposed term limitations on legislative service, reflecting the public's disenchantment.

In this environment, the Centennial Leadership Symposium in Government called student participants to provide public leadership in the next generation. The discussion addressed the issues that leaders will face, the kind of preparation that is needed in order for them to do it, and the nature of leadership itself. The symposium's keynote speaker, Admiral William J. Crowe, former chairman of the Joint Chiefs of Staff and distinguished professor of geopolitics at the University of Oklahoma, set the theme.

May You Live in Interesting Times

Admiral William J. Crowe

In 1989, at the conclusion of a military career that spanned five decades, I came to the University of Oklahoma as a new professor of geopolitics. While the university was kind enough to give me a fancy title, I was in fact as raw a recruit as the newest assistant professor on the faculty. When I entered my first class and looked out on the faces of those bright and expectant students, I was as nervous as I had been in briefing my superiors in the government hierarchy. At least I knew something of what they expected of me; but what would these young men and woman ask of an old soldier who had not quite yet faded away?

It did not take me long to learn that I did have something to offer them, but as importantly, they had much to offer to me. The discussions in which we engaged were often spirited, and I found myself pressed to challenge these students to think seriously about the world around them as much as they challenged me to rethink my own suppositions. Dealing with young American men and women was, of course, not entirely new to me. One cannot be a leader of any rank in the American military today without coming into contact with the young men and women of the service on a daily basis. I learned at the University of Oklahoma that the same spirit of interest, commitment, and dedication to the country that is so common among the young men and women whom I knew in the navy is shared by a new generation of young Americans in the nation's heartland.

It was, therefore, with enthusiasm that I accepted a role in the university's Centennial Leadership Symposia. These symposia brought together leaders from various walks of life with several hundred of the most motivated students at the university. The discussions in which I participated at the Government Symposium reflected fully the experience that I had as an instructor at the university. The remarks that follow are based on those made at the symposia before several audiences, later revised for publication in this volume. My subject is leadership, its nature and requirements, and the role that leaders must play if the United States is to continue its role in the world and provide the kind of life that we want future generations of Americans to enjoy. These thoughts are based on my experiences as a leader in the armed forces of the United States, but I hope that they may serve useful to young Americans who aspire to leadership roles in other areas.

When the Chinese say, "May you live in interesting times," I think that they have in mind just exactly the period that we are experiencing right now. Our world is truly in flux. It is moving so rapidly that many goals and strategies that seemed appropriate, even a short time ago, like six months, will now have to be rethought and reshaped. Certainly the global political picture has altered dramatically in an extremely short period of time.

I believe that all of us, in our hearts, were confident that at some time the illusion of communism would crack wide open, but I suspect that not a one of us anticipated that it would happen in our own lifetime. Hasn't it been amazing? Absolutely stunning. In essence we are witnessing, firsthand, one of the great watersheds of history. We are actually experiencing it and reading about it in our newspapers and seeing it on our televisions. As the facade of communism shatters and the Soviet empire crumbles all together, Eastern Europe is literally throwing off its shackles and moving, in a very halting way, toward pluralism, freedom, and a free market.

As Americans, of course, we applaud these developments. I should caution you that breaking down one wall, throwing out one dictator, et cetera, will not solve all of our problems for the future. It will not secure the future. It will not necessarily make the world wonderful. I submit that we are in for a protracted period of uncertainty and struggle. As these countries sort out the wreckage that they have now caused and look to the future, I predict that we will see new political parties in each of these nations vying for power, seeking new solutions.

There will be new pockets of poverty, new pockets of wealth. There will be a great deal of confusion, trauma, frustration, and even disillusionment before the necessary institutions are in place and new responsible governments take hold of their destiny. All of these nations are going to have a protracted period before they can get their arms around their destiny. Make no mistake, we do not know as yet what the replacement regimes will be or what they will look like. While their future is essentially their problem—in other words, a European problem—the United States as the leader of the free world will undoubtedly be deeply involved in this very revolutionary process.

This example, while a most prominent one, is not the only serious challenge that we are currently facing and that our entire society faces. Simultaneously, we are being besieged on a number of other fronts. Technologically we are on the brink of another industrial revolution. For example, modern electronics has brought computers, televisions, robotics, spacecrafts, and instantaneous global communications. Our ability to calculate, our ability to harness complicated processes and control them, and literally to shrink the world has been revolutionized just in the last two decades. I read the other day that in the next ten years, we will see more inventions than we have seen in the proceeding thirty thousand years. That's mind boggling. Bear in mind that the United States has no corner on these developments. U.S. leadership in each of these fields is being threatened from many directions.

Complicating our situation is an alarming deterioration in our industrial and public infrastructure. To turn around this depressing trend will require foresight, imagination, untold investment, but above all, courageous business and governmental decision makers. Environmental concerns, as you are all aware, are mushrooming. In fact the physical quality of our planet is being threatened. Closer to each of us personally is the drug addiction problem, which threatens our younger generation and saps the self-confidence not only of us as individuals, but our nation as well.

This matrix of challenges forces us to examine our educational system and to examine it deeply and thoughtfully. Many say that it is in crisis, but more importantly and frankly, it is the educational system that, with proper attention, offers us the best prospects for overcoming our problems and for easing our transition into the next century. Our schools cannot be reoriented or improved easily or quickly. It will require a national effort involving each and every one of us over the next several decades. We are facing unprecedented demands and if we are to meet them successfully, it will require a high order of statesmanship, political courage, innovation, perseverance, sensitivity, and knowledge. In every facet of our national life—political, technical, business, professional, educational, social—we will desperately need women and men who are prepared and willing to take responsibility. People to dare, to risk, to enter the lists, and to get out in front, in other words, genuine leaders, quality leaders.

In no area is this more important than in government service. I believe the quality of our governmental leaders will be more important at this point in our history than any other. During forty-seven years in the navy, I watched time and again how a skillful leader could inspire people to perform above themselves, to turn around an organization on the brink of defeat, to adjust smoothly to new and changing circumstances, and to make people feel good about themselves, about their work, and about their comrades. These are no mean achievements, but good leaders can do these things. I can assure you that no military organization, platoon, squadron, regiment, fleet, or army can be successful without talented and selfless leaders. It is a law of gravity in the service world, and I genuinely believe it extends to every field of endeavor that involves group efforts or the combined efforts of men and women.

Let me expand on today's challenges for leaders, their important role in our society, and particularly in our future. I will also make a few comments on the preparation of tomorrow's managers, chief executive officers, commanders, politicians, and professionals.

Nothing strikes a more appealing chord in America than peace and prosperity, and by this measure we are doing very well indeed. History is shaping up in the Soviet Union, Eastern Europe, Central America, and South Africa, much as we have wanted. For over fifty years we have been pressing the case for self-determination and arguing the merits of pluralism. Now our wildest dreams are coming to pass. In fact, I find it almost fun to read the newspapers again. Every day we see stunning events in Eastern Europe.

Our gross national product continues to increase at a rate of some 2–3 percent annually. Inflation and interest rates are far less burdensome than in the early 1980s. And American jobs are being created, not only by Americans, but also by foreign investors in our economy. Beneath the veneer of today's satisfaction, however, is a world that is shifting, changing, and growing at an unprecedented pace. And I use that term precisely—an unprecedented pace, unprecedented in all of world history. We are at a crucial turning point in our own international life, there are hosts of troublesome problems on the domestic side of the house, our technology is on the brink of another industrial revolution, and world demographics are exploding.

It is one thing to enjoy peace and prosperity from one year to the next. It is another for each generation to leave America as good, if not better, than they found it. On that score, not one of us can be entirely satisfied with the status quo; in fact, there are even some grounds for alarm. While we applaud and welcome recent events in the Soviet Union and Eastern Europe, the real tests are still ahead of us. President Gorbachev is courageously pressing ahead to reform his society, but he is beset with a broad spectrum of problems—ideological, social, and economic. (Speaking of leadership, a study of President Gorbachev would be very much in order.) I have had several opportunities to visit the Soviet Union and on my last visit I found myself depressed by what I saw there.

The trauma is not over in Russia. Rejecting seventy years of history and redirecting a huge multiracial nation in an entirely new direction is a shaky enterprise at best. The prospect for serious instability and economic collapse is still very much alive. In turn, managing the U.S.-USSR bilateral relationship with these uncertainties in the background will require American statesmanship of the highest order and require quality leadership in the coming decade.

In Eastern Europe, the wall has come down, the past has been dismantled, but the structure for the future (frankly, the most important task) has yet to get off the ground. There will be confusion for some time, and frustration, and perhaps, disillusionment. While our country is 3,000 miles away, it will nevertheless play an integral part in the rebuilding process—politically, economically, and psychologically, as well as with respect to security. For forty-five years, we have been waiting for this window of opportunity. Are we up to it? Are our political, military, diplomatic, and technical leaders up to this significant and unique challenge?

On the domestic side of the house, we likewise have some truly tough problems which must be addressed. Let me run down some of the key problems:

• a massive three trillion dollar national debt and heavy reliance on foreign creditors to keep the federal government afloat;
• an overloading of our highways, air traffic system, and municipal utilities, due not only to heavier demands, but also lagging investments in basic infrastructure at all levels of government;
• controversy over the benefits and risks of nuclear power plants and the risks of nuclear fission in general, complicated by

the fact that nuclear waste is piling up without adequate means of permanent disposal;

• the high cost of medical care for our senior citizens and the overtaking of our public health system by the national drug crisis and the AIDS epidemic.

Solutions to each of these complex challenges will involve huge investments, technical knowledge, long-range planning, decades of effort, and thousands of governmental and private citizens. We are talking about unprecedented scale, scope, and complexity here. By definition, these types of undertakings will require world-class leadership.

As we attack these specific real-world issues, there are some fundamental processes that underline everything that our society does, that will, at the same time, deserve a great deal of attention if we are to enter the twenty-first century in a healthy and competitive posture. First, the lagging quality of education in our primary and secondary schools, as seen in verbal and math achievement tests; the surging costs of a college education; a general decline in advanced degrees awarded to American students; and a shortage of technically trained graduates. All of these threaten our ability not only to develop the necessary technology, but perhaps most importantly, to produce leaders of sufficient skills and numbers. These shortcomings strike at the very heart of our ability to keep pace with the world and to resolve the issues that still lie ahead of us over the horizon.

Similarly, the role of our government in making things right requires thought and perhaps action. One thing we do know, government service is not as attractive or rewarding as it once was. We are expecting people to do a lot more with less. For example, since 1975, we have gained thirty million people, put forty million more vehicles on our highways, and added thirteen billion passenger miles in domestic air service. Yet, we have seen little or no growth in the number of people employed by federal, state, and local governments.

Meanwhile, funding for domestic programs has barely kept pace with inflation. In virtually every sector of our government, we are still meeting the requirements of the 1970s, not the demands of today, or especially those of the 1990s. The picture is virtually the same throughout the country.

The attitude of our young people toward government has changed over time. Fifteen years ago, a majority of college freshmen (66–75 percent) wanted to develop a philosophy of life and to help people in difficulty, usually through public service. Now, they want to be well off financially and to disappear into a corporation or profession. This trend is bound to continue if more of our young people have to borrow their way into or through college to the tune of twenty to fifty thousand dollars.

Please understand, I am not convinced that we need more policy planners in our federal, state, and local governments. Surely, however, we have to think about how we are going to recruit and retain the engineers, social workers, educators, medical professionals, and law enforcement officers required to provide an adequate level of public service. And we expect these same people to lead the public in support of enlightened policies.

Also, the relationship between business and government needs rethinking. All over the world, our main competition (e.g., Japanese, Korean, and German businesses) are subsidized and directly aided by a close connection between the bureaucracy and business. Yet Americans cling to the belief that government must police industry rather than aid it. Perhaps this anachronistic philosophy makes us feel better, but we pay a very high price for this belief.

No matter what its persuasion, liberal or conservative, the federal government cannot provide for the common defense, the general welfare, or the domestic tranquility without a healthy and growing economy, fueled by jobs and revenues provided by the private sector. That fact of life is built into the woof and warp of the free enterprise system. No matter what their size, large or small, private industries cannot uphold their share of the bargain unless government is willing to invest in our national transportation system, provide adequate and reliable sources of energy, tend to the education of our young people, maintain the overall health of our society, and develop methods to dispose of our hazardous and nonhazardous wastes.

One more basic issue should be cited. Daniel Boorstin, in his award-winning trilogy, *The Americans*, describes in great detail our tremendous technical achievements and the republic's success in putting together enterprises of phenomenal complexity and scope, such as the building of nuclear weapons and the conquering of space. In the end, he concludes that the "advance of science and technology, whether guided or vagrant, now controls the daily lives of Americans." In other words, our future is no longer primarily governed by statesmen or our own decisions. This is a rather depressing conclusion and perhaps our most terrifying challenge, to get man back into the decision-making loop, to control our own destiny. But do not underestimate this task. In this age of technical specialization and rapid change to get the roller coaster under control will require leaders of unprecedented breadth, understanding, and sensitivity.

Let me now turn to the role of leadership. As we confront this exciting but trying future, it is vital to understand that leadership can and does make a crucial difference in every successful undertaking and organization. The examples are limitless: Arturo Toscanini, knitting together the New York Philharmonic; Colonel Travis at the Alamo; Henry Ford, introducing mass production; Gail Borden, conducting hundreds of experiments before he successfully condensed milk; Abraham Lincoln, inspiring the nation in a time of peril; Dwight Eisenhower, bringing together disparate allied armies to liberate Europe; Admiral Nimitz, using audacity to overcome the Japanese superiority after Pearl Harbor; General Matthew Ridgeway, turning around a dispirited U.S. Army in Korea; Thomas Watson's tremendous drive creating IBM; Martin Luther King's fight against prejudice; Dr. Salk's peerless drive and determination; Neil Armstrong, setting foot on the moon; and the list could go on and on. Each one a gifted leader in his field and in his time; each one made an unforgettable contribution. It is difficult to overestimate the importance of quality leadership.

Successful leaders differ greatly in their styles and techniques.

In fact, social scientists have failed miserably in their efforts to develop a formula or a recipe that will identify great captains. Instead, there are a variety of views on what traits are the most important, what education or experience is the most valuable for a top executive, what techniques work best. The combinations are frankly infinite—two individuals with completely different mixes may be equally successful at the same task. We see that time and again in business executives, scientists, and military commanders who have distinguished themselves.

There are, however, I believe, some generalizations worth noting. Successful leaders, without exception, are well founded in the mechanics of their business or profession, whatever it may be. They possess the ability to inspire others to accept the leader's vision, to follow his example, or to make extraordinary efforts on behalf of the larger enterprise. This characteristic is manifested in many forms, but it is always present. They have the facility to relate their endeavors to fundamental goals, in other words, to understand and to fit their efforts into a larger picture of society's needs, the constitution's requirements, national strategy, et cetera. This capacity to see the larger picture is perhaps the rarest quality of all.

As for techniques, successful leaders appreciate that different tasks, groups, and individuals require different approaches. Leadership of a combat unit varies from that of a business office, a school situation, a manufacturing company. Professional people, politicians, businessmen, laborers, secretaries, enlisted men—all have their own way of looking at the world. If you are to lead them or merely deal with them, you will do well to understand their sensitivities, their biases, their strengths, their weaknesses, and mold your leadership approach accordingly. There is considerable room for style, drama, and imagination. But whatever combination or nuances you employ, they should include, in some fashion, the fundamentals I have just mentioned.

Two other comments appear appropriate. These are personal views, but germane to this vital topic. I am personally persuaded that "brilliant success" attends those who look to the fundamentals, but then ultimately marry them to ingenuity, boldness, and even to audacity. Timidity has no place in great endeavors. Risk-taking goes with the territory. I don't mean unreasonable or irrational risks, but as the old saw says, "Nothing ventured, nothing gained." The examples are legion in industry, combat operations, diplomacy, and research, where leaders, trusting their own assessments and judgment, departed from the norm with phenomenal results.

Let me cite a personal experience. About ten years ago in the U.S. Navy we were faced with a terrible drug problem that literally threatened the future of our service. The chief of naval operations at the time was a man named Tom Hayward. He was told that if he outlawed drug usage he would destroy the navy, because it was so deeply rooted in the young people of our country that they would leave the navy rather than give up drugs. After considerable soul-searching, he resisted and ignored that advice and laid down a staunch policy of no drug usage. Although he was told that it would be a disaster, he was right. The policy has proved tremendously successful, and today we don't have a drug-free navy, but we have one with extremely small amounts of drug usage, the lowest of any service or any other organization in the country.

My experience suggests that exceptional leaders normally believe that their education is never complete. They make it their business to study not only their own profession for all their lives, but to expand their competence in other fields and attempt to profit from the experience of leaders in other activities. They study not just theory, but how politicians, jurists, managers, academics, and military commanders have managed challenges in real situations. Quality leaders never cease to learn.

It is often asserted that "leaders are born, not made." As with most folk wisdom, there is something to that proposition. It is difficult to deny that some individuals seem naturally to belong in the front of the parade. But when you have lived as long as I have, you discover that leading parades is just one kind of leadership (in fact, probably not the most important form), and that the subject is a great deal more complicated than that old saw suggests. Life is a marathon, not a sprint—or a parade—and what is needed most desperately are leaders who cannot only start the race, but finish it.

I have time and again witnessed men and women who initially didn't believe they had the talent to persuade others, to issue orders, to persevere in adversity, to inspire others. I have watched them change into determined and successful leaders under skillful tutelage. Often an experienced teacher, drill instructor, shop steward, supervisor, or manager has the ability to detect something in another individual that the individual himself cannot detect, something that signals leadership aptitude. Then, using a careful mix of increased responsibilities, encouragement, high standards, and rewards, transform that individual from a follower into a productive leader. It is an amazing phenomenon. I can assure you that process is at the heart of your military services, and my belief is that it is replicated in every sector of our national life.

Once the fire is lighted, once you experience the thrill of building a winning team, or triumphing in an election, or seeing a difficult project through to completion, or selling your unconventional suggestions to the main office, your life is probably never the same again. People who have had such success employ their new-found confidence to attack additional challenges and then turn their eyes to the next rung of the ladder. In essence, new vistas have opened up to them, because there are few thrills equal to those of successfully leading other men and women.

If we are interested in developing leaders, our schools and workplaces must not only supply substantive and technical knowledge for performing specific tasks but also convey the importance of leadership. We must shape curricula, organizational responsibilities, and assignments so that aspiring leaders can be identified and encouraged to hone their techniques and talents. Our nation must actively work at this task rather than passively wait for leaders to rise out of the mist. Today's world demands more than that of our schools and of our way of life.

Similarly, the breadth of our professional education must be critically reviewed. Too many educators prefer to deprecate bureaucrats while ignoring the processes of government. The problem in Washington, D.C., is not a lack of good ideas but rather of good people who understand the structure and nuances of the executive and legislative branches, who can identify a good idea and then shepherd it through the Washington labyrinth, developing sufficient consensus that the idea can be translated into action. These individuals are rare jewels.

The environmental expert must understand how restrictions he is advocating impact not only the ozone layer but also the community, and often the livelihood of men and women. The professional diplomat today may be involved in arms control, trade policy, foreign aid, and international communications. Politicians may have an excellent command of the technicalities of lawmaking, but if they don't understand free market economics or the intricacies of defense budgeting or farm subsidies, they may be shortchanging their constituents. The space project manager who is at home with laser beams and rocket propulsion, but doesn't appreciate the legislative process, is severely handicapped, because no matter how innovative or advanced his technical ideas, if he can't sell them to the White House or Congress, they will come to naught.

In this day and age of complex, multilayered projects and firms, broad-gauged leaders are a must. Moreover, they must have a sure grasp of human interactions and motivations and the social pressures currently driving the nation if they are to regain the initiative and restore human control over our technology. I am told that when President Kennedy interviewed nominees for his cabinet the questions he personally asked did not concern the area for which they were being considered. Kennedy concentrated on what were the candidate's outside interests, what books he read, what he knew about sports, about politics and life. What was his experience with people? It is wise to think about these things in training leaders. These are demanding requirements, but we have entered a demanding world which cannot be wished away. Our hope lies with better and better education and training, which accommodates both abstract theory and real-world concerns and situations.

Yes, we do live in interesting times. Interesting times imply change, stirring, uncertainty, and even trauma. It is in such a period when we most desperately need leaders at all levels. Franklin Roosevelt, in describing his own experience in the depression years, commented, "Without leadership, alert and sensitive to change, we are bogged down or lose our way." He was dead right. The Marine Corps has a more earthy prescription. In training young officers, they have a phrase they stress, and I watched my son grapple with it, "Lead, or get the hell out of the way for somebody else to do it."

Admiral Crowe speaks with the voice of a practical man. Leadership demands that we identify the main problems facing us and act with boldness to address them. The future is in the hands of those who will choose to shape it. We must demand of ourselves that which our circumstances necessitate. Our perspective must be global, our ambition broad, our determination firm. Pericles, in the early years of the Peloponnesian War, said the same thing; after he died, Athens squandered its advantages and lost the war, bringing to an end the Periclean Age of Greece. Does America stand on the edge of a new "American century," or is it on the edge of a precipice leading to its demise as a great power? This question lingers in the background of Crowe's remarks.

In a much ballyhooed book, historian Paul Kennedy traces *The Rise and Fall of the Great Powers* and concludes that the United States seemed likely to commit the same mistake that had brought earlier great powers to their knees.[1] To make a short summary of a long book, Kennedy concludes that this mistake lay in the overextension of imperial reach, followed by a concomitant overinvestment in military power, leading to a decline of economic infrastructure and ultimate ruin. After World War II ended, the United States did not unilaterally disarm, as it had after every previous war. Instead, it assumed the burden of leading the free world by providing a protective umbrella of military might. In the nuclear age, this required substantial investment in nuclear technology and in conventional weaponry, while maintaining a large standing army. The combination brought America's defense budget to 7 percent of the GNP by the 1980s, compared to about 2 percent in Japan and 3–4 percent in West Europe, our two main economic rivals. The result was declining economic competitiveness and a declining economic base. This trend, which Kennedy appears to believe is inexorable, means that the United States is a society in *relative* decline, when compared to other powers such as Germany and Japan. In the next century America will occupy an important role in a multipolar world, but it will be a diminished role from that which the country has played in the twentieth century.

Kennedy makes a convincing case to the reach of his data. Unquestionably, other nations are experiencing faster rates of economic growth than is the United States. In all probability the twenty-first century will witness the emergence of a multipolar world in which the United States will be among a handful of major players on the world stage. Still, there is much to question in Kennedy's analysis, even assuming its main empirical contentions are accurate. In comparing the impact of military investment on economic strength over time, for example, Kennedy assumes that the economic impact of money invested in defense expenditures is less productive than would be the investment of similar dollars in non-defense-related areas. This may be true, but it remains to be proven. In an era of high-technology defense systems, the investment of taxpayer dollars in military research and development may have important multiplier effects on the economy. Furthermore, even if military investment is less productive than other research and development, it does not follow that this is the most critical comparison. One might wonder whether the transfer of wealth from production to consumption through the various byways of the welfare state does not have a greater impact on GNP than does investment in military technology. These are empirical questions, and not new ones. They lie at the heart of the issue that Kennedy wants to address. To compare Japanese and American military expenditures as a percentage of GNP without at the same time comparing other expenditures on the same basis gives a unidimensional picture of what is actually happening in the two countries.

The demise of communism in the Soviet Union and Eastern Europe offers lessons about the past and new prospects for the future. Perhaps the near half century of the cold war, during which the United States overinvested in defense while underinvesting in economic infrastructure, would have been hot rather than cold had we not chosen the course we did. Perhaps historians with a longer perspective will write that it was this very investment that ensured that nuclear war did not occur. Perhaps it will appear to future generations that the investment in military power ensured the survival of the free world until the communist regimes collapsed. And perhaps, in the "new world order" of which President Bush speaks, American military power will ensure the global stability that economic growth will require.

Of course, to argue that the investment in American power was necessary is not to vitiate the thesis that, due to it, the country is on the verge of either absolute or relative decline. But what does decline mean? If one measures it by America's share of global GNP, then it seems evident that as the nations of the world recovered from World War II, America's relative share of the world's wealth would decline. If one measures decline by military power, then it seems evident that America will soon stand alone as the only military power possessing the material and moral resources to ensure the peace. Predictions about whether America will rise or decline, then, depend upon one's assumptions about the nature of the world in the post-cold war era. By focusing exclusively on economic and military resources, Kennedy reduces the equation to two evidently important but significantly limited variables. History will record that what people believe is often more important than what they have. An interpretation of the decline of the Roman Empire that left Christianity out of the account would surely be inadequate.

Notwithstanding these possible shortcomings in Kennedy's analysis, his book does touch the dilemma confronting the students who participated in the government symposium.

They are called to leadership by Admiral Crowe, but what kind of world will they lead? In the patriotic decade of the 1980s, young Americans wanted to believe in their country's greatness. They must now wonder, in listening to voices like Paul Kennedy's, how great their country can be. In a panel discussion at the government symposium, visions of America's role in the newly emerging world order were given by Oklahoma Senator David Boren and Fourth District Congressman Dave McCurdy. Senator Boren, the chairman of the Senate Select Intelligence Committee, and Congressman McCurdy, the chairman of the House Select Intelligence Committee, both bring a global perspective to the question of the nation's future.

Senator Boren takes Paul Kennedy's challenge seriously; he recommended the book for the symposium reading list. In his position as chairman of the Senate Intelligence Committee, he has access to the various political and economic data collected by America's intelligence agencies. Already, the changing character of America's role in the world is evident in the government's intelligence estimates. Boren believes that we must come to a new understanding of our role in the world.

The whole world has changed and our biggest challenge right now is to change our thinking with it. One of the real functions of a leader is to explain to the American people the new environment we are in. America faces new challenges and we must be prepared to make the sacrifices that are needed to adjust to it. It is the function of the leader to tell the people what they really need to know, to give them enough information that they can understand the changes in the world. One of the things we have to realize is that we are going through a period of change as dramatic as any period of change in the last three or four centuries. The difference is that this time the change has not come principally from the force of arms. As Lech Walesa said, the whole Polish revolution was carried out without a single windowpane being broken.

The world has changed just as much in the last twelve months as it changed in the twelve months following the end of World War II, when a whole series of new political relationships developed. At that time we realized that we were in a dramatically different environment and we reached out to create new institutions in the United Nations, NATO, regional security agreements, and the Marshall Plan. These were steps taken to deal with a totally different world. I think it is urgent for our leaders to convey to the American people that the changes that are occurring today are just as dramatic.

In a sense we might say that we have defeated communism and have won the cold war, but we have to understand that the decline of the Soviet Union could lead to a decline of the United States as well. We must understand and tell the American people that it is going to take new and different assets, different strengths to play a leading role in the twenty-first century than were required in the twentieth century.

Many countries, including the countries in Western Europe and Japan, have been willing to follow our lead during the cold war era. They have deferred to us on matters of international importance, even though their economies are as strong as ours. The European Community has a bigger GNP than we have. Japan, as we all know, has a higher per capita income than we have. Why have they followed our lead up to this point? Because they needed us. As long as they perceived the Soviet threat or felt vulnerable to the Warsaw Pact nations, they needed us. They needed the shield of American military protection, especially when we were paying so much of the cost for maintaining it. Now do they still need us? Not to the degree that they did, even twelve months ago.

I had a very interesting experience a couple of weeks ago. Dave McCurdy and I both serve on the intelligence committees of the House and Senate and I asked some of our operatives from around the world to come in and tell us what was going on. They told us, "When are you people going home? We do not need you any more. There is not a Soviet threat for you to protect against. Why don't you go on home?" We heard from people at the operational level with whom we have worked for years on joint intelligence operations in places like Western Europe. We must recognize this new reality. Of course, we must maintain the right kind of military strength and we must be able to deal with regional conflicts.

More than anything else in this next century, our influence in the world is going to depend more on our economic strength and the strength of our system as a model for others to follow, than it is going to depend on our military strength. That means that we really have to develop a whole new set of assets in this country.

When the cold war began, we had nine of the ten biggest banks in the world. Now we do not have any of the top twenty. We had a 70 percent share of world assets, now we have a 19 percent share of world assets. If we are going to have political influence in the world and be more than just a bit player in the twenty-first century, then we have to rebuild the economic strength of this country and regain our economic vitality and our ability to compete.

I heard one of the panelists say that if we reach out to Eastern Europe and other areas of the world we have to do it in a way that also promotes our own economic advantage. We do need to be a player in Eastern Europe. We do need to provide technical help and economic assistance. We do need to be helping in Nicaragua and Panama and many other places. Yet, according to the last *New York Times* poll, 80 percent of the American people are strongly opposed to any increase in American foreign aid. We have the most opposition to increasing foreign aid at a time when there is the greatest need for us to be involved. How do we get over that?

I have proposed that we undertake a Buy-American Plan. When Japan and West Germany gave help to Poland and Hungary, they did not give cash, they gave credits. Most of their aid could only be used to buy products produced in Japan or produced in West Germany. Similarly, a Buy-American Plan could help the countries of Eastern Europe, while at the same time creating jobs here at home. In other words, foreign aid credits could only be used to buy American products. American goods would be used to build new factories, the transportation system, and the telecom-

---

munications system. When spare parts are needed in the future, they will buy American spare parts, produced by American workers, creating American jobs here at home.

To get U.S. taxpayers to support politically a role in the development of emerging nations, we have to show it is also to our advantage. We need a new approach.

Other critical changes are also required if we are to rebuild our economic strength. Our tax policy must be changed to provide incentives for investment and saving. Our educational system must be rebuilt. The federal government needs to assist in attracting the best and brightest individuals to the teaching profession and reducing our dropout rate. We cannot compete with Japan if 29 percent of our students drop out of school before they finish high school, compared with only 1 percent in Japan. We cannot waste a third of our human power and compete with the rest of the world.

To compete in the twenty-first century, we must internationalize the thinking of the next generation. The University of Oklahoma in its next one hundred years can continue to play an important role in this area. We have to speak the world's languages. We have to understand the world's cultures. We are woefully insular right now in our educational system.

For example, how many Japanese high school students speak English? One hundred percent. They have to take six years of English to graduate from high school. How many American students are studying Japanese? Two one-hundredths of 1 percent. In Africa last year, I saw a Japanese trade delegation closing a contract. They were in the lobby of the hotel, shaking hands, and signing documents. Were they speaking Japanese? No, they were speaking Swahili. I have seen them in Central America, closing a deal. What were they speaking? Not Japanese, they were speaking Spanish. By the year 2000, the European community has as a goal that every sixteen-year-old in those countries will speak two foreign languages in addition to his or her native language.

Senator Claiborne Pell of Rhode Island and I will soon propose a major expansion of our student exchange programs, beginning with at least 10,000 college undergraduates placed in the Soviet

Union, Eastern Europe, and Central and Latin America, where we have very special interests and special problems.

We need such a program for two reasons. First, we need to build a bond between the next generation of leaders in those countries and the United States. Second, we need to get American students overseas to expose them to other cultures. They will learn the languages and be sensitized to the fact that they are going to compete in a world environment. We had 356,000 foreign students studying in the United States last year. A huge majority of them came from the Orient. How many American students studied abroad last year? 24,000. Our students simply are not venturing out. They are not going into the other environments. They are not living in the other cultures. They are not forcing themselves to learn other languages. Malaysia, with a population of 14 million, has 25,000 students studying in the United States. We have only 24,000 Americans anywhere else in the world.

We have to change our attitude. We have to really create an international learning environment in our universities. We have got to really encourage these sister relationships to send our students to other places to study.

So that is another challenge as we look at the twenty-first century. We need new assets if we are going to be a major player. We have got to be economically strong. We have to rebuild our educational system. The next generation of young American leaders must understand they are in an international environment in a way that we have not been in the past.

Senator Boren is concerned about America's future, and his view is Churchillian. He finds Paul Kennedy's analysis of America's situation plausible, and accepts the norm implicit in Kennedy's argument: America should want to be a great power. Not all peoples think this way. It is hard to imagine, for example, a symposium on leadership in Australia, Costa Rica, or Bhutan in which this topic would dominate the conversation. Some European nations might not be preoccupied with the world power equation either. Indeed America, in its isolationist past, would not have worried about its comparative greatness as much as its absolute growth. Yet now the mantle of world leadership has fallen our way and our own prosperity and happiness seem to depend on our maintaining the role that history has thrust upon us.

When a leader of Senator Boren's stature and experience speaks to us, we should listen. What is most significant in his remarks is not the feasibility of each of his prescriptions as much as the way in which he goes about identifying the problem. Take, for example, his proposal to put our foreign aid program on a "Buy-American Plan." The idea has strong appeal to Oklahoma Symposia students, who seem to reflect the national sentiment against foreign aid of any sort. During the government symposium several students reacted strongly in favor of the Buy-American Plan and against U.S. foreign aid programs. As senior communications major Johnny E. Pate expressed, "This is a key factor in our ability to create economic growth at home. Foreign countries are buying foreign goods with American money. By giving them credit we can keep our money at home, stimulating our economy and reducing the trade deficit." That which appeals to the common sense of OU students runs smack up against the realities of Washington politics, however. Senator Boren, joined by three of the most powerful members of the United States Senate (Lloyd Bentsen of Texas, Robert Byrd of West Virginia, and Max Baucus of Montana), introduced legislation to establish the Buy-American Plan, but the bill was sent to a possible early death in the Senate Foreign Relations Committee, "whose members generally oppose converting to tied aid because they believe it forces developing countries to invest in large-scale projects often ill-suited to their needs."[2] Congressional resistance to the Boren plan reminds us of the great complexity of the issues confronting leaders today, as well as of the equally great complexity of leading in the milieu of American politics.

Not all students were attracted to the Boren plan. The emphasis given to Japan as both an international competitor and as a country whose foreign aid program is tied to the purchase of Japanese goods and services led sophomore marketing major Ron A. Schaeffer to see a tension between the resistance to foreign aid and the appeal of the Buy-American Plan, on the one hand, and the appeal for an enhanced international and multicultural perspective, on the other hand.

It is remarkable that ethnocentrism and egocentrism are so common in a country which preaches acceptance and pluralism. Contrary to popular opinion, this problem will not go away by itself. The "Me Generation" of the 1980s does not automatically become the "We Generation" of the 1990s just because a Miss America hopeful says it will in the question-and-answer competition. Again, this problem stems from our inability to use a long-range perspective in decision making. Such a deeply rooted cultural flaw can only be corrected through effective moral leadership.

Japan-bashing is the nativistic response to America's diminishing global influence. While it does nothing to solve the problem, Japan-bashing does at least give us the temporary pleasure of a national ego-boost. "Our country is best no matter what, so there!" is obviously not an effective response to the problem. It is, however, the most common response.

Senator Boren sees the problem of foreign aid from two perspectives. He recognizes the value of foreign aid and the desirability of continuing the program, yet he sees in the public's "nativistic" response to it a threat to its continuation. The Buy-American Plan seeks to find a more solid political footing for the program that will have the ancillary benefit of helping the economy. One is reminded, here, of Tocqueville's contention that the American moral compass finds its gravitational force in the concept of "self-interest, rightly understood." Americans, Tocqueville argued, are saved from a life spent entirely in the pursuit of naked self-interest by a saving sense that their own long-run interest may be well served by some short-term sacrifices. This, he says, is why they go to church. It may be too much to expect the next generation of Americans to give selflessly (despite the national debt) to help impoverished foreign regimes, but it may be possible to convince them that it is in their interest to do so. If they listen to Dung Tran, a senior mechanical engineering major, they will see the view from the other side. Tran is from Vietnam.

It is especially hard to understand why we must give millions of dollars away as foreign aid to countries that we hardly ever associate with. It is true that we badly need the money for our domestic problems, such as the homeless, drugs, education, etc. But it is our kindness and hospitality that have drawn men and women with ideas and determination from all over the world to come to America; and this is what makes up America and her greatness. This is the very reason I have chosen to stay here and become an American. I, like many other immigrants, am proud of my heritage. But now I'm an American and a proud one at that. America has given me my dignity and freedom, an opportunity of being the best that I can be. I love America, not only for what it has given me, but also for what it stands for.

Congressman Dave McCurdy sees in the demise of communist regimes in Eastern Europe an opportunity for America to play a unique role in shaping the post–cold war order.

The challenges we face today, of course, are very real, but it is an exciting time to be alive. Certainly, it is an exciting time to be an American. Much that we have recently seen—the crushing blows to communism, the failure of Marxist ideology around the world, and the striving for freedom by people throughout the world—is, I think, a result of the resolve by the United States and our NATO allies in trying to contain the Soviet expansionism since the end of World War II.

When we talk about leadership, I think we have to talk about the generation of World War II leaders such as General George Marshall, who happens to be one of my personal heroes; Presi-

dent Truman; and diplomats such as George Kennan. George
Kennan, for instance, was a primary architect of the policy of
containment. Containment basically sought to contain the Soviet
aggressive behavior and to put a check on communist expansionism around the world. That strategy guided our overall defense and foreign policy for over thirty years, and proved to be
successful.

Today we have seen the success of containment, and we
need now to move beyond it to a new doctrine more appropriate
to the new world that is now emerging. We need to recognize
the nature of the changes that are taking place before our eyes,
and appreciate the opportunities that are afforded us.

In my opinion, the changes that are taking place in the
Warsaw Pact countries are irreversible and I find that most
informed people with whom I speak about it share this view.
There is a widespread recognition that, because of these
changes, we are entering a new era of uncertainty and many
challenges. I think it is time for us as Americans to go beyond
the policy of containment and try to establish a new policy—
a new strategy. I have named it the era of attainment. By that
I mean that we need to consolidate our victories over communism and develop a policy where we can have freedom and
democracy around the world. We must seek to establish economic prosperity for all human beings on this planet and to
do so in a stable, secure environment. I believe that we can
do that.

We must build upon our political experience to promote democracy around the world. That is going to take active leadership.
We in the United States cannot be spectators on the sidelines
watching events unfurl in Eastern Europe and around the world.
We need to be engaged. Many of my constituents would like to
say, "Well now that we have won the battle against communism,
perhaps we ought to withdraw into our own borders and not be
engaged internationally." I oppose this position of isolationism.
I think it is shortsighted. Our long-term gains and our long-
term interests economically, socially, politically are best served
by participating actively in the global economy and the global
environment.

Congressman McCurdy's emphasis is somewhat different from that of Senator Boren. Senator Boren stresses the factors that will permit America to remain a player in the geopolitical game; Congressman McCurdy emphasizes the goals that we should seek, and they echo the call of John F. Kennedy. In his inaugural address, President Kennedy spoke of an American idealism in which some have seen the roots of our entanglement in Vietnam: "Let every nation know, whether it wishes us well or ill, that we shall pay any price, bear any burden, meet any hardship, support any friend, oppose any foe, in order to assure the survival and success of liberty." Kennedy's rhetoric was intended to be a reflection of Lincoln's call at Gettysburg, "that we here highly resolve that these dead shall not have died in vain—that this nation, under God, shall have a new birth of freedom—and that government of the people, by the people, for the people, shall not perish from the earth," with, however, the important difference that Lincoln was calling America to preserve the prize of liberty in America and not to seek to enshrine it elsewhere. The clarion call of liberty is a tantalizing one, and once it is unleashed in the national psyche, it will not go away. In the fifteen years following World War II the country, led by presidents Truman and Eisenhower, followed a policy that was in stark contrast to George Washington's "no foreign entanglements." The theory of global internationalism that guided America's foreign policy establishment in shaping America's postwar foreign policy led to, if it did not require, John Kennedy's pledge to "bear any burden."[3] Eventually, Kennedy's idealism was crushed against the reality of the Berlin Wall, and Lyndon Johnson, sunk low by the burden of the Vietnam War, watched idly as the Russians smothered the new shoots of the Prague Spring.

If America permitted one-half of the potentially free world to bear the weight of communism, in the other half it did seek to nurture the conditions under which free regimes could develop. McCurdy sees in the Marshall Plan a precedent to guide American policy in the 1990s. The Marshall Plan had no

Buy-American attributes. Truman's goal was to get the aid to those who needed it, and to do it quickly. According to Congressman McCurdy,

One of Kennan's original precepts was to have military containment while allowing Western Europe to grow and prosper based on a free market economy. That policy and the freedoms that ensued brought the shining light of democracy and free economy in contrast with the centrally planned economies of the Soviet and Warsaw Pact. That stark comparison, I think, eventually led to the demise of communism.

So now, according to McCurdy, America must act decisively to affirm its role in shaping the new world order about which President Bush speaks. It is no surprise, then, that McCurdy finds Paul Kennedy's argument problematic.

Even though I do not subscribe to the declinist theory of Paul Kennedy in his book *The Rise and Fall of the Great Powers*, I do accept the proposition that we must have a new strategy for an era in which economic power will assume more importance. Kennedy stated that the United States is overextended militarily and will inevitably decline as did Great Britain. I believe that the collapse of communism came none too soon for the U.S. economy, and I think that now we must shift from a posture emphasizing military security to one focusing on economic security. We must get our own house in order and consolidate our gains as we try to prepare for the next challenge. That challenge, I think, lies in competing in a global economy while being mindful of the needs of Eastern Europe and those countries that still need some assistance. Our obligation is to nurture freedom in Eastern Europe and other places where it has a chance to grow, just as we did after World War II.

At a time when scholars are proclaiming the "end of history" and commentators are declaring that "democracy has won"

its war against totalitarianism, Congressman McCurdy sees
the difficulties in the path that lies ahead.[4] Democracy is at its
best a messy business, as those countries aspiring to it will
soon discover. As McCurdy put it in a speech to the George
Marshall Foundation in January 1990, "in all the euphoria . . .
we must caution our friends in Eastern Europe about the
potential for disillusionment with democracy . . . for they will
soon find, just as we in the United States have always known,
that democracy is glorious in the abstract, but often difficult
in practice."[5] McCurdy's call for a pragmatic idealism beckons
Americans to accept moral responsibility for the fate of the
formerly communist regimes. The challenge facing McCurdy
and other American leaders, however, is that the moral consensus upon which the Marshall Plan rested no longer exists
in America today. One need look no further than the students'
opposition to foreign aid to see that this is so. John Kennedy
may well have been the last American president in a position
to call unambiguously upon the national conscience.

The similarities in the views of Senator Boren and Congressman McCurdy are matched by similarities in their careers.
Both are from Oklahoma, both received degrees from the
University of Oklahoma, both studied abroad (Boren at Oxford as a Rhodes Scholar and McCurdy at the University of
Edinburgh on a Rotary Foundation Fellowship), both are moderate to conservative in political outlook, both chair their
chamber's intelligence committees, and both have been mentioned as potential candidates for the presidency. Both emphasized the need for Americans to be better and more broadly
educated and to become familiar with other cultures. They
called upon the students to extend their horizons beyond the
borders of Oklahoma, and in doing so, asked them to consider
their own aims in life; for their lives will surely be touched by
the global concerns that Boren and McCurdy addressed. The
reaction to the issues raised by the two legislators echoes this
fact.

Victoria Allred, a senior history major, accepted Senator

Boren's version of the challenge facing America. "The United States has come to a point in its history where it will have to change its policies and perspectives if it wishes to remain a world leader. The reign of most world powers lasts a very short time, and unless the United States addresses its ills, it will be forced to relinquish control." But what will facing this challenge mean to these future leaders? Fourth-year pharmacy student Grover L. Compton stated this dilemma succinctly:

Individualism has to be balanced with a sense of community identity. People's private lives need to be sacrificed in favor of the public needs. This is especially true concerning the young people of this nation who are gifted in some talent, leadership skills being one of these talents. America needs its "best and brightest" at the helm guiding the way, not quietly accumulating a fortune. This is not to say that a man should not strive to improve the quality of his private life, but that an equilibrium is the ideal situation.

How to find this equilibrium? To a generation of students nurtured in the individualism of Ronald Reagan's America, George Bush's call to civic virtue requires educated ears. That education, of course, is precisely what Senator Boren, Congressman McCurdy, Admiral Crowe, former American Ambassador to El Salvador Edwin G. Corr, and other symposium speakers sought to provide. John A. Basinger, a senior letters major, found in Senator Boren and Congressman McCurdy models of the kind of leaders America now needs, each seeking to educate the next generation by the example set.

The speakers and panelists at the symposium, asked to discuss leadership, instead demonstrated it to a large extent. While nearly all of the panelists addressed the general topic of leadership at least in some token fashion, they tended to turn the discussion to issues rather than the overarching theme of the conference in its generality.

Senator Boren and Congressman McCurdy were especially notable for their use of leadership qualities. Boren, when asked about almost any subject, would tailor his answer to the issue dealt with most specifically in his vision—education. McCurdy likewise steered his responses toward his issue of international policy and defense. Both demonstrated identity with followers (Oklahomans and Americans as well as humans in general), a vision for society which addressed needs on several levels (increased prosperity as well as more knowledge and satisfaction as humans), and an appreciation of the constantly changing relationship with their constituents. Each also communicated clearly his vision and outlined means of attainment.

Not all students found the discussion so satisfying. To some, the definition of the problem seemed unfairly put; to others, the solutions proposed seemed inadequate. James Barnett, a senior marketing major, felt that Senator Boren was implicitly blaming American students for the fact that so few study abroad.

It was very discouraging that both Senator Boren and Rep. McCurdy recognized the problem of educational decline, but they were not really willing to state any viable solutions. Boren went so far as to suggest that the decline in education is basically caused by unmotivated students unwilling to learn. For example, Boren stated that not many students were willing to study in foreign countries. I sharply disagree. Students would be more than willing to study abroad if the costs were not so high. Students, especially in college, have enough money problems trying to pay for their education and daily living expenses. Just trying to pay the continual rising tuition is enough of a headache, much less paying thousands of dollars a semester to study abroad. Every foreign student that studies in America for a year is financed by their respective home countries.

The whole problem with the decline in education is funding. Whenever the budget is cut, education is usually included in that package. Listening to Boren's comments really upset me . . .

because not once did he mention that we needed to devote more money to education. On the topic of foreign affairs, however, the first thing that he would mention was our need to be more active in the areas of foreign affairs, especially those in the Eastern Block—"short-term sacrifices in taxes and investments, for long-term gains." I would ask our leaders to have this same attitude with education. Short-term sacrifices for education would mean long-term improvement and advancement for society as a whole. As Dave McCurdy put it, "We need to get our own house in order."

Junior letters major John J. Barto also thought it unfair to blame the students for their lack of opportunity.

As much as I appreciated the ideas of Boren, McCurdy, Crowe, and Corr, it seemed as though there was an abundance of ideas, with little or no mention of actual plans or legislation. For example during the satellite link-up panel discussion, Boren and Corr had everyone in the forum convinced of the growing need for the United States to produce international students. Not once, however, did any of the panelists mention any programs implemented or any strides made towards this goal. Ambassador Corr went so far as to tell our congressmen that he had observed, here at OU, a lack of desire from students concerning overseas studies.

Ambassador Corr had not, in fact, said that OU students had a general lack of desire to study overseas, as he later noted; he merely said that he had in his diplomatic career encountered difficulty in satisfying the demands of Central and South American countries for American exchange students. It may be the case that American students do want to study abroad, but in places like Oxford and Edinburgh, and not in places like Montevideo and San Salvador. A preference for First World instead of Third World experiences would be consistent with the disapproval that many students expressed toward American foreign aid programs, which direct most of their funding to Third World countries that do not draw large numbers of American exchange students. The internationalization of the university, if it comes, will have to sweep more broadly than the aspirations of many of its students. It is in part for this reason that the university seeks to infuse its general education curriculum with a multicultural emphasis.

Eden B. Gillespie put a different interpretation on Senator Boren's statistics. If more students are coming from other countries to study here than are going from here to study in other countries, she reasoned, then perhaps it's because our schools are better than theirs.

Senator Boren emphasized that many foreign students study in the United States, yet few American students are willing to study abroad. Even tiny Malaysia sends many students. We should send more of our students outside, they argue. "It would be a dramatic statement to exchange students with the USSR," Boren said. "We need to send more students abroad to build the warm bonds of friendship [with the leaders and citizens of other countries]." Encouraging foreign study *could* do that. And we *are* behind other countries in number of students sent outside. But rather than seeing this as a terrible malady and hanging our heads in shame, we should recognize these figures as a compliment to our education system. Yes, Malaysia does send most of its student-age population to the United States to study. But isn't that because they want their youth to achieve a good education, and our resources are better than theirs? Couldn't it be that America has more power and wealth than the student-sending Oriental countries do, and that they merely want a share of it? Senator Boren said that 356,000 of the 386,000 foreigners studying here come from poor Oriental countries, upholding my point. If educational opportunities in other countries are worse than ours, why welcome those lesser opportunities merely because they are foreign? . . . we continue to cry over the "brain drain," and moan that our "best and brightest" minds are leaving Oklahoma, a complaint common nationwide. Won't pushing good students out the door just further this problem?

Hard questions, these, questions that reflect the hard choices that we face as a society and as individual members of it. The students do not accept the notion that parochialism in American higher education is their fault—give them the money and they will be glad to study overseas (although perhaps not in Malaysia). If the students do go abroad, they will become more cosmopolitan; but then, they will be less likely to return to Oklahoma to live and work. Students believe that the country should make sacrifices now to create a better future, but they think that the sacrifices should be made through higher taxes (spreading the burden to society as a whole) rather than through higher tuition (visiting the burden upon them and their families). Politicians can exhort students to expand their horizons, but when these same politicians are unwilling to support more spending, the exhortations seem hollow. The students want society to bear more of the burden of the education so that they can be better prepared to serve their state and country as adult leaders. But would the students repay this public investment in their country's future, or merely succumb to the temptations of a more cosmopolitan private life?

To Jackie Follis, a senior political science major, society's emphasis on short-term rewards robs youth of the incentive to take a longer view.

What incentive is there for a young man or woman to join the Peace Corps or participate in some other international character building experience? Those people cannot pay off their huge student loan debts, support their families, or build their resumes for the jobs their self-serving counterparts will grab right out of school. We are taught to take what we can now, and then later, when we get enough, we can sit back and ponder the universe. Our approach to the world and our lives needs to change now. We need to offer our children—through example—the values they will need to become strong leaders in a global community. What good is this "perspective" we gain from a strong liberal arts education if we don't practice what we preach? It cannot simply start with America's youth—they are enculturated; there must be a simultaneous shift in cultural norms.

Recognizing what needs to be done is not the same as doing it. Why should a young person today make a sacrifice to serve his or her community or country when other young people are intent upon taking advantage of the opportunities that the selfless pass by? Why should young people sacrifice at all when the country's leaders in Congress refuse to balance the nation's budget? How do they (and we) balance a concern for self with a commitment to community?

The students acknowledge the need for sacrifice and blame those who are now in charge for having been too unwilling to do so in the past. They respond when leaders such as Senator Boren and Ambassador Corr call for short-term sacrifice for long-term gain, but wonder why all of the sacrificing is being imposed upon their generation. Sophomore marketing major Ron A. Schaeffer indicts American culture generally for the live-now syndrome.

Society places the most emphasis on immediate gratification, causing us to choose environmentally dangerous but convenient disposable diapers, quarterly profits over long-term fiscal stability, and unhealthy fast food over well-balanced meals. It is the lack of long-term thinking which seems to be at the root of most problems facing our country today. The Japanese have captured much of our automobile, electronics, and video industries because they plan for the distant future while American companies have traditionally planned quarter by quarter. Toyota might have as a goal 30 percent market share by 2001, while General Motors is worried only whether its stockholders will be pleased with an upcoming dividend.

That which is characteristic of American business is also typical in American government.

A primary example of governmental shortsightedness is the legislature. Instead of engaging in productive debate, legislators too often simply criticize and cower. They are too concerned with protecting the immediate interests of the voters in their districts and thus their seats; they are unwilling to make small sacrifices for a better future. For example, nearly everyone agrees that the United States spends far too much on defense at the expense of social programs and that expenditures must be slashed—until it means closing a base in a congressman's hometown. Voters, a primary part of any democracy, grow to share the attitudes of their elected leaders. . . . More than just improving government operations and our national standing, long-term thinking by leaders in government would set a positive example for the people of the United States.

Letters major Camille Richter, a junior, shares Schaeffer's view of politicians.

The United States is an affluent nation, and most Americans want to have their cake and eat it, too. Therefore, one of the first challenges a leader faces is convincing his/her followers to sacrifice now in order to achieve a future goal. How to master this challenge is still an unanswered question; the first step, however, is having leaders that understand people and are motivational. This problem is especially difficult on the political scene, where a leader must risk losing popularity in order to implement effective solutions.

What are we to make of the fact that the politicians who participated in the symposium in government agree with the students about the nature of the problem, while the Washington political establishment of which they are members appears incapable of solving it? This problem is complex, and it is a mistake to attribute it primarily to political timidity, as some are inclined to do. The problem lies not within each politician but rather in the dynamic that occurs when they come together in pursuit of

their particular policy aims.[6] Admiral Crowe appreciates the
difficulty of the task facing public leaders in a democracy.

How can a leader get people to make short-term sacrifices in
order for long-term gains? The real answer to the question is that
I don't really know, particularly in a society such as ours. I think
you have to pick your issue carefully. You have to throw your
whole being behind it, your charisma, your reputation. You have
to lay out what you are trying to achieve, why it is important.
You've got to demonstrate that the long run outweighs the short-
term gain and you've got to press and use every persuasive skill
in your body. Then you may not be successful.

In a peaceful society that is acquisitive, materially oriented,
people are reluctant to make short-term sacrifices. They are not
sure why they have to do it. And certainly if you try and get them
to do this on a whole range of issues across the board, your
credibility is going to disappear and they are not going to do it.
So you've got to pick the issue carefully. It's got to be an important
issue and you've got to make sure that they understand that
you are committed to it, willing to risk your reputation or your
integrity, willing to risk defeat or reelection in order to try to get
a success on that particular issue. What makes it so hard is that
when you start you never know you will succeed. It's sort of like
winning an award, you never know whether you are going to
win. The only way you know is to fight and find out.

Leaders must, then, chose their issues and strategies carefully. They must understand the character of the American
people, and seek to take advantage of opportunities as they
come along. How should they appeal to the people they are
called upon to lead? Perhaps Tocqueville had the best answer
in his concept of self-interest, rightly understood, echoes of
which may be heard in this comment by senior journalism
major Laura M. Moxley:

Our society is a very hedonistic society. We are pleasure-
oriented people. I enjoy and want things that give pleasure

such as money, prestige, vacations, and the like. We can't blame ourselves for wanting what has been instilled in us from birth to want. It is, after all, what this great country was founded on, "life, liberty, and the pursuit of happiness." However, we're not going to be able to maintain this system if we don't take steps to protect it. We must focus on educating the masses, providing opportunities for everyone to receive better education, education that consists of knowledge on local, national, and perhaps even most importantly, international levels. Therefore, money should be poured into our education system, not taken from it and placed elsewhere. . . . This is a cultural problem that will take a long time to correct but the time to begin making changes is now.

There is little that one might call idealism in this statement, but perhaps unabashed hedonism may lead to the same result. Only by straightening out our cultural problems will we be able to sustain a level of productivity suited to our material desires. In the process, we will also regain the competitive edge in international trade, strengthen our educational institutions, and stand tall on the world stage. And what of the idealism that drives Congressman McCurdy's attitude toward the countries of Eastern Europe? Here principle and interest go hand in hand. As Congressman McCurdy himself put it in his speech to the Marshall Foundation: "Besides our moral interests in helping Eastern Europe get on its feet, though, we have an economic interest as well. We should see in Eastern Europe a huge, untapped market opened for American products, technologies, and investments."[7]

We may take some solace in the fact that neither Admiral Crowe nor Ambassador Corr rests his hopes entirely on the principle of self-interest. Each believes that the American public is capable of responding to an appeal to the collective good. According to Ambassador Corr,

We must appeal to people on the basis of a higher good that transcends our short-term gratification. In a sense, we have to inspire people on moral and historical grounds. I think it is also incumbent upon the person who's asking people to make those kinds of sacrifices to try to convince them that it will be worth it in the longer term for themselves and particularly for their children and future generations. . . . People give a lot of lip service to that until it comes down to whether I myself will make that sacrifice or whether someone else will. We are all in favor of it until it gores our own ox; then it gets a little bit different.

Admiral Crowe found himself in full agreement, and cited two prominent examples, the space program and the war on drugs.

This country will do a remarkable turnaround once you succeed in selling this notion of public good. Of course one of the more graphic demonstrations of this in peacetime in your memory is the space program. It's incredible that the United States of America actually funded the necessary investment of not only monies but also material and people to put a man on the moon. Once the conversion was made, once the decision was credible to the American people, politicians could successfully implement it, and in retrospect the space program really amazes me. I wonder if we could carry out another one today.

The drug problem in my view is a graphic example of where we should take some near-term hits in order to solve a long problem. At this juncture, I don't see the willingness of our people to do that. It's a good case study. The leadership in every sector of your country is beginning to get behind doing something about the drug problem. We are beginning to see some changes, modest changes in attitudes. I don't think you've seen enough to really make the progress we want as yet. I am not terribly pessimistic that in the long run we won't make the decisions that are necessary to solve that problem. Of course, the American way is you let the problem degenerate until it is so horrendous that you can't live with it and then you go out and solve it.

Whether enlisted in the cause of national power or global mission, leadership has its own requisites. But what are they?

In his address to the students Admiral Crowe challenged them to "Lead, or get the hell out of the way for somebody else to do it." This Annapolis ethic reduces the qualities of leadership to very simple form but states an essential truth. Leadership requires in the first instance a willingness to lead, to take risks, to get out in front. As we have seen, these University of Oklahoma students regard themselves as leaders; they were selected on precisely this criterion. Admiral Crowe arrayed a number of qualities relevant to the task of leadership, but his larger message to these aspirants was that a capable leader can make a crucial difference in shaping events. From the drill instructor to the virtuoso, it is the exceptional person who takes advantage of the opportunities that circumstances afford.

Admiral Crowe is a man of action and his view of leadership is appealing to students who conceive themselves in that mold. When he spoke of the qualities required of a good leader, he began with the active person's best friend, good luck.

If you had your choice of any one particular trait, I think you should take first of all being lucky. There is nothing that beats being lucky. Unfortunately, you can't depend on that . . . we're talking about leadership in terms of a single issue maybe, or a single decision, but your effectiveness as a leader is built not on a single decision. A president, an executive, a labor leader, or a politician builds on conduct over a long period of time. He's got to be honest as much as he can; and when he has a problem, I agree strongly with the ambassador, he must lay it out and relate it to larger causes and explain what he is doing and why.

A leader has got to establish a record of success if he wants followers. Frankly, in a sort of Machiavellian way, a leader has got to pick issues to build up this reservoir of capital, issues on which he knows he can be successful, so that when a hard one comes along, people will follow, take his advice, take his word, and support him because of his record of success. In addition, I think consistency is terribly important, as is integrity. People in the long run do appreciate integrity even if they don't always agree with you or the decisions you make. If you are consistent, then you can prevail. Finally, people appreciate frankness and candor. Sometimes frankness may inspire the very opposition you are trying to avoid, but I think in the long run building a track record on being candid and straightforward will yield more pluses than concealing your objectives.

In the comments of Senator Boren and Congressman McCurdy, on the one hand, and Admiral Crowe and Ambassador Corr, on the other, we see exemplified two variations of American pragmatism. Each set addresses the question of leadership from a particular perspective. The two elected representatives exemplify what James MacGregor Burns, in his book *Leadership*, calls "transactional leadership."[8] Transactional leadership is the give and take among elected politicians as they seek compromise on difficult and divisive issues. They may have individual visions of the future and they certainly do have individual policy preferences, but in the end they must practice the political version of Donald Trump's "art of the deal." Senator Boren's Buy-American Plan, for example, may be an excellent idea; but several powerful members of the Congress oppose it. When Congressman McCurdy seeks an example of American leadership in the world, he cites the Marshall Plan. The Marshall Plan was, of course, named after a bureaucrat and was driven into law by President Truman. Admiral Crowe and Ambassador Corr are both career civil servants—Crowe in the military, Corr in the State Department. Their conception of leadership is essentially functional. The qualities they seek in leaders are those requisite to the command of troops at war, organized governmental units, and so forth. A member of Congress who possessed these qualities would be a good leader of his or her office, but would not necessarily fare as well in dealing with the voters. There, a certain ambiguity is sometimes required.

None of the four leaders stressed what seems most important to Burns. His book, which was required reading for the symposium participants, stresses the need for "transformative" leadership, the kind of leadership that is capable of reshaping a polity. Transformative leadership has about it a certain charismatic quality. It is typically demonstrated only by leaders of nations, in democracies, by elected political executives. Burns has always had a fascination with the American presidency, conceiving of it in terms of one of the great presidents about whom he wrote, Franklin Delano Roosevelt. The Rooseveltian model of the presidency shaped the perceptions of the postwar generation of presidential scholarship until about 1968, when many liberal scholars came to have doubts about the "imperial" presidencies of Johnson and Nixon. The student leaders were, like the scholars of the 1950s, taken with the notion of transformative leadership, but embraced it with a healthy caution. They understood that the transformation could be either good or bad depending upon the moral fabric of the leader.

Appropriate to her history major, senior Victoria Allred placed the problem of leadership in perspective.

Perhaps it would be useful to investigate what characteristics leaders possess, and what is required of a leader. Ambassador Edwin Corr, during the panel discussion, gave some characteristics that he had found to be helpful to leaders: definition of a leader's mission; empathy for followers; knowledge and intelligence; willingness to take risks; creativity; and persistence. Admiral William Crowe had a few ideas of his own about what is necessary for a successful leader: luck; honesty; goal-orientation; success; consistency; integrity; and frankness. However, these traits only define responsible leadership such as those found in democracies and constitutional monarchies. Neither man addressed the question of how individuals such as Hitler become world leaders and have a significant control over people and events. Burns attempts to explain how such people gain leadership although they might not be the most democratic or competent. His best explanation is that of charisma. To be an elected official requires some personal charm in order to attract voters, but the vital element in a totalitarian leader's race for power is his ability to manipulate the minds of the masses. Despite his mental instability and far-fetched ideas, Adolf Hitler was able to gain control of Germany, captivate the hearts and minds of most Germans, and lead a nation into world war. Adolf Hitler did follow some of Ambassador Corr and Admiral Crowe's advice; he did understand the needs of the German people, realizing their desire to regain their pride. He used the German economic depression, and the apparent success of certain Jews, to inflame racial hatred. Even his choice of scapegoat exploited an ages-old prejudice of Christians. His aggressive and forceful foreign policy regained Germanic honor, and that feat allowed him to continue on his destruction of an entire race. He was certainly a risk-taker, and his early successes in the Rhineland and in the Sudetenland gained the respect of his followers. Maybe Admiral Crowe and Ambassador Corr are right about both authoritarian as well as democratic leadership.

Senior letters major John A. Basinger saw clearly the relationship between charismatic leadership and the moral foundations in which it is set.

The relationship [between leader and mass] is another important aspect of leadership. It is related to, but different from the empathy and understanding of the follower society—in other words, the identity. The identity is a cultural and historical phenomenon, while the relationship between leader and followers deals with the dynamics of the mindset of the masses. It is a function of the degree to which the leader has succeeded in universalizing his or her vision in the society. The leader must realize the state of mind of the group in order to influence it further in embracing the utopia which has been created in the mind of the leader.

This utopia leads to a fifth property of leadership. The leader's vision of utopia must not only recognize the base needs of the society such as abundance of food and material wealth, but also address higher needs. This was described by Burns as a morally uplifting quality, and in its ideal sense leadership would be on a higher moral plane. However, the use of higher needs has too frequently been perverted for the causes of leaders. Hitler not only restored employment in Germany during his rise to power, he also gave the German people a renewed sense of pride and group solidarity and belonging. He moved up Maslow's hierarchy of needs, but certainly not in a manner frequently described as morally uplifting. To use these characteristics of leadership in a positive manner is the challenge we face today.

Sophomore Elizabeth A. Calvey connected this dilemma to the American problem of short-range vision. Leading the public to make short-term sacrifices for long-term gain is, for Calvey, a moral problem, since the public's penchant for quick satisfaction is a reflection of its declining moral values.

An effective leader. What does this mean? To define this we must first define leadership. In his book, *Leadership*, James Mac-Gregor Burns explained leadership as . . . "the capacity to transcend the claims of the multiplicity of everyday wants and needs and expectations, to respond to the higher levels of moral development, and to relate leadership behavior—its role, choices, style commitments—to a set of reasoned, relatively explicit conscious values."[9]

To put it more simply, leadership is the ability to direct people physically and morally to higher levels, to achieve something in a positive manner. . . . In describing what a leader should be, Admiral Crowe stated that a leader is someone willing to put off the immediate gains and make sacrifices for a higher goal tomorrow. A leader must be able to look forward and make sacrifices knowing that in the long run success will be achieved. Being a leader is not always a popular role. This is one area where persistence plays a vital part of leadership. A leader knows that he/she will be unpopular for a while but in the end if he or she sticks to it the goal of success will be eventually achieved.

Listening to our guest speakers I got the sense that our value system in America and Oklahoma is no longer an ideal state. That is, compared to what other countries value, we as Americans and Oklahomans are slipping into mediocrity. We are no longer on top of the world. . . . Our panelists were concerned because most Americans will no longer sacrifice the short-term for more favorable long-term results. We are captivated and motivated with the prospect of earning the "quick buck."

The speakers suggested that a way to alleviate this problem of preoccupation with dollars is to show people that a higher good is possible if we just sacrifice a little. I feel that if we can realign people's values we can achieve this high good. People need to realize that a small sacrifice now will make for a better tomorrow.

An adjustment in values is needed, but how will it be accomplished? Cori M. Hook is a senior language arts major, and she traced the problem's solution to the place where all paths seem to lead, education.

In the last decade of the twentieth century, a new shortage has emerged. No, it is not an energy or labor crisis but a leadership crisis. The United States is currently facing some of the most complicated and pressing problems in its history—problems that are threatening to its citizens, natural resources, environment, and economy—yet, the number of people willing and capable of leading the country through these dilemmas is perilously low.

The main reason for the falling production of leaders is that it has remained an aspect of the American culture that has gone undefined and unnoticed. Historically, leadership has been taken for granted in this country. In times of distress and emergency someone has always risen out of the pack to help the nation regain stability. We, the citizens of this country, have accepted and heralded our leaders as heroes without giving very much thought to the circumstances and influences that allow such people to ascend to greatness. With the recent boom of the "talk show" mentality and the trend towards probing and prying into our public officials' private lives, not to mention the disappointing failures of some of our most prominent leaders, Americans have become distrustful and skeptical of their leadership . . . but we have still failed to correctly pinpoint the source of our problems. J. Irwin Miller hits the nail on the head:

"We talk more about the decline of America than ever before in our history. We are discouraged about our capacity to deal with the great new forces of our time. We ask: Is someone doing something to us? Is it the Russians, the Japanese, the West Germans? Are there new circumstances that are beyond human control? It is clear to me that none of these is to blame. We are doing it to ourselves."[10]

"We are doing it to ourselves" is exactly right. No supernatural force or foreign country is to blame for our lagging leadership. We, as citizens of the United States, are responsible. American culture condones greed and emphasizes wealth as the ultimate symbol of success. We set money and prestige up as goals to attain and fail to promote happiness and charity as the ultimate ends for which to strive. We totally disregard ethics and morals and too often use the bottom line on a financial statement as the only consideration in the decision-making process. We produce leaders who choose to lead for their own benefit rather than for the common welfare. We erroneously accept the notion that leaders are limited to government officials and fail to recognize the leadership qualities of other innovative and dedicated citizens.

What we as Americans need to do in order to produce more and better leaders is to undergo a radical moral reform and consciousness-raising era. . . . But how can we accomplish this?

The most feasible way is through education. We need to start including ethics courses in school curriculums as early as grade school to foster and promote the moral development of people. We can no longer rely on the church to fulfill this need. Leadership symposiums similar to the one at Oklahoma University need to be held on a regular basis to demonstrate the significant, immediate, and continual demand for good leaders. . . . It is imperative that we educate people on the qualities and duties of a good leader by any means possible such as courses, seminars, movies, newspaper articles, and media blitzes.

The role that a broad, liberal arts education plays in the development of leadership should also be stressed. . . . Because of the technology boom and the influx of vast amounts of information, specialization in education has become the trend, but educators, politicians, and students all need to realize the importance of receiving a well-rounded education.

Sociology, psychology, and political science courses need to focus on the relationships between a leader and a follower. Naturally, leaders need to understand and communicate effectively with the people that they intend to lead. A good leader possesses empathy for his/her followers and can look at issues from their point of view regardless of the leader's own personal ideas. A knowledge of the intricacies of the society in which they are a part is vital to leaders. John Gardner put it this way: "Leaders had better comprehend the values of our common culture, past and present, know how our political and economic systems work, and understand how and why science has changed our world."

The government symposium's morning discussion focused on the qualities of leaders and the challenges facing the nation. The afternoon session addressed leadership issues in state and local government, and voluntary associations. The future of Oklahoma was much on the minds of the participants. While there was a great affinity in the issues addressed during the morning and afternoon sessions, there was a decided difference in tone. The dialogue during the morning discussion had surrounded American preeminence in the world and the country's capacity to maintain it. The state of Oklahoma has, however, always reflected the soft underbelly of American confidence. More than perhaps any other state, Oklahoma is identified with the Great Depression and the dust bowl. The circumstances of its founding in territorial days have combined with the facts of its history to produce an inward doubt in the Oklahoma psyche about the state's prospects. Its reliance on oil, gas, beef, and agriculture, industries that have experienced wide swings from depression to prosperity within the memory of most living Oklahomans, has contributed to Oklahoma's peculiar attitude. Leadership in Oklahoma, then, has meant convincing Oklahomans that they have a future for which to fight. The present generation of leaders faces a more difficult task than their depression-era predecessors. In those bleak days the circumstances themselves represented a call to civic duty. Now, amidst relative plenty, leaders must persuade citizens that the state's future welfare depends upon present sacrifice. This same principle is enunciated by national leaders, but in a rather different and more parochial context.

Panelists Robert H. Henry (former Oklahoma attorney general), Virginia Austin (businesswoman and civic leader), Jenkin Lloyd Jones (editor of the *Tulsa Tribune*), Roger A. Randle (mayor of Tulsa), and Timothy D. Leonard (U.S. attorney for the Western District of Oklahoma) outlined the challenges facing the state.

Robert Henry: The first major challenge facing both America and Oklahoma is the crisis in the lack of enlightened leadership, of leadership with courage. I'm the reason that *Profiles in Courage* was on your reading list. You see in that book some enlightened, educated leaders who took a course of action that was going to almost certainly mean political doom for them. I recently heard Senator Daschle from South Dakota comment on the president of Czechoslovakia, who was attending Washington and talked about how much this book had meant to him. So there is a crisis of enlightened leadership, particularly in Oklahoma where we are at the crossroads of whether we are going to become a modern member state of the federation known as the United States of America or whether we are going to become a Third World country like Guatemala.

The second crisis is the collapse of the American infrastructure, particularly education. We are all rejoicing and pounding ourselves on the chest these days that Eastern Europe is finally reading Jefferson, and it strikes me that maybe we ought to start reading Jefferson ourselves. In many senses their educational infrastructure is better than ours. My friend George Singer, who is one of my modern heroes for his efforts with Task Force 2000 and House Bill 1017, just returned from Saudi Arabia where they are building a university campus for four billion dollars. We can't seem to agree on a couple hundred million dollars here.

The third crisis is the environment—global warming, ocean pollution, toxic hazardous waste, and atomic waste. Atomic wastes take many thousands of years, as you know, to decay and correct themselves. In Oklahoma we battle to preserve our scenic rivers, our hunting, fishing and recreation lands, and endangered species. We are trying to turn the clock back on some very damaging pollution to what was at one time a very, very beautiful state. In Oklahoma we lag behind on most of these social causes, but it is almost all right to be for the environment now, and we will rely on you folks to carry that leadership forward. As Dr. Lewis Thomas points out in *The Lives of a Cell*, all we have to kill are the little one-celled green organisms in the ocean and then we shut off the oxygen. And so I leave you with these three issues: the crisis of enlightened leadership; the collapse of the American infrastructure, particularly education; and the environment.

Virginia Austin: I think it is really important when we talk about leadership, especially in a room that is half full of women who are going to enter the career market and also parent tomorrow's children, to really recognize that there are role models for women as leaders and we should be celebrating those too. I would mention women like Benazir Bhuto, Margaret Thatcher, Corazon Aquino; American women like Eleanor Roosevelt, Marion Wright Edelman, Helen Keller; and (in our own state) women like Hannah Atkins, your regent Sarah Hogan, and Mary Frates, who made the opening remarks last night.

I come to you as a volunteer who has had a twenty-plus-year career in the public arena always as a volunteer. I have learned that citizens can assume leadership roles and advocate and move issues into the public arena and on the public agenda in a very powerful and forceful way if they take the time to understand those issues. Most of you in this room aspire to leadership of some sort. I think it is extraordinary that so many of you want to seek public office. We have certainly seen some outstanding role models of leaders in the national/international scene as well as on the state and local level here today. But the vast majority of you, in all candor, will probably end up as private citizens, and I think it's very important that you remember that we need leaders at every level of government, not just leaders who head the military, our Congress, our nation, our state, or cities. We need citizens involved at every level.

With that in mind, I would like to speak about an overarching challenge that I see for the 1990s, and that is the survival of the American family in any recognizable facsimile of what we know today. Beyond that, the very well-being of the children of America is on the line. You in this room are going to have careers and you are going to parent children. I am raising this issue not, as you might expect, because I am a woman, but rather in spite of it, because I feel the challenge to the American family is not a gender-specific issue. Because government increasingly is involved in these issues, the challenge to you as citizens in the next decade will be to successfully manage the interface between governmental regulation, legislation, business obligation, and volunteer initiatives in the social welfare issues affecting families—your families and those of the children of the growing underclass of poor. The family as we know it will either flourish or not depending on how these issues are addressed.

Consider these facts. Today about 74 percent of men work but 79 percent of women with no children under eighteen work as well. So do 67 percent of women with children. That's almost as high a percentage as men already. One-half of all women with young children work. According to the new popular book *Megatrends 2000*, this next decade is going to be the decade of women in leadership and, now I am quoting from the book, "as workers, professionals, and entrepreneurs, women already dominate the information society. . . . 30 percent of small businesses are owned by women" (Naisbitt, 217, 226).

Now what does this really mean? It means that issues like day care and parental leave are of increasing importance. Thirteen states already have mandatory parental leave. Issues like flex-time employment increasingly will be a part of the public dialogue. So will issues of drug prevention and adolescent pregnancy prevention, not to mention child abuse and domestic violence. All this week the *New York Times* has featured a series of articles discussing care for the elderly. What will be the quality of all this care? With an increasing number of two-wage-earner families with elderly parents and children, how will these responsibilities be divided between public employer and private citizen? Beyond these, there lies an even more complex set of problems. We've talked a lot about education, but in the most comprehensive picture of education we face the fact that many children tòday face significant issues related to poverty.

Consider the following: 20 percent of all children in the United States live in households with an income below the poverty line. Nearly half of all black children under the age of six live in poverty and 40 percent of Hispanic children do so as well. In addition, large numbers of children come from broken homes, single-parent families, and a full 50 percent of the children born out of wedlock are born to teenage mothers. When you think of these families, more often than not headed by single women, think of the issues I just mentioned and add to them issues like welfare reform and workfare, homelessness, day care for homeless families, and Head Start.

We have to ask ourselves, What is government's legitimate responsibility here? What is government's legitimate responsibility for those people who can't help themselves? What is our responsibility as citizens and how can we manage the interface of government, private business, and the voluntary sector in the decade to come?

Jenkin Lloyd Jones: I want to congratulate the audience because they haven't contributed to the "brain drain" of Oklahoma. Some of you may have enrolled in OU because you couldn't get into Harvard or MIT or Stanford. Some of you may have enrolled because it is cheaper to go to OU. But I like to think that most of you decided to go to OU because you thought it would contribute to the polishing of your lives, which is what a university is supposed to be. I am worried about the number of bright Oklahomans who leave, and I must confess that none of my children went to an Oklahoma school, but I am nevertheless worried about the fact that it is considered chic to go elsewhere for an education. Yet, when I see some of the gyrations in the state senate of Oklahoma, I can understand there is a rationale behind that.

After you have lived in Oklahoma for seventy years, you develop one great characteristic, and that is an almost total imperviousness to panic, because if there ever was a state that has had a lot of good reasons for panic, it's been Oklahoma. When I came down here from Wisconsin as a child in 1920, this was a state renowned for a low level of public education. Oklahoma was renowned for relatively low level of public health, and in the cities children died of what we called "summer complaints" all the time. There was no recreation. You had to travel for miles over flint roads to get to mud in Arkansas. We had none of the amenities that we now take for granted.

But I want to point out one thing. While life in many American cities and in some American states is less salubrious than it was in 1920, almost everything in Oklahoma is better. If you think about this a minute, you realize that we haven't failed but rather that we must have some genius. We have some reason for self-congratulations. Ever since John Steinbeck wrote the book *The Grapes of Wrath*, we have been haunted by the Okie image. But it isn't so much what they thought of Okies in California, it's what Okies think of Okies in Oklahoma that is very, very important. And there has been a tendency to consider ourselves "second-class," which I think is undeserved.

One night at a banquet in New York I sat at a table with John Steinbeck. Naturally, we got to talking about Oklahoma. He said, "You know, I ought to write a sequel to *Grapes of Wrath* because the fascinating thing is that in these smaller California towns, the chief of police, the head of the fire department, the school board, and the city council are, more often than not, Oklahomans." They got dusted out in 1934, 1935. They were ruined. They started on a low base but when they got to where the rains were falling again, they flowered just like drought-stricken flowers will bloom again. I wish we would get over this *Grapes of Wrath* complex.

I am worried about the fact that, like practically all rural states,

our small towns have dried up. I am talking about the sucking
out of the lifeblood of the small town, first, because of the trend
to move into the metropolitan areas, and second, because of the
trend to move out of the state. Granted, the city has amenities
that the small town can't offer, but the exodus is largely because
of our self-image. Until we quit thinking about ourselves as a
drying up state, we are going to do things politically that are self-
defeating.

I think Oklahomans are great people. We have a high percentage of what I like to think of as America-loving people. If we can
ever tell ourselves that we are not a colony of Texas and we have
our uniqueness, then we'll have a future. We can't do it if the
gap between urban Oklahoma and rural Oklahoma continues to
widen. Rural Oklahoma maintains much of its political influence
but has lost most of its bright people.

I think the future looks great. We are the last southwestern
state that has a surplus of surface water. Regardless of what
happens to our punched out oil fields, this gives us a great
advantage. I think we have potential in almost every respect, but
if you don't believe in yourself you are not going to behave with
greatness. I hope you will help reverse this attitude.

Roger Randall: From the time when I grew up, in contrast with
the kinds of experiences that most of the students in this room
have had, the world has changed a lot. I grew up at time when
the United States was the unequaled leader in the world, the
unquestioned leader in the world. We were morally dominant in
what we stood for compared to what anybody else in the world
stood for. Certainly that is a more debatable proposition now.
We were militarily dominant, unquestioned in our dominance.
Today with the changes that we are seeing in the world, military
superiority may become very different in its definition and in its
significance.

We were economically dominant and we were the envy of all
the world. The balance of payments surplus that we enjoyed was
a problem because of its continuing size. What we were able to
achieve in the United States economically for working-class people was the envy of the world because someone who built a car
in the United States and worked all day in the factory line could

go home to a quality of living that would have been equally traded for by many, many people in the world whose position in life was higher. Today there are fewer and fewer areas in which we lead in world economic activities and our standing in the world has declined. I was brought up when we were repeatedly told that we have the highest standard of living in the world in America. We, of course, do not today have the highest standard of living in the world.

A natural question for you to ask is what difference does it make whether we are economically prosperous or not? We should not evaluate our lives by the material standards by which we live. If our standard of living falls as a consequence of not continuing to be competitive in the world market, our economic ability to pursue environmental quality programs will decline. If you haven't got the dollars to put into clean air and clean water and quality environment, then you don't do it. The most polluted countries in the world, of course, are the poorest countries; the two go together. If we do not keep our competitiveness, we will no longer have the dollars to provide for cultural advancement. We will no longer have the dollars to provide for educational quality; our education standards will weaken. Our country usually lags behind much of Western Europe. The social caring level in this country will not reach to higher standards if we do not have the dollars to provide for higher standards. These are all consequences of our competitiveness and the profitability of American companies. In Tulsa, Oklahoma, today the companies that are doing well (and we have lots of companies doing well) are competitors in the national and international economy. The companies doing less well are those who are competitive with other companies in the local Tulsa market. Those companies that do well are those who participate in the broader economy.

So, what can you do to help us become more international? First, as citizens you can help us as a state and as a country to set being international as a public policy goal. You can participate by your own career choices. What is the career that you are contemplating contributing to the success of the United States of America and to the success of Oklahoma? What are you doing individually to be comfortable in your mastery of foreign language? How many students here can carry on a minimal conversation in a foreign language?

It is very difficult, when you are located so distant from foreign cultures as we are in Oklahoma, to become conversant in a foreign language. We have few opportunities to talk to anyone in the foreign language which we are seeking to master except for other students of that language or a professor or a tape recorder in the language lab.

We all recognize that one of the easiest ways to learn a language is to be immersed in that language. I throw out to the university a thought: schools in Oklahoma might try to create a place on campus that allows for immersion—a location where you have television with entertainment tapes and news tapes in the language; newspapers, books in the language; where people talk the language; where you could eat meals and be with people in the cafeteria who speak that language; and where no one in that immersion room was allowed to speak anything other than the language. That would be interesting to try. Being adept at a foreign language, being comfortable with foreign cultures, being up on foreign affairs as we relate to foreign countries—those are examples of the kinds of things that you can do.

One of the great heritages that we have in Oklahoma is a kind of frontier entrepreneurial heritage. When we became a state, we had the largest population of any state outside of the original thirteen to join the union. It is not only significant that we were a large state in population at the time that we joined the union, but also that our population had been amassed in a very, very short period of time. We had in Oklahoma a great diversity of people who settled and came here from the North, the South, and all over. All kinds of people came to Oklahoma, so we were a very cosmopolitan state.

This is partly the reason why so many Oklahomans have succeeded in the international field, Admiral Crowe being an example. I think that success in the international area is a by-product of having grown up in a community of such diversity. We learned that people of other cultures were people with whom we could easily deal. We were accustomed as a people to dealing with diversity and not put off or intimidated or made to feel uncomfortable in dealing with diversity.

If America is going to succeed, we have got to be successful internationally. For America to be successful internationally, it has to be an international competitor. You have a heritage in Oklahoma that I think facilitates your ability to do that. What you have to have is a recognition that this is important to you. You have to have the self-confidence in your life that you can be a contributor to our successful competition in the world economy.

Tim Leonard: First and foremost on a national and international scale is the question of how we as a country and we as citizens react to the dramatic changes that have happened on our globe this past year. How we react in the next few years could have lasting effects. Certainly this is the most dramatic year in my lifetime, and there are few years in this past century which have changed the face of the world all in one period of time like this past year. Our actions as a country will have consequences for each of you through most of your lifetime.

Second, I'm also concerned about the environment. It is really easy to blame past generations for the environmental problems that we have. My generation and the generation before mine did what they thought was the right thing. They tried to protect the environment, and many significant gains were made, particularly in the areas of agriculture, preserving the soil, and preventing wind erosion, which caused the dust bowl and led many Oklahomans to leave the state. We've made some dramatic changes and we have a new awareness. But I think we as a state have to make some decisions. Some of them are major decisions, but many of them are small decisions. One of the problems with our environment is the convenience of disposing of our waste products, whether they be hazardous waste or our household papers and other recyclable things. It is very convenient just to throw it all out. As a nation and particularly in Oklahoma, we are going to have to forgo that convenience in the future, not just your generation but your children's generation. We're going to have to make some tough decisions. We're going to have to weigh the advantages of bringing in business and industry to this state, which may create jobs in the short period of time and be a boon to our economy, but in the long run may not be industries that are kind and gentle to the environment. Our children and your children may pay a price.

The third area of tough decisions is education. In addition to the many problems already mentioned, I am concerned that we have asked the schools to do a whole lot more than just educate children. We have asked them to teach things that children probably should learn at home. We as parents should be teaching our children values and responsibility. We as parents should be spending the time, and believe me it takes time, to guide our children towards more responsible lives. It is going to be harder and harder for your generation if both parents are in the work force.

The fourth and last issue that I want to address is one that I have become particularly aware of in my new job as United States attorney. That is the issue of drugs. Law enforcement is not going to win the war on drugs. The war on drugs is going to be won by the youth of America, their parents, and in the schools of America with a realization of the tremendous damage and harm that drugs are doing to this country. If the war on drugs were won today, the impact of drugs on this country and to your generation would still be immense. Already the hundred thousand babies who have been born to crack-addicted mothers have cost our medical and social welfare systems over five billion dollars, and that is just the beginning, because those crack-addicted babies are going to have mental and physical disorders and antisocial behavior for the rest of their lives. I've heard much about the legalization of drugs. This is probably the craziest argument that I've heard. Whereas in alcohol abuse only about 10 percent of alcohol users become addicted, we already know that over 75 percent of people who try crack cocaine become addicted to it. The reaction is much more violent. We would not eliminate the criminal problem if we legalized drugs, but we would focus even more on the numbers of violent crime which are the result of drug use. That is an issue with which all of us are going to have to continue to deal.

In the area of leadership I would like to mention several things. First, you do not have to hold political office to be a leader.

Generally I have found, and I think Rodger Randle and Robert Henry and those of us who have served in various elective positions would agree, that most people in political office are followers. They react to the problems; they react to the leadership of communities, of special groups, and other organizations of citizens who are involved and who want something done. The person in the elective office usually reacts to problems rather than leads. It is important for the elected officials and those of you who strive to be in elective office to be leaders.

It also is important in leadership, whether elective office or not, to be able to disagree without being disagreeable. Rodger Randle served as the [president] pro tem of the senate for two years. I was the Republican or the minority leader of the senate. We had been friends before, but it had been traditional that the minority leader and the pro tem of the senate usually got engaged in very fierce battles both on the floor and off the floor. An interesting thing happened: we became very good friends in those two positions. We had our disagreements, but we did it as much as possible in an honorable way. We tried for the most part to work on those things that we could agree on. That is what is really important—to work on the positive and not accentuate the negative.

In leadership, whether it is in or outside of politics, I always look more at someone's actions than at his rhetoric. I always watch to see if someone is as nice to the receptionist as he is to the CEO that he has an appointment with. Leadership and true movement occur because the masses are involved, not because the CEOs, or elites, or some other organization is involved. It is the masses that want change. Some of the greatest leaders in the world have arisen from the masses because they heard, they listened. So if you aspire to be leaders, whether in politics or not, always remember to listen and always remember to be attentive to those who you may feel are not at your level, perhaps even more so than to those who you are striving to please or gain support from. It will pay off a lot of dividends.

Finally, I want to comment on the question that Dr. Peters asked about how many of you are leaving Oklahoma. One quick story: I was raised in the large cultural center of Beaver, Okla-

homa, in the Panhandle. I left Beaver to come to Norman and the
University of Oklahoma. When I saw Beaver in my rearview
mirror, I can remember thinking, "Boy, that's the last time I'm
going to have to live in this place." I spent seven years in Norman,
and when I left Norman in the mid-sixties, I was ready to leave
Oklahoma and see the world. Well, I had an obligation to the
United States Navy and spent three years in New England and
Washington, D.C. I thought that the nation's capital was where
I wanted to be. It was in the center of the world that I had an
interest in, the world of politics and government. I met my wife
there and got married there. About a year after I'd been married,
I walked by an inner-city school, and I saw this little school with
an asphalt playground; it just kind of triggered a whole thought
process of my roots. I remembered the fresh air and the playground at my little grade school. I thought, "I don't want my
children having to play in a fenced-in asphalt playground." I
came home and told my wife Nancy, "We're going to move back
to Oklahoma, if you agree." Well, Nancy was from Illinois and
she had visited Oklahoma, but she was used to trees, water, and
things like that. Of course, I'm from the western part of the state,
where there aren't many trees. And so we came back to Oklahoma
and I went to work in the attorney general's office in Oklahoma
City. We spent a couple of years there, and our first child was
born in Oklahoma City. Then all at once this old tug came back.
I thought I wanted to raise my children in a small town, and the
first thing I knew I was coming back to Beaver, Oklahoma. We
had three children there, and here's the irony. We had been out
there about two years and my daughter was getting ready to start
first grade, and you will never guess what the school board in
Beaver, Oklahoma, decided to do. If you now go by the grade
school in Beaver, Oklahoma, you will see that the playground is
asphalt.

I think it is important to go out and see different parts of the
world, different parts of this country. Then perhaps you will
come to the realization that I came to, having traveled all over
this country: Oklahoma is a very special place. You will find
people in California who may still consider themselves Oklahomans when they get together. I find people all over the world in

all kinds of important positions who are still Oklahomans. There is a special independence and a uniqueness about the people in Oklahoma. I see us having a very bright future. We do have to overcome some hurdles.

I hope that each of you will carry with you a positive attitude. The biggest hurdle that we have in this state is the negative attitudes that probably originated with the dust bowl. We can be proud of the accomplishments we've made. We've come a long way in this state through the fierce independence that we have. I think another danger is the negative attitude that we have toward public officials. Most of the people who I met at the state capital and in Washington, D.C., are well-meaning, hard-working, good people. We may disagree with them, we may want to get our own ideas and those of our friends presented, and sometimes we will be frustrated. . . . But I think we need to have a positive attitude about our state. The continual tearing down of our state and our public officials creates a real disrespect for our form of government. We have an excellent form of government. It is burdensome, it is cumbersome, and it is frustrating. But it is a good system, and most of the people out there are very dedicated public servants.

The issues addressed by the panelists run the gamut from the family to the environment, but there is a common sublimi-nal theme: they all care deeply about Oklahoma. Unlike the panelists in the morning discussion, whose orientation is shaped by national and global experience, these Oklahoma leaders view the rest of the world with Oklahoma eyes. They are not concerned about the family; they are concerned about Oklahoma families. They are not concerned about the environment; they are concerned about Oklahoma's environment. Their concern is with their state and its people. And they are worried. They are worried about the problems facing the state, and perhaps more important, about the more severe problem that is posed when young Oklahomans choose to make their lives elsewhere.

Persons who migrate to Oklahoma today cannot but be

struck by what can only be characterized as the state's self-prepossession. The *Daily Oklahoman's* brand of political conservatism reflects a kind of nativism. Very often when the paper rails against the government it poses the issue as the people on the one side and the state on the other. Its editorial cartoonist's main protagonist is a homey-looking character representing John Q. Public who is alternately bemused and befuddled by the latest actions of the government. His reactions to the government range rather narrowly from skepticism to incredulity. The *Oklahoman's* usual political opponents are the "liberal" Democrats who control the legislature. Not all of the Democrats are liberal, but both liberal and conservative Democrats typically espouse populist themes. The Democrats have always been for the "little guy" who is somehow different from the *Oklahoman* cartoon character. On all sides, one hears that Oklahomans are a great people whose problems are caused by political or economic elites who are leading the state astray. The enemy is either big government or big business, depending upon one's perspective. In virtually the same breath, both sides claim that the state's problem lies in a low self-image. Jenkin Lloyd Jones states eloquently the dilemma of a state mired in a dust-bowl image that has penetrated the inner recesses of its consciousness. This self-image causes the "brain drain" of successive generations to the greener pastures of the bicoastal economy. Tim Leonard appeals to the students to value their cultural roots and the state that nurtures them.

It seems possible that the two Oklahoma self-images are directly related to each other. A state that was crushed by the privation of the Great Depression and dwarfed in national image by its neighbor to the south had no other solace than to tell itself that it was great. "Oklahoma is OK" is the motto of a state in which many citizens apparently feel that all is not ok. It also seems possible that the entire question of Oklahoma's self-image is largely irrelevant to the students of the next generation, very few of whom say they plan to be living in Oklahoma in five years. When asked what might keep them here, they respond in unison: economic opportunity. Senior political science and economics major Kimberly Clinton's response was typical.

Within our group we discussed reasons why the majority of the symposia participants planned to leave the state. These reasons included: a lack of economic opportunities, poor economic environment, lack of cultural events, and a lack of emphasis, by the state, on education. The members of the panel seemed to realize that these are real problems facing our state. However, few real solutions were offered to encourage us, the future leaders of the United States and the state, to stay in Oklahoma. After evaluating my experiences with the panel, I would argue that a great deal more must be done to ensure that outstanding individuals, such as those participating in the Leadership Symposia, stay in or at least come back to the state. Some ideas that were developed by our group to encourage this include: increase funding for both secondary and higher education, increase funding for and support of events such as Ballet Oklahoma and the Oklahoma Symphony, and improve the economic incentives which encourage business and industry to come to the state.

Law student Tomme Jeanne Fent also connected the problem of low self-esteem to education.

Jenkin Lloyd Jones gave the need for self-esteem a local emphasis when he asserted that until Oklahomans change our image of ourselves, we will continue to do things that are politically and socially self-defeating. Jones urged, "If you don't believe in yourself, you are not going to behave with greatness." As a state, our lack of belief in ourselves is manifested most greatly in our youth. Our defeatist attitude and low self-image surfaces every time a child drops out of school, or "graduates" from high school without knowing how to read or without knowing enough math to balance a checkbook. It shows its head every time an adolescent picks up a cigarette or other harmful drug. It is embodied in every teenager who is forced into early adulthood by an unexpected pregnancy.

Each of these problems is a result of an entire society with low self-esteem. Each of these problems is magnified and multiplied many times over throughout the remaining forty-nine states in this country. It is no coincidence that the staggering growth of these and other problems decimating the ranks of tomorrow's leaders is concurrent with a disturbing decline in public support and enthusiasm for education. A challenge for tomorrow's leaders will be to regenerate that support and enthusiasm.

Sophomore zoology major Kristin Ockershauser agreed.

A large part of Oklahoma's economic hardship is directly due to Oklahomans. The lack of pride in our state is reflected in our speech and attitude. Our poor educational system is largely to blame also. Several policies have been proposed to bring into Oklahoma large corporations, which would bring much-needed jobs and money into our economy. Yet the companies don't come due to our poor educational facilities. They are able to get comparable benefits and cuts in other states with a better educational system. This is causing us to remain in economic trouble. We must begin with education for we cannot regain power internationally until we become strong nationally.

There is simply no similarity between the Oklahoma from which these students plan to escape and that which drove a previous generation to California. Oklahoma is obviously a better place than it was during the dust bowl and offers its citizens a good environment, many leisure-time activities, major college sports, advanced forms of art, and many other aspects of the good life. Why, then, should anyone (much less 95 percent of these students) want to leave it? The students' aspirations outpace the opportunities that the state affords. Oklahomans of the dust bowl generation would look upon the Oklahoma of today as a paradise; the Oklahomans of the next generation want more. In part, the aspirations of these students reflect the natural desire of youth to conquer the world, or at least experience it. If they did not want to go someplace else at some time in their lives, something would be wrong with them. But when asked specifically about their plans and concerns, the students make it clear that their main motive is the pursuit of a life plan suitable to their material tastes. They want to have successful careers, they want to live a prosperous life, and they want to have new experiences. They figure that their opportunities are better elsewhere.

The relationship between Rodger Randle's emphasis upon internationalizing Oklahoma culture and the aspirations of these students is evident. Randle's remarks, which reflect the views of many panelists and speakers during the Centennial Symposia, reveal a significant difference in outlook compared to the Oklahomans of Jenkin Lloyd Jones's generation. The older generation has patience because it has perspective. The present generation of leaders is impatient because it believes that Oklahoma will fall behind unless it takes dramatic steps now to enter the stream of international commerce. It took the great public Big 10 universities almost two centuries to build the foundations of their greatness, but civic and educational leaders in Oklahoma want the state's universities to reach parity in the next decade.

These students are, in the end, the product of a new American culture that transcends the borders of Oklahoma. They have more in common with students in other states than they do with their parents' generation of Oklahomans. It is precisely because that their prospects will be determined elsewhere that they plan to leave the state. If 85 percent of Oklahoma students will be educated in Oklahoma, many of the brightest of these will seek careers outside the state. The state's goal must be less to retain them than to ensure that it attracts others to take their place. These are not mutually exclusive goals, and both can be met if the state offers opportunity and an attractive quality of life. The dilemma resides in the fact that making the state more attractive will require policy decisions that many in the state will not support. Jones's concern about the death of Oklahoma's small towns is based upon a harsh reality. Even if Oklahoma were able to hitch a ride on the international economic train, these communities would be left at the station. Why, then, should they and their elected representatives support public policies that have the ultimate consequence of ending their way of life? Many schools and small colleges that serve rural needs in Oklahoma would have to be closed or would be dramatically underfunded if the state were to channel sufficient resources into its major population centers and universities to make them nationally and internationally competitive. The only alternative way to pay for it would be by major tax increases. Robert Henry spoke eloquently to the need for political courage, and he is correct. To political courage, however, should be added the wisdom of Solomon and the patience of Job.

The Centennial Symposium in Government ended, therefore, where it had begun, with the problem of leadership. Robert Henry fears a lost generation of leaders in Oklahoma. He believes that

we have a crisis of leadership, but it only takes a few good leaders to pull us out of this. We need enlightened courageous leaders with liberal arts education, with a vision for the future and the courage to be able to say we need to do something controversial.

Tim Leonard connected the crisis of leadership to a parallel crisis of followership.

Our government is only as good as the people who are involved in the process and how enlightened those citizens are. I am most pessimistic about the number of people in this country who don't want to have anything to do with government. They don't want to be involved; they don't want to find out what the issues are and where candidates stand on issues. They are turned off by the entire process. That then leads to the election of people who would never be chosen by an enlightened electorate. If there is a lack of leadership, we as private citizens have to share that blame. We can't blame those who are in office, because after all those people are representatives and it is the citizens who put them in office.

Rodger Randle agreed with Tim Leonard that when citizens criticize their government they are really criticizing themselves.

When we look down our noses at who is representing us, we're really looking down our noses at the kind of job we have done ourselves as citizens. Because we, in our form of government, are responsible at the grass roots for how it functions. When we question the quality of who is in office, we're really calling into question the success of our own role as citizens because that is what people in office reflect. When the *Daily Oklahoman* runs down, as it does in unmerciful terms, people in public office, it is really admitting its poor job of contributing to the kind of educated citizenry that would produce the quality of people in public office who attract praise.

Virginia Austin is more optimistic than Leonard and Randle. She sees the problem of leadership from the point of view of a citizen who has chosen to become involved. She spoke of a group of private citizens who have sought to provide leadership for Oklahoma.

I am both hopeful and distressed. I spent a lot of time away from Oklahoma in the last ten years, but I was born in Oklahoma City and have lived there the majority of my life. At the end of the seventies and the beginning of the eighties, there was lots of talk in the community that our traditional leadership was very closed, that those leaders were aging, and that there wasn't anyone around to fill the gap. So we followed a model that was common in cities beyond Oklahoma and developed a program called Leadership Oklahoma City. Leadership Tulsa, I believe, had been thriving for years before that. From that effort has grown a statewide leadership program. I am really so pleased and proud of the numbers of young to middle-age men and women who are very interested in what is going on in the state and who are very committed to what is going on in their local communities. In fact alumni of Leadership Oklahoma City sit on the majority of boards of directors throughout the Oklahoma City community. So I think there are plenty of people available to fill those roles and plenty of citizens who really want to get involved.

Virginia Austin's optimism and Robert Henry's pessimism are two sides of the same coin. Their common currency is a belief that leadership will make the difference in Oklahoma's future, if only it can. Tim Leonard and Rodger Randle share the belief that leaders cannot lead until followers are prepared to do their part, both in choosing leaders and in facilitating their task. In downtown Oklahoma City one of the tallest buildings is called the Leadership Building. There is Leadership Oklahoma City, and before it, Leadership Tulsa. There are the University of Oklahoma Centennial Leadership Symposia. In Oklahoma, leadership is in the air. That air is, however, often fouled by political charge and countercharge. Political invective in Oklahoma is often *ad hominum*. Many of those who are most active in civic leadership are most mistrustful of their elected political leaders; many elected political leaders are mistrustful of the business community from which most civic leadership is derived. As the panelists in the Leadership Symposium in government made abundantly clear, the state faces difficult challenges, some of which it will face side by side with other states in the union, others of which it will face mostly alone. In facing these challenges it will require all of its human resources. One aspect of leadership lies in the capacity to find common ground. Oklahoma will be well served if its next generation of leaders can find it.

CHAPTER 3

THE MATTER OF CULTURE

IN 1784, A WHITE EUROPEAN MALE named Immanuel Kant wrote an essay called "Idea for a Universal History with Cosmopolitan Intent."[1] In it, he proposed that human history may be viewed as a progression of the species from barbarism to civilization occurring as an unintended consequence of the antagonisms of people and states. The vehicle of the human transformation was what Kant called culture, "the social value of man." Culture, in this sense, denoted civilized man's moral capacity, that which set him apart from beasts and barbarians. According to Kant,

All man's talents are gradually unfolded, taste is developed. Through continuous enlightenment the basis is laid for a frame of mind which, in the course of time, transforms the raw natural faculty of moral discrimination into definite practical principles. Thus a *pathologically* enforced coordination of society finally transforms it into a *moral* whole.

Prerequisite to the completion of human culture, thus defined, was the development of civil society, ultimately "a completely just civic constitution." This conception led Kant to speculate that "the history of mankind could be viewed on the whole as the realization of a hidden plan of nature in order to bring about an internally—and for this purpose also externally—perfect constitution; since this is the only state in which nature can develop all faculties of mankind." Such an interpretation of history would have to take the long view, he held, since "this revolution seems to require so much time that from the small distance which man has so far traversed one can judge only uncertainly the shape of the revolution's course and the relation of the parts to the whole."

Let there be no doubt about it: the history of which Kant speaks is that of *civilized* (i.e., for Kant, European) man. When Kant writes of "taste," "enlightenment," and "morality," he means the taste, enlightenment, and morality of higher European culture. When he writes of the "perfect constitution" embodying the idea of "right," he means the notion of right that the Western political tradition produced. Today Kant's philosophy would be regarded in some academic circles as an example of Eurocentrism, the belief that the Western tradition is the standard against which other traditions should be understood. Some who would find Kant's view Eurocentric believe that the culture that the Western tradition has produced in Europe, North America, and a few other places, is merely one culture among many; no better and perhaps worse. Often those who believe this favor "multiculturalism," a view that holds that all cultures are valuable; that Western culture is not better than other cultures, but simply different; and that there is decidedly no millennium in prospect in which Kant's Eurocentric civilization would or should become universalized. If one examines the manner in which the term *culture* typically is invoked today (for example, at various points in this chapter) one sees that the newer conception of culture has worked its way into the vernacular of most people. It has become a part of our culture.

What is most interesting is that the concept of culture that is invoked by some against Kant is one that he himself, or his contemporaries, seems to have invented. Etymologically, the word *culture* derives from *cultivation*, as in the cultivation of the soil. It also referred to animal husbandry and, among the

Greeks, to the development of the human body. It was not until the eighteenth century that the term was applied to human intellectual development or to society generally. Then the term referred specifically to the "training, development, and refinement of the mind, tastes, and manners."[2] Unquestionably, those who gave the term this connotation meant the mind, tastes, and manners of European man, and not those of aboriginal tribes, which, to them, would have seemed wholly lacking in culture. Guided by his understanding of culture, Kant argued that a specific kind of political regime was requisite to its completion. The highest form of human culture could only occur in a perfectly just society. By introducing the concept, however, Kant let the cat out of the bag. Little could he have anticipated that two centuries later the concept of culture would be used by those whose aim was to criticize the liberal regimes that he thought necessary to society's moral completion. Little could he have guessed that some modern thinkers would transpose the ordering of culture and regime, arguing that only by affirming the relativity of all cultures could a truly just regime be founded, and that a truly just regime would necessarily deny the primacy of any particular cultural values.

In 1990 another white male, of near-eastern ancestry, spoke to the Centennial Leadership Symposium on the Arts and Humanities. Vartan Gregorian is of Armenian heritage and was born in Iran. His scholarship has been devoted largely to the history, politics, and culture of the former Soviet Union and of that part of the world that was once the Ottoman Empire. His vitae reveals him to be an intellectual citizen of the world, having won honors and held appointments in places stretching from Palo Alto to Teheran. Yet in his administrative career he has had a special responsibility as a custodian of the Western tradition. He has led colleges of liberal arts at the University of Texas and at the University of Pennsylvania, where he also served as provost. He was for eight years the head of the New York Public Library, a repository of

Western culture. He now serves as president of one of America's elite private institutions, Brown University. This man, whose life and career spans East and West, chose to address the students of the University of Oklahoma about American culture. He explored the problems posed for the men and women who will lead America in the twenty-first century by the tendency of democratic culture toward a stifling uniformity. He emphasized the necessity of maintaining our ethical bearings in a world that encourages a concern with self and with a materially satisfying existence. Drawing his text from Alexis de Tocqueville's *Democracy in America*, a quintessential product of the Western tradition, Dr. Gregorian challenged the students to rethink their own fundamental commitments.

Modern Individualism

Vartan Gregorian

My friend and former colleague, the late Loren Eisley, responded to the wonders of the universe, to suffering, to loneliness, to the fear of death, but above all else, to human dignity and human spirit when he wrote in *The Immense Journey* that "looking across the centuries and the millennia toward the animal men of the past, one can see a faint light, like a patch of sunlight moving over the dark shadows of a forest floor. It shifts and widens, it waits out, it comes again, but it persists. It is the human spirit— the human soul, however transient, however faulty man claims it to be. In its coming man had no part; it merely came. That curious light and man, the animal, sought to be something that no other animal had been before. The light has followed us all the way from the age of the ice, from the dark borders of the ancient forest into which footprints vanish. It is in this that Kierkegaard glimpsed the eternal, the way of heart, the way of life, which is not of today, but is of the whole journey and may lead at last to the end."[3]

"Through this," Eisley thought, "the future may be conquered. Certainly it is true. For man may grow until he towers to the skies, but without this light, he is nothing, and his place is nothing. Even as we try to deny the light, we know that it has made us, and what we are without it remains meaningless."

The Centennial celebration of the University of Oklahoma provides us an opportunity to celebrate the human spirit, human dignity, human reason, human potentiality, knowledge, and learning, as well as to celebrate our community with mankind and to celebrate America. Our great universities are a manifestation of our belief that man's surest path to his or her fullest state of being lies in the enlightenment of the mind.

During the past three centuries colleges and universities in America, especially since the foundation of the land-grant colleges under the Morrill Act of 1862, have been the backbone of our nation's economic, cultural, scientific, technological, social, and political progress. Without American universities, the United States would never have achieved its current preeminence. The American university has been able to accommodate so many in so many ways, and educate so many as well as possible, for the nation's labor market, its managerial and professional force. It has democratized access to higher education and nationalized opportunity for the first time in our nation's history.

At the same time, it has provided for us a breeding ground for generation after generation of American leaders. It is a great accomplishment of American civilization to have taken this musty, medieval institution, so closely tied as it was to the class structure of the Old World, and transformed it into an instrument of democratic culture and governance. The European universities nurtured and were nurtured by aristocratic culture. They were not designed to produce leaders alone; they aimed to create a leadership class. The American university, in serving the broader public, fosters the ambition and skill demanded of leaders in a democratic society. At the same time, it shapes and is shaped by the unique culture of American democracy. That culture is strongly shaped by and committed to the principle of individualism, the belief that people should be left alone to "do their own thing." Thus, the American university plays the ironic role of preparing our leaders and fostering a sense of individualism that makes leadership in a democracy so difficult.

The special circumstances in which American culture has

shaped its leadership are best understood by considering another birthday, namely the 150th anniversary of Alexis de Tocqueville's *Democracy in America*, and through this to revisit the American individualism. In 1831 Alexis de Tocqueville, a young French aristocrat, came to the United States to obtain a view of the future. He published his findings in two volumes, one in 1835 and the other in 1840. Reading his classic work some 150 years later, we cannot fail but to be amazed at his foresight. *Democracy in America* has continued to command the attention and respect of scholars and students of history, political theory, political science, and sociology, and all those who write and study the strengths and limits of democracy in general and the American democracy in particular. Today, when political theorists are concerned about such issues as mass cultures, the realities and prospect of the tyranny of the majority, issues of authoritarianism and totalitarianism, Tocqueville is hailed for his sagacity and foresight. In discussing for a moment the nature of his insight into democratic government we may easily see why.

Tocqueville believed in a democracy built on the foundation of a republic and a republican political system based on small property holders. He believed in a democratic society in which there were political checks and balances, in which religion would provide a moral cohesion and moral checks and balances between equality and liberty, in which voluntary associations representing the diversity of popular opinion would play a unique role, and all of the above would provide a countervailing force against the dangers of the potential advent of the tyranny of the majority. He had, he tells us, "only one passion—the love of liberty and human dignity," and he sought to explain to the emerging modern world what would be required to preserve liberty and dignity. He warned us of the cultural consequences of social leveling, a reign of mediocrity that would undermine human potentialities and possibilities for greatness and excellence. He warned against the possibilities of democratic despotism and administrative centralization. However, he did not advocate law and order as ends in themselves. He wrote, "A nation that asks nothing of its government but the preservation of order is already enslaved in its heart," for force in the defense of privilege angered him even more than force against privilege.

In a society it was "not sufficient," he said, "to have good laws and good institutions." In this, he reminds me of St. Augustine's *City of God*, in which St. Augustine pointed out that Rome had law and order and was well run indeed, but what was the goal of Rome? *Quo vadis?* Where are you going? What are your aims?

Tocqueville believed that we should judge a society in terms of whether or not its laws, institutions, and mores fostered a free society. A product of the late-eighteenth-century and nineteenth-century European cultural and intellectual traditions, Tocqueville had philosophical affinity with Montesquieu even though he rejected what he perceived to be Montesquieu's advocacy of geographical determinism.

He was fascinated with Rousseau's social contract and his views on how a society may be virtuous and its citizens good and free; but he rejected Jean Jacques Rousseau's concept of the general will and the indivisibility of the concept of sovereignty because he feared it might contain in it the seeds of absolutism and totalitarianism. He rejected Condorcet's materialism and his uncritical belief in the inevitability of progress. He liked and respected John Stuart Mill, who formulated one of the first comprehensive concepts of liberty. Yet he took issue with him on the question of aristocracy, aristocratic autonomy, and the social and political role of religion.

Jean-Claude Lamberti, in his recent first-rate scholarly work, entitled *De Tocqueville and the Two Democracies*, characterizes Alexis de Tocqueville as the last great puristic embodiment of civic humanism.[4] He is right. Civic virtue has primacy in Tocqueville's political choices, for he was convinced that liberty would expand with civic virtue. He believed that the relentless quest for material wealth (the middle class's preoccupation with profit and private pleasures) was inimical to civic virtue and would erode, sooner or later, the civic spirit and citizens' active and direct participation in the public affairs and politics, which were so crucial for the health and welfare of a democratic society. A materialistic individualism would unleash civic apathy, he thought. It would undermine artistic creativity, cultural originality, and possibilities of national greatness.

Tocqueville saw in America a new phenomenon. He described it as "individualism," a term that he coined to describe the American character. "Individualism is a word," he said, "to express a new idea. Our fathers only knew about egoism, whereas what I would like to provide in describing the American character is individualism." During the same decade that de Tocqueville visited America, America was also visited by an Englishwoman, Harriet Martineau, who agreed with Tocqueville that Americans have great respect for men as individuals. She wrote, "The puerile and barbaric spirit of contempt is scarcely known in America. The English insolence of class to class, of individuals towards each other, is not even conceived of except in the one highly disgraceful instance of the treatment of people of color. Nothing in American civilization struck me so forcibly and so pleasurably as the invaluable respect to men paid by men to men."[5]

Tocqueville agreed: he, too, objected to American enslavement of African men and women and the conquest of Indians. Race relations in America inspired his most negative statements about America. He believed that slavery produced moral degradation in both the slave and the master. He was equally appalled by the character and the ferocity of racial animosity, not in the South alone, but in the North as well.

However, in *Democracy in America* Tocqueville predicted that modern social economic developments would, by necessity, promote the cause of equality among individuals. The legitimacy of power would be based on service to the people and the extent to which the government was free. Although he did not view America, or any state, as having completely actualized the principles of freedom and equality, he did believe that America approximated these ideals more closely than any other country. More than anywhere else, America provided for him the principles upon which a responsible democratic society may be constructed. He welcomed the presence of such stabilizing expedience in our democracy as local self-government, separation of church and state, a free press, indirect elections, and the unique and vital role of our many voluntary associations. The latter, he believed, were a bulwark against oppressive conformity; a means to protect individuals from subordination to impersonal administrative machinery; a vehicle for the expression and satisfaction of sectional needs, as well as a counterweight to state authority.

This and the checks and balances in our system of government, particularly in independent judiciary, were necessary safeguards for man's natural passion for freedom. The power vested in the American courts of justice of pronouncing a statute to be unconstitutional "forms one of the most powerful barriers," he said, "that has ever been advised and devised against the tyranny of political assemblies."

But Tocqueville had several worries. The number one worry was the balance between equality and freedom. He foresaw many fundamental problems and potential conflicts inherent in the fabric of democracies in general and the American democracy in particular. The question that preoccupied him most was the ability of democracies to maintain the delicate balance between freedom and equality. In democratic and modern egalitarian regimes he observed that there is a strong tendency toward centralized administration and concentration of power. These regimes, he feared, in the name of fostering equality, threatened to destroy individual independence, independent thought and action—in short, individual liberties.

Tocqueville was convinced that the ruling passion of democracy is equality. It tends, however, to overpower every other sentiment, even the concept of liberty. Liberty, therefore, requires constant effort and vigilance, for it is difficult to attain and is easily lost. "Its excesses are apparent to all," he wrote, "while its benefits may easily escape detection. The pleasures and advantages of equality on the other hand, are immediately felt and require no exertion. Democracy awakens in us," he wrote, "the kinds of anxieties and desires with which we cannot cope. The soul is excited, forever battered and hopelessly relentless, and in this relentlessness, the individual is pressured always to choose between equality and freedom." The quest for equality and peace of mind often pressures us to surrender our freedom, or as Erich Fromm would say later, "to escape from freedom."

The second worry that Tocqueville had about America was the

balance between individualism and community. He worried that American society, like any democratic society, tends to fragment, to atomize itself. Each individual becomes the center of a small and private world of one's own, preoccupied with one's family, one's self, one's friends and one's narrow community. As a consequence, the individual loses sight of one's community, one's society at large, and the greater universe. His focus and energies are directed towards improving his own personal lot, his own conditions of life, and the result is a combination of self-centered, dangerous, and divisive force in a democracy.

The third concern about Tocqueville was the balance between private interest and public interest. He points out that the tendency toward an exclusive and persistent preoccupation with personal well-being and material comforts inevitably diverts the attention and talents of individuals of superior intellect from politics to business and from public life to private life (private affairs). As a result men find other outlets for their talents and freedom, avoiding "conformity and vulgarity of political life." This phenomenon is potentially dangerous, for it downgrades the importance of public interest, downgrades the importance of public service, downgrades the importance of the community and politics, and worst of all, it downgrades political process and politics, which are so necessary for the running and governing of a democratic society. Unless checked and balanced, it can lead to the formation of the nucleus of new aristocracy, who will try to govern America. In a modern world, because of pacts, lobbying, and so forth, people of intellect and people of wealth will shy away from politics and thus downgrade politics as not worthy of their time. Of all the things that Tocqueville worried about, that is the one aspect of American politics and democracy that preoccupied him most. He feared that America would entrust its future to persons who were not worthy of leading the nation. The hoi polloi would dominate the American democratic regime.

Thus, Tocqueville's final great concern was with the propensity of democratic regimes to be dominated by the culture of the masses. He analyzed the delicate balance between individualism and conformism and underlined one of the central ambiguities of

American individualism, its paradoxical compatibility with conformism. According to him, typical of Americans is the notion that one must always rely on one's own judgment, rather than on authority, or tradition, in forming opinions. At the same time, in the absence of tradition or authority, one inevitably looks to others for confirmation of one's opinions. Refusing to accept established opinions and looking to one's peers for affirmation can turn out to be the two sides of the same coin. Of all the elements of conformity in America, he described "peer pressure, public pressure," as one of the most important elements. Under the guise of individualism, Americans sought conformity.

The apparent homogeneity and unity of a democratic society conceals two possible sources of heterogeneity, namely intellect and wealth. This intellectual capacity is distributed unequally—the majority often demands conformity. Nonconformity becomes imprudent. The tyranny of the majority over the minds of those who are its intellectual superiors poses a direct threat to a democracy and often leads to the advent of mediocrity.

The democratic predisposition toward conformity manifests itself, according to Tocqueville, even in the one area of our lives in which we might expect diversity to prevail—the arts. The consumptive concern for self, the self-interested concern for consumption—these are the primary passions of democratic man. The more cultivated among us aspire to artistic taste, but our taste typically exceeds our means of satisfying it. Consequently, in America, the culture of art sacrifices quality to quantity; art becomes more pervasive just as it becomes less artistic. Instead of seeking to capture the essence of the human spirit, artists in democratic societies tend to focus on that which serves the commercial markets best. Artists in democratic times, he says, "employ their talents in the exact delineation of everyday life . . . they copy trivial objects from every angle, though nature provides only too many examples."

If we cannot transcend the commercialization of life we may at least aspire to rise above the taste that it serves. The arts today stand shoulder to shoulder with the humanities in their potential to soften the sharp edges of our culture. But like the humanities, the arts must struggle against the same cultural predisposition toward conformity that threatens to rob us of our humanity just as it buries us in the mass graveyard of modern civilization.

Tocqueville's *Democracy in America* was both an analysis and prescription about the nature and the prospects of our democracy. It was his ardent belief and hope that the delicate balance between freedom, equality, and social order must be weighed by enlightened self-interest, public morality, patriotism and a variety of voluntary associations, long-term self-interest, and cultivation and growth of a spirit of compassion. He hoped, especially through education, to moderate, if not override, short-term gratification and excesses of materialism. He hoped individuals would recognize thus, as a result, that while the right to property is important, so is the protection of integrity, privacy, and independence of the individual. He hoped they would also recognize that the individual is not an economic being, but also a moral and political being.

Hence, he hoped that members of a democratic society will come to see the desirability of postponing the urge for immediate gratification of their desires in the expectations of more certain or greater degree of satisfaction at a later time. This, he expected, would enable individuals, through moderation and compassion, to reconcile their well-being with the common welfare of the people and recognize that what is right can be also useful and socially beneficial.

Now, what if Tocqueville were to come to America today? We have just celebrated the bicentennial of our Constitution. We are ready to celebrate, not only this great university's centennial, but the bicentennial of the Bill of Rights. Tocqueville would, I think, hail the durability and resilience of the extraordinary document whose two hundredth anniversary we celebrated. He would applaud America's continued pluralism and regionalism, its unity and diversity, the separation of church and state, the multiplicity and variety of its voluntary associations, such as teacher-parent associations, historical associations, local associations, preservation societies, and hundreds—thousands—of associations that he thought were peculiar in America and one of the best ways of bringing democratic spirit to America. He would also hail the freedom of the press and the strength of an independent judiciary.

At the same time he would note, with apprehension, in my opinion, the levels of concentration of power, the difficulties of holding together our pluralistic society, rampant materialism and the preoccupation with material goods, and special interests at the expense of our collective welfare. No doubt Tocqueville would also express anxiety over the disintegration of our shared values, lingering racism, extremes of poverty in the midst of ostentatious abundance, the ravages of the environment, the homelessness, the nuclear threat, the state of our public school system, the national disgrace of having twenty million Americans functionally illiterate, our ignorance about our heritage, history, and the world.

He would surely express disquietude over the corrosion of public and private ethics and civic morality, the decline of the quality of our citizenship, our care of the republic and the current manifestations of his concept of individualism as an American attribute, which he had hailed in 1835.

Though today we continue to speak of ourselves as "individualists," the reality of our life seems to have grown more collective and more anonymous. Modern individualism is facing the danger of becoming a mere slogan and abstract ideology divorced from reality. The decline of the traditional family unit, of social rituals and self-transcending ideals and ideologies combine to force the individual now to create his or her own meaning.

The tendency of modern individuals facing the dilemmas inherent in complex socioeconomic structures and mass culture is submission to conformity, a smooth absorption into the group, rather than taking on the arduous task of self-discovery and self-realization. More and more we seem to be impatient with, if not hostile towards, nonconformist individualism. Such individualism stands for maladjustment, for deviation from the norm, and for dissent from the group. It stands therefore, for conflict, for heresy and for heterodoxy. In short, it is deemed to be undesirable. We are, or we seem to be, obsessed with the notion of eliminating conflicts from positive thought.

"Peace of mind" has become our chief concern, and production of techniques to eliminate conflict a major industry. I am sure that Tocqueville would agree with Albert Einstein that the perfection of tools and the confusion of aims are characteristic of our times. Nowhere is this more apparent than in the *crise de concience* of corporate America during the last three years.

In 1987, the year that we celebrated the Constitution, books were being published about leading American businessmen such as Iacocca, Ueberroth, and Getty. These books had enticing titles such as *Leadership Difference, Passion for Excellence*, and *The Big Time*. They were promoted as handbooks for success, efficiency and corporate virtue. Typically they portrayed the corporate leader as teacher, mentor, exemplar, and forger of values and meaning.

Then suddenly a virtual tidal wave struck America, a wave of scandals—scandals on Wall Street, scandals at every level of government, scandals in the ministry. Whether coincidental or not, the aggregate impact of these revelations undermined the public trust in individuals and institutions thought to represent the highest standards of ethical and moral behavior. I am sure Tocqueville would be shocked to learn that, before his fall, Ivan Boesky was resoundly applauded at a commencement address at a major university (not the University of Oklahoma) for extolling the virtues and advantages of greed. He said (before going to jail but not after): "Greed is all right; greed is healthy; greed is American. You can be greedy and still feel good about yourself."

People are being told now that if they find their own spontaneous feelings and act on them, all will be well. Subjectivity, ladies and gentlemen, nowadays has been raised to a level of idolatry under the guise of "individualism" and "fulfillment." People are encouraged to focus exclusively on themselves at the expense and exclusion of the greater community. Needless to say, this would dismay Tocqueville, too. So would the vulgar commercialization of God and religion—a religion that preaches, sometimes, by its malpractitioners, the imperative that the almighty dollar or buck does not stop outside heaven's gates, but is a necessary ticket into them. When graduates of a major university business school in New York tell a distinguished journalist that they are not only "willing to sacrifice their private lives" (that is fine; some of us have done that by going into higher education), but also "to sell their souls" in order to advance their careers, that, too, would alarm Tocqueville.

Felix Rohatyn, of Lazard Freres and Company, described the Wall Street scandals as a cancer called greed, and 56 percent of a cross section of the American public polled by Lou Harris in May 1987 agreed with him. However, when asked what they thought most Americans would do in similar situations, 82 percent of the group polled replied that most Americans would buy stock, even though they knew it was illegal to do so. When the same people were asked what they themselves would do, 53 percent replied affirmatively that they would buy it, too, even though it was illegal. Most surprising, for me at least, was that of the 53 percent, 64 percent of them earned $50,000 a year or more, and 60 percent were college graduates. Apparently the more affluent people are, the more privileged they are, the higher the status they have in society, the more likely they would be to engage in insider stock trading. I hope this is not the right conclusion one must draw from the above polls.

In the May 25, 1987, issue of *Time* magazine, the cover story was entitled "Whatever Happened to Ethics? Assaulted by Sleaze, Scandals and Hypocrisy, America Searches for Its Moral Bearings." "Not since the reckless 1920s," held *Time*, "has the business world seen such searing scandals. White collar scams abound, along with insider trading, money laundering, green mail, etc. Greed, combined with technology, has made stealing more tempting than ever. What began as the decade of the entrepreneur is becoming gradually the age of pin stripe outlaws."

The apparent lack of ethical concern of our future business leaders is a most disturbing phenomenon. At the New York University business school a professor recently gave his class a hypothetical case study, the Panabla Case. The students were asked to serve as members of the Board of Directors of a drug company. One of the company's products had been found to kill fourteen to twenty-four Americans annually, and the FDA [Food and Drug Administration] wanted to ban the drug. The drug, however, represented 12 percent of the company's profits. The students were asked the question, As a member of the board, what would you do? Over 80 percent of the class decided to keep the drug on the market, and if banned in the United States, would sell it to a foreign country. Ten years ago, when the same class test was given at New York University only 40 percent took the position "my company, right or wrong."

It is clear, and I am sure Tocqueville would agree with me, that "healthy individualism" means a balance between the personal component of the self and the social component of the community. Neither can exist by itself. If separated, each is an abstraction. It is an individual's social role that defines one's character, and it is through choices that one becomes an individual. The absence of intelligence, commitment and choice, morality and ethics will always weaken our social bonds, and hence, weaken our society and our democracy. For, ladies and gentlemen, we cannot privatize public morality, nor relegate it to the realm of private choice—what students of today call "life-styles," whatever that means.

The tension between morality and politics is real, and we must confront it. We cannot retreat from the big issues of society in our time to the "pygmy world of private piety." We cannot be social, political, and moral isolationists. Nor can we reduce ourselves into plain Social-Darwinistic, atomized, sociobiological consumer units. We cannot be bullish on ethics either—as a newspaper editorial stated, "Let's be bullish on ethics"—because ethics has no bottom line. It is not commodity; you cannot buy and sell it; ethics is acquired, and you don't acquire it by taking one course in business school or law school.

We have to build meaning into our own lives and build it through our commitments. Beware of manuals and fast-track recipes because, ladies and gentlemen, unlike *Fifty Great Moments in Music*, by Milton Cross, there are not fifty great moments on ethics. We have no choice but to end the imprisonment of the self and concern ourselves with those outside of our moral enclosure. We need a moral center, not a moral enclosure. We need to be capable of moral outrage and sensitive to the pain and sorrow of our fellow men and women. It is important, not only to be able to engage in new ideas, but to be willing to make public declarations of one's convictions and one's commitments, and then translate them into action and deed.

Oliver Wendell Holmes said it so eloquently, "A life is action and passion. It's required of a man that he share the passion and action of his time, at peril of being judged not to have lived at all." True individualism, therefore, is a means to affirm and enhance our humanity and our potential as moral and social and political beings. In the words of Albert Schweitzer, "Affirmation of life is the spiritual act by which man ceases to live unreflectively. To affirm life is to deepen it, to exalt the will to live." Such affirmation does not mean the cult of narcissism, exaltation of cynicism, or aloofness from society. Affirmation means more than personal gratification, because a democracy needs a committed, enlightened citizenry.

My message today is not one of doom and gloom; if that were the case, I would not have become an educator. I would not be an educator if I were not an optimist; my call today is for reflection and action.

I am heartened by the current national concern and debate about the role of ethics, the role of law in our society and the fact that many business leaders are concerned themselves and are trying now in many ways to set, not only themselves as examples, but many of their firms and associations as examples of ethical behavior and ethical standards. There is a great deal of concern about the role of law in our society, the scope of our shared values, the necessary balance between self-interest and public interest, parochial interest and national interest, and most will be delighted to learn that apparently it is no longer all that good to be "cool."

If the 1980s was the decade of the yuppies, than the result of the Lou Harris survey poll recently released is most encouraging. It reports that 57 percent of yuppies find themselves unappetizing, and 90 percent find egocentric tendencies to be singularly unattractive. The study also reveals that, as a symbol of an ascendant new generation, yuppies appear to be fading fast. But though the symbol may be diminishing, it is highly unlikely that the materialism of this new generation will disappear overnight. It will be with us in the future, as it has been with us in the past.

Therefore it is incumbent upon all our educational institutions and our intellectual and educational leaders to assume a leadership position in the current national debate on the role of ethics in our culture, our notions of citizenship, individualism, mutualism, social obligations, and how they affect the health and welfare of our democratic society.

At a time when we face awesome national and international challenges, when the social fabric of our democracy is undergoing severe strains, when we face, not only an explosion of information and knowledge, but also dangerous levels of compartmentalization and fragmentation of that knowledge, our universities and colleges have a fundamentally historical task to educate, to give us not just training alone, but education; not just education, but culture; and not just information, but its distillation, knowledge. Education must endow us not only with a life view, but also with a world view. It must help us to recover a sense of the wholeness of human life, to assist us to rediscover and redefine our larger cultural legacy, and to remind us, along with Emerson, that we learn nothing until we learn the symbolic character of life. It must instruct us to see the best our culture has taught, said, and done, as well as to see the dead aberrations that clutter our history. For a society without a deep historical memory the future ceases to exist, and the present becomes a meaningless cacophony. Education should nurture in us individualism, true individualism, and give us the strength to choose.

The philosopher Henri Bergson once remarked that man has a tremendous reservoir of indetermination, and that our power of choice for good and evil is enormous. It is through choices that one becomes an individual. As educators, we must remain mindful that moral values and social ideals do not take root in the dry sands of materialism. Tocqueville's concept of enlightened self-interest makes it incumbent upon us to create a moral climate in which public interest and common good are fostered as necessary extensions of enlightened self-interest. As rational, moral and spiritual beings and as educated citizens, we must be able to distinguish between right and wrong, right and might, justice and injustice, end and means, personal gain and public good.

We must always be mindful that our forefathers founded a land of opportunity and not a land of opportunists.

The founding fathers wrote the Constitution with the faith that the ordinary citizens were committed to the accomplishment of extraordinary acts. The Talmud also expresses the same belief, that in every age there comes a time when leadership suddenly comes forth to meet the needs of the hour. And so there is no man and no woman who does not find his or her time, and there is no hour that does not have its leader. Because you must always know, on that occasion of the centennial, that society, regardless of its size and complexity, will always turn on the act of the individual, on the act of the leader; therefore, on the quality of that individual.

One last thought: Alexis de Tocqueville did not deal with American higher education. He did not see in American higher education, a system, a stabilizing system, the guardian of equality and freedom; an element that strove for excellence in order to become the intellectual guardian of our American democracy. That is one of the reasons that today American higher education has a tremendous role to play, in addition to all voluntary associations with historical roles, to preserve all democracy, to preserve our democracy, to preserve our freedoms, and to give meaning to our equality.

That is why now, in the midst of an explosion of information—for all available information doubles every five years—in the midst of the explosion of knowledge and complex challenges facing us, the American universities cannot afford the luxury of transforming their first two years of instruction to meet the woeful inadequacies of our public school system. We cannot afford, and therefore we need leaders to say so. We cannot afford to relegate 50 percent of our universities' time and resources to remedial work.

We must help rescue our public school system; we must reach the core of our culture in its unity and diversity. We must teach our students science, logic, mathematics, and biology. Universities, in two years, cannot do justice to twelve years of neglect in learning. We are our high schools' keepers. This nation must take preventive measures to reform, strengthen, and in some instances, rescue our high school system.

Our major universities, such as the University of Oklahoma and Brown University, cannot afford to be complacent about their or their country's future. We are national institutions, and therefore we have national responsibility to do something, collectively, as well as individually. At the time when we graduate 750,000 functionally illiterate high school students, at a time when 850,000 of our young drop out of school, and others are ill-prepared for the complex society of the twenty-first century, we cannot condemn our youth to economic and technological subjugation or witness passively the emergence of a permanent underclass.

We also cannot afford to see our society and our educational system drift apart into two separate but unequal worlds; nor can we afford the luxury of having twenty to thirty million functionally illiterate Americans and rank forty-ninth amongst 160 members of the United Nations in literacy. Both of these problems present our nation with both moral and economic imperatives.

Some 150 years ago Edward Everett, minister, scholar, orator, politician, president of Harvard, and a leading conservative of his day, delivered a major speech, and if I may be permitted to quote one paragraph, he said, "There are two roads by which a society can travel when it comes to the question of education. One, the route most other nations have followed, was to treat education as a luxury for a small privileged class of wealth and leisure. By that reckoning, the fortunate few let learning creep in with luxury and dispensed its blessing to those it chose worthy of the honor. They would do so out of the surplus of their vast fortunes." That, Everett intoned, was not the American way. The American way was to "make the care of the mind, from the outset, a part of its public economy and the growth of knowledge a portion of its public wealth. This must be done because we cannot afford to fail."

The other area in which Tocqueville would sympathize with me and with all my colleagues who are educators is the extent to which American universities have begun to take academic freedom for granted. On many college campuses today there is a mood to "do the right thing, to say the right thing, to do politically the right thing," and thus abdicate what higher educational institutions are all about. Academic freedom is and must remain a central policy of the American universities.

Thomas Jefferson was an early exponent of intellectual freedom as a foundation of our modern universities. "The University of Virginia," he said, "would be based on the illimitable freedom of the human mind, for here we are not afraid to follow truth, wherever it may lead, nor to tolerate error so long as reason is left free to combat it." Even though Jefferson was unable to implement that freedom fully at the University of Virginia, throughout the last two centuries American universities, with various degrees of success, have attempted to uphold the principles of free inquiry and the tenets of academic freedom.

The universities of our nation must be guarantors of the First Amendment. The courts alone cannot guarantee the First Amendment and the right of free speech. Some students tell me that this is a free country, that we can say anything we want. My response is simple: If you have nothing to say, it doesn't make any difference whether it is a free country or not. The university must remain a sanctuary for ideas, even the unpopular ones. We cannot and will not compromise, and we should not compromise on this principle. Freedom of speech cannot be rationed—it cannot be dispensed piecemeal. The right is a single entity that belongs to all.

The hallmark of a university must not be a little bit of intellectual freedom, not freedom behind closed doors, not freedom just for liberals, nor just for conservatives; not just for radicals or for organized groups but, as Bertrand Russell put it so well, "It should be also for a minority of one."

The free discourse and debate fostered in our universities is our best hope for nurturing in each succeeding generation a respect for the right of each individual to form, espouse, and defend his or her beliefs and thoughts. The universities must encourage the examination and challenges of all ideologies, all theories, all theses, and all assumptions. To resolve such debates is not the point—simply to have them is exactly the point.

Charles W. Elliott, one of the foremost American educators of

his time, observed with great eloquence, "The very word education is a standing protest against dogmatic teaching. The worthy
fruit of academic culture is an open mind; trained for careful
thinking, instructed in the methods of philosophical investiga-
tion, acquainted in a general way with the accumulative thought
of past generations and penetrated with humility."

Freedom of thought, freedom of speech, freedom to publish,
freedom of press, freedom to disseminate are fundamental fea-
tures of a true and open democratic society. Justice Hugo Black
pointed out so forcefully that "freedom of speech, press, petition
and assembly guaranteed by the First Amendment must be ac-
corded to the ideas we hate, or sooner or later we are denied the
ideas we cherish."

In two landmark cases in 1957 and 1967 the Supreme Court
affirmed these principles as they related to the university. To
impose any straitjacket upon the intellectual leaders in our colleges and universities would imperil the future of our nation.
Teachers and students must always remain free to inquire, to
study, and to evaluate, to gain new maturity and understanding;
otherwise our civilization would stagnate or die.

Upholding the notion of academic freedom which the Supreme
Court called of transcendent value to all of us, it ruled that the
classroom is particularly and peculiarly the market place of ideas.
The nation's future depends, it said, upon leaders exposed to the
robust exchange of ideas which discovers truth out of a multitude
of tongues, rather than through any kind of authoritative selec-
tion. The alternatives otherwise, ladies and gentlemen, are Or-
wellian and therefore unacceptable. As Nien Cheng wrote about
the cultural revolution in China in her book *Life and Death in
Shanghai*, "When the penalty for speaking one's mind is so great,
nobody knows what anybody else thinks."[6] At our universities
we want to know, we need to know, what everybody thinks; to
think without prejudice, and to teach without fear are central to
the mission of our great universities, including yours.

That is why I would like to conclude this evening by saying
what America needs for its higher education systems is not to
provide personalities who will entertain you, but to provide true
individuals who care for the nation, who don't want to take as

much out of this nation and return as little as possible, but who do care for the future of our youth, the future of our nation, the future of our country. I know it is old-fashioned, and I don't want to misquote or reiterate Kennedy—we also have to ask once in a while what can we do for our nation, for our country, rather than confine our thinking to our own immediate gratification.

We have to postpone, we have to cherish, we have to cultivate our nation's garden, because this nation is too precious for us to squander it now. And for that we need you, all of you students, to become leaders of this country. Individualism and social commitment are compatible. True individualism has both private and social components. Education can bring the two together. Compassion can expand it, and enlightenment can be helpful, not just for you, and for your nation, but also for the future of your children, their children, and their children.

So let us think for once not about tomorrow's bottom line, but about the nation's ultimate destiny; because you, ladies and gentlemen, have a rendezvous with leadership and a rendezvous with the destiny of this nation.

In preparing to meet this rendezvous, Vartan Gregorian challenged the students participating in the Leadership Symposia to escape from the culture of individualism, to merge their own life plans into the larger context of the future of their country. He called for them to set for themselves a higher ethical standard than has been set for them by the examples of unethical conduct in the business, governmental, and even the religious realm today. He asked them to embrace the aesthetic as well as the material dimension of life, to seek a higher meaning. In sum, he calls upon them to become citizens in a republic of ideals, rather than participants in a culture of individualism. Gregorian, it is clear, shares Kant's conception of a higher culture, one that could produce a morally complete and just society. In proposing to the students that they transcend the culture in which they are likely to live, Gregorian implies that there is a standard against which that culture can be judged.

What does this mean to these students? Unquestionably, they responded to the exhortation; they want to be the kind of person that Gregorian calls upon them to be. But what kind of a society does Gregorian's speech call to their minds and what role do they see themselves playing in it?

By way of example, let us consider the prospect of a more meaningful role for the arts in American society. The topic was raised, curiously enough, at both the Arts and Humanities Symposium held in the spring of 1990 and in the Business and Technology Symposium the following fall. At the latter event, the entrée was gained by futurist John Naisbitt's claim that the twenty-first century would see a rebirth in the arts in which art would surpass sport in laying claim to Americans' leisure time. More people would participate in and more money would be spent on art than on sport by the century's end, Naisbitt claimed. Venues for art would proliferate around the country, bringing high culture to places where it had not been before.[7]

To students at the University of Oklahoma, this is a striking proposition. They are accustomed to the ongoing national debate about the proper role of athletics at a public university, and happen to attend a university with a major and successful athletic program. They have been raised in "football country." In the years after World War II, the university sought to build a successful football program in order to bring national recognition and to counteract to a degree the dust-bowl image from which the state suffered. The effort was remarkably successful, leading longtime President George Lynn Cross later to say that he hoped to build a university in which the football team could take pride. That the university and state do take pride in the athletic programs of Oklahoma's major universities is without question; but is the prominence of athletics in Oklahoma culture merely a step along the way to a higher form of civilization such as Naisbitt predicts for America?

To senior journalism major John C. McKinney, who studies

radio, television, and film—three venues for modern art—
the prospect that art would supplant sport in the preference
schedules of Americans is ludicrous.

The biggest gripe I had with *Megatrends 2000* was the renaissance in the arts. There are many numbers to support the rise in
attendance to theaters and museums but the idea it will replace
sports as society's primary leisure activity is going a little far. I
understand the view of reexamining life through the arts. . . .
But the day we see the kind of ratings on TV for an opera that we
see for the Super Bowl or the World Series, then I'll believe Mr.
Naisbitt. Can anyone really see the number of children enrolled
in music classes equal to the number of children playing little
league sports? Will drawing or dance ever become an Olympic
event? I feel the emotion of victory through competition cannot
be equaled in art.

McKinney sees sport as responding to a different human imperative than art. Sport is competitive, and the competitive
instinct drives American culture. McKinney is correct. When
television networks purvey art, they do so for competitive
reasons—they want a larger market share in order to maximize
profit. This will lead them to present the kind of art that
the public will watch—Roseanne Arnold art—and to preempt
regularly scheduled programs for major sporting events—the
World Series—in order to make money.

To senior letters major Julie R. Harvey, who shares John
McKinney's skepticism, the competition between art and
sport that Naisbitt presumes carries a social implication.

I remember reading in psychology class in high school that
sports are the chosen entertainment of the less educated while
art is the entertainment of the better educated. I always wondered
how such a sweeping generalization could actually be supported;
it sounded so denigrating. While I think art is more cerebral than
sports, I do not think of it as elitist. Entertainment should not be

used as an instrument to categorize people. I must admit I enjoy and understand art more than sports, but I do not see art superseding sports entirely. You cannot think that and live in Norman, Oklahoma. When the University of Oklahoma, an institution of higher education, gives greater emphasis to the quality of education than to its athletic prowess then I will believe that art has reached its renaissance.

Harvey appears to believe that art is a higher form of culture than sport. To say that there is a positive correlation between art and intelligence and a negative relationship between sport and intelligence is a sweeping generalization indeed, one that George Will would surely deny as applied to baseball. Yet how can it be denied that, in America, the arts are supported primarily by well-educated upper-middle-class people, while sport makes its profit from commercial television broadcasts geared toward the average viewer?

An answer seems to lie in greater precision in the definition of art and sport. Bincy Yohannan perceived that art and sport are not alternative forms of expression in competition with each other, but instead alternative ways of expressing the human spirit. She shares the Greek conception of sport as a form of art.

Sports, in a way, is itself a type of art. It is certainly symbolic of the exact global economic trend that Naisbitt promotes. Its competitiveness is representative of the competition brought about by worldwide free trade while its team unity is representative of the interdependence of future national economies. Yes, I am certainly optimistic that today's citizens (as well as the young people who will be the leaders of tomorrow) are becoming more involved with and interested in reading literature, attending museums, etc.; however, I also hope that we will correct those problems within our sports events (for example, athlete drug use, sexual misconduct, the fierce contract battles) that have spoiled our outlook on the sports world.

Yohannan sees sport as a microcosm of life, just as modern artists, in Tocqueville's apt phrase, engage in "the exact delineation of everyday life." Both sport and art are reflections of our culture. For art to transcend sport is as meaningless as for sport to transcend art; they are two sides of the same equation, each a measure of the human type they produce. This view is shared by panelist Michael D. Anderson, senior minister at Oklahoma City's Westminster Presbyterian Church.

I frankly do not see much difference, at their best, between athletics and aesthetics. I think the Greek ideal is still the ideal that we ought to aspire to. . . . The planning, the preparation, the discipline and, let me emphasize, the beauty of a Joe Montana to Jerry Rice pass pattern is an aesthetic act. I also saw the first time there was a ballet on the stage of the Metropolitan Opera House, and the first great dancer to grace that stage was Mikhail Baryshnikov. I have talked to Baryshnikov about his life in America, and I have also talked to Lynn Swann, who danced ballet on a New York stage even though he was noted as one of the best wide receivers in the NFL. Neither sees much difference between an artist and an athlete, at their best.

What ties art and athletics together? For Yohannan and Anderson, as for the Greeks, it is the aesthetic value of the human form, a universal phenomenon. In our appreciation for art and sport we reflect our faith in a human ideal.

If this is true, then the analysis of the role of art in society presents an angle from which the rest of society can be viewed. Tocqueville teaches us that democratic societies will succumb to mass culture, that art will be trivialized, that the quest for a higher and better life will be sacrificed to the demands of modern individualism. The participants in the Symposium on the Arts and Humanities joined with Vartan Gregorian in saying no to mass culture and yes to an enlarged role for the arts. Their hope is given promise by Naisbitt's prediction. In discussing the role that art should play in American society, however, and the manner by which that role can be enhanced, it becomes clear that the meaning of the term *art* is democratically understood. Just as Julie Harvey seemed to find it difficult to say outright that her appreciation for art is a product of her intelligence, so too were the panelists reluctant to advocate that art should play a transcendent role in democratic culture. These leaders in the arts appreciate art as an aspect of democratic culture, and not as a challenge to it.

"The first question we want to ask ourselves," said panel moderator and OU President Emeritus Paul F. Sharp, "is whether, in a society such as ours, pluralistic, with numerous ethnic groups and many cultures, the concept of the arts and humanities and their role is elitist?" Oklahoma City businessman and art patron James R. Tolbert III thinks not.

Often purveyors of arts and humanities are elitist individuals and they project an elitist image, but clearly the arts and humanities themselves are not elitist. They are the broadest possible base in our culture, in our condition, and more particularly in our need to relate our world's past into the base of knowledge with the previous human experience and to develop means of creatively communicating among ourselves. So I don't think the arts and humanities are the least bit elitist. I think the problem has been that many people who practice them and many people who purvey them to you are people who are determined that that separates them from others. As a consequence they have not always been properly appreciated and they project an elitist image. I think that's unfortunate and I think it is up to those who care about the arts and humanities to overcome that. I have a peculiar vantage point because I own a bookstore which is, I hope, the best bookstore in Oklahoma and maybe in the Southwest. As a consequence I see people who care about the humanities. People come into my store on a regular basis, and they are not the elite. They are very much a cross section of Oklahoma. They are very interesting people, but they do not hold elite positions or hold themselves out in an elite manner.

To Jim Tolbert, the arts are not elitist, but artists and art dealers sometimes are. There is, in his perception, a tension between the artistic community and the broader culture. Yet Tolbert's vision of the role of art in society is essentially democratic. The aim of art is to communicate creatively. Art must be rooted in culture and history. Art is a reflection of society and helps us understand ourselves. Democratic art has a democratic appeal. Bookstores, even the best bookstores, are not frequented by intellectual elites but rather a "cross section of Oklahoma." What they sell is presumably what a cross section of Oklahoma will buy.

Mary Y. Frates, founder of the Oklahoma Arts Institute, agrees with Jim Tolbert but wants to see the democratic culture of art expanded. "I think it is a shame that there aren't even more opportunities for all of us to participate," she said, although "opportunities abound for those of you who seek them out, or who simply walk through the door of opportunity." This call for participation in the arts was echoed by Anita Rasi May, who as executive director of the Oklahoma Foundation for the Humanities has played a leading role in the efforts of the foundation to disseminate culture in Oklahoma. "I cannot understand why it is not elitist for a person to appreciate football even when one cannot play it, but elitist for a person to appreciate an opera even though one cannot sing it." Perhaps it is as Mary Frates says, that there is simply more access to football than there is to opera. Said May, "When I started work for the Oklahoma Foundation for the Humanities, it was my goal to have as many humanities programs as there are football games in Oklahoma, and I think I'm coming close to achieving that goal."

One reason Anita May has been able to fulfill her ambition of making the arts and humanities more accessible to the public is because the foundation that she heads is funded by the federal government and draws support from private contributors, many of them wealthy. However much the arts and humanities may appeal to most Oklahoma citizens, they are typically patronized by the wealthy. Michael Anderson said,

The first time I was taken to a symphony I noticed that the front row seats went to patrons at a $1,000 and the seats behind them went to supporting members of the aristocracy of the community for $500 and so on. You, as a student participant in some of the best cultural events in Oklahoma City, will get a picture of elitism simply by being there. You will be in a second balcony, wearing your dungarees, and the patrons will be in the front rows wearing black ties. In our publicity of the arts, we also have made them look elitist. You look at the society pages of large city newspapers, and the arts look kind of elitist. But, unfortunately we tend to deny that which we haven't experienced.

Notwithstanding the fact that the arts are patronized by the rich, they have their appeal to all. It is in the marketplace of democratic art that the essence of democratic culture is to be found. Jim Tolbert, whose bookstore makes humanistic culture available at a reasonable price, understands the paradox of the rich patronizing the arts in populist Oklahoma.

One of the problems in our country has been the way we finance the arts and the way we present the humanities to people outside of the university setting. In Europe it is generally done with state funds. In this country it is almost universally done with private funds. Private funds tend to be in the hands of rich people and so we solicit rich people and give them status for having given money to support the arts. That has created an environment of elitism in the arts. One of the answers is to alter that financing system. Another answer is to acknowledge the problem of access and the barriers that creates. One of our healthy examples occurs in Oklahoma City and Tulsa both, where we have a great outdoor art festival. It's a phenomenal thing when you think of the 650,000 or 700,000 people who in six days will come through a park setting to look at nothing but visual art in downtown Oklahoma City. And more remarkably they will spend two million dollars and buy over ten thousand pieces of art. These are Okies doing this, and the reason they will do it is because it is accessible. There are no barriers to walking through a park—you don't even have to go through a doorway. For those who have been raised with a great deal of anti-intellectualism, it can be psychologically threatening to go into an environment when you have to go through a closed door. I think as a society we have to recognize that and devise mechanical and other ways to overcome that.

Making art accessible is the key to the development of an artistic culture. Oklahomans will buy objects of art, and more Oklahomans will attend an outdoor art show in Oklahoma City in six days than attend an entire schedule of football games at the stadium in Norman in an entire season. It is a matter of making it easy to do. Tolbert's faith in the capacity of his fellow Oklahomans to appreciate the arts is reassuring. Insofar as buying artistic objects implies an appreciation of art, he is no doubt correct. It remains to be seen, however, what the cultural impact of a broad dissemination of artistic objects might be.

Jackie Follis found an element of humor in the attempt by these cultural elites to disseminate an appreciation for the arts to the masses. To Follis, art is a reflection of life that can only be grasped from the ground up, not from the top down.

Of course, the purpose of the panel was to promote an integration of arts and humanities into everyone's lives—to encourage participation and the development of self. But this was an elitist panel of "States Arts" people. These were people grappling with questions of how to get the ordinary folk to realize what it means to understand an opera, or to appreciate Shakespeare. I felt the strong elitism present in their assemblage and in what they felt their purpose was at the symposia.

I think that one reason the arts are viewed as elitist is because our society, and people like this panel on the "Arts and Humanities," think that they [the arts] need to be taught. They are imposing. We, perhaps, wonder if we *can* understand them if someone doesn't explain them to us, hence, we have classes in Shakespeare, music and art appreciation, poetry etc. But the arts are humanity, they are us, we participate in them daily. Someone mentioned the enthusiasm of the audience at a football game and wondered why that enthusiasm was not applied toward "the arts." I assert that it is because we are trained to be spectators in the arts, not participants. We are not encouraged to be involved as at a football game where participant and spectator are melded toward appreciating the entire experience. It is when the arts are segregated and placed on a high-society pedestal that they become intimidating and inaccessible.

Michael Anderson thinks that art must serve a higher purpose than mere aesthetic enjoyment. Its aim is to raise the human spirit. But toward what vision should the human spirit be aimed? He believes that the twenty-first century will witness a homogenization of culture, in part through art.

I think that in Oklahoma we need to experience more of the arts, and then we will suddenly discover the significance of this way of expression of the human spirit that reaches out and brings a beauty and symmetry and cohesion to our lives. Even when words fail us, the arts can sometimes bridge that tremendous gap in an otherwise rather incoherent world. John Donne said, "We live in two worlds, one world that is dying and one that cannot afford to be born." I think at times we find the artists making the bridge for us to the new world and certainly we are moving into a new century of tremendous excitement. For the first time in all of the history of humanity we are going to see Asians, Africans, Americans, Latin Americans, and Europeans experiencing the common life in a way that's never been experienced before. It is a brilliant future that I predict will first be seen by some artists who will portray it in painting, or in a dance, or in music.

Contrary to the current fetish over cultural awareness and multiculturalism with which so many universities today seem preoccupied, Anderson endorsed an older, Western notion that the final development of the human race must be a "common life" in which man's essential humanity is the tie that binds each to all. Unlike Tocqueville, who believed that all democratic art must be derivative of democratic culture, Anderson finds the particular strength of the artist in his or her capacity to foretell the future, a John Naisbitt of the human spirit. The world awaits a twenty-first century Wagner and a modern rendition of *The Ring of the Nibelung* in which a new kind of man emerges from the ashes of an older and weaker society. This new man will not be the product of a particular culture, but instead an amalgam of many cultures.

To senior letters major Bobby Cater, the arts can have a transformative effect on culture precisely by challenging the status quo. It is precisely by being different that art has its main impact, but it is precisely because it has an impact that it threatens. The problem with democratic art, in Cater's view, lies in its propensity to reinforce rather than to challenge prevailing dispositions.

In antiquity and the Renaissance, the role of the poet (synonymous with artist) was to teach as well as to entertain. The satires of Aristophanes produced laughter but also insights into the absurdity of Athenian society. Arguably in our modern, secular society, many artists fail in their didactic responsibility (some in the entertainment also). However, especially in totalitarian societies but certainly not exclusive to, the burden as the dissenting, rational voice insisting on personal liberty and dignity falls on the artist.

Whether they like or realize it or not, the artists will produce a work with some kind of social impact. The significance can range from revolutionary doctrines to insignificant paintings. Unfortunately many artists do not fully appreciate, much less exercise, the social responsibility they have. These type of people claim their work does not have to signify anything, and in our type of democracy, they certainly have the right to believe and behave this way. Yet, society shall define a work in some kind of social and often political terms.

Indeed society often looks to the artist for leadership. The poet is in a unique position to provoke and challenge the thoughts of his audience. He can express the frustrations and the hopes of people in a way that touches a broad spectrum of people. In a totalitarian society, the artist is the only voice for the powerless. He has the courage to articulate the mood of the oppressed and oppose the actions of the government.

Even in a society such as ours, the artist constantly questions the norms and conventions of his community. The observations and assertions an artist makes, often find him at odds with the "community elders and powers." Most societies strive for unity and to a great extent a uniformity of ideas. But social conventions are a rich source for the poet's inspirations. This is why governments and the influential sectors of society many times label artists as dangerous since they question and undermine that uniformity.

Indeed the poet raises the issues that the majority does not want to confront or are too oppressed to verbalize. The artist becomes identified as the symbol for hope. When Czechoslovakia transferred from its communist government to a democracy, the country turned to dissident playwright Vaclav Havel to preside over the new government. Havel, only months before, was in political detention for his plays, which criticized his society. His courage to speak and write against the injustices in his country was interpreted as leadership.

Thus there emerged from these discussions four views on the role of art in society. There is the aesthetic view, that art should be appreciated for its own sake and should be widely disseminated. There is the cultural view, that holds that art teaches us about our culture and should be widely understood. There is the metaphysical view, that art is ennobling of the human spirit and should call us to a higher understanding of self. There is the political view, that art challenges the prevailing norms of culture and power and should stand in opposition to the preferences of the mighty and the masses as well. The former two visions are essentially egalitarian; the latter two visions are essentially elitist. It is possible that a properly structured curriculum in the liberal arts might bridge the gap between the egalitarian and elitist views, indeed, that only a liberal arts education can.[8] What is most striking about the discussion is the tension between the concept of art itself, which beckons us to a universal aestheticism, and the democratic tendency to think that all matters of taste are relative. In Oklahoma, for example, much of the readily accessible art reflects or celebrates the various cultures of the American West during the nineteenth century. Some people like this kind of art more than do others, but it doesn't make any difference to those who think that art is intrinsically good. All four explanations of the relationship of art to society are valid; anything that causes an appreciation of art is good; all forms of art are valuable; and if a half-million people attend an art exposition, then this demonstrates that art appreciation is alive in Oklahoma. One wonders, however, whether the dissemination of art celebrating these aspects of Oklahoma culture will lead to the creation of a new and transcendent form of Oklahoma culture based in significant part on the appreciation of art, or merely reinforce a nativist attachment to the culture that now exists.

A second challenge that Vartan Gregorian posed to the students was to rediscover a sense of community, an attachment to the society around them. Tocqueville's emphasis on the value of community traces itself to Rousseau, Montesquieu, and the Roman thinkers. It embodies a vision of what was once called "republican virtue," the virtue of the good citizen in a free society. Tocqueville recognized that, in the democratic age, the ties that bind individuals to their community would become weakened by the pull of self-interest. He thought that only through a supporting network of cultural norms that were essentially independent of democracy's influence could democracy be made civilized. He perceived in the American experience the kind of cultural foundations that could compensate for democracy's weakened ties.

The society that Tocqueville witnessed was based largely on local institutions and communities. There is very little resemblance between it and the society in which these students will lead their lives. Twentieth-century mass culture is little conducive to the sense of community spirit that Tocqueville found in the American towns of the 1830s. Today, it is all too easy for individuals to disappear into the culture of the mass. What, then, is there in the life experience of these students that will enable them to heed the call to civic duty? Gregorian's answer lies in part in the breadth of vision that is provided by a liberal education, traditionally defined. Gregorian stresses that such an education must find a place for an understanding and appreciation of other cultures, much in the same way that the cultivated gentleman of Victorian England might have patronized the Royal Geographic Society. But the ultimate goal of a liberal education is to produce a liberal person, a person whose broader intellectual horizons make for a more enriched life. Gregorian believes that it must be the goal of American higher education to produce liberally educated men and women, but he observes much in the environment of American higher education to prevent that from happening. In a morning address, Gregorian elaborated his view of the relationship between education, culture, and the individual.

There Will Never Be Another You

Vartan Gregorian

This morning I would like to talk with you about yourselves and the world that you are going to inhabit. Each of you is unique, each a different personality. In the entire history of the world there never has been nor ever will be another like you. When we consider that uniqueness, that individuality of the person, we can define you as an isolated person, in terms of your individual characteristics. Individualism, the way that Tocqueville described it, goes beyond personality. It considers the individual as a rational, spiritual, moral, historical being, while remaining cognizant of one's tradition, cognizant of one's inner world, of the fact that each person is taking a unique journey through this earth, this planet. Each must decide how to manage one's time and how to contribute to our human species through compassion, through sharing our common human destiny. We must not feel pity towards people, but sympathy, empathy, toward our fellow men and women.

Those are some of the principles I discussed last night, but also I stressed one thing that Tocqueville had mentioned, that there are certain stabilizers in American society protecting both aspects of democracy—equality and freedom, individual freedom and collective freedom. Those were separation of church and state, an independent judiciary, and checks and balances, with an independent judiciary, executive branch, and the legislative branch. Tocqueville also stressed the importance of small property, that gave a base for you to protect and to pass along to the next generation. He is perhaps most famous for having emphasized the special American habit of participation in all kinds of voluntary associations, from local self-government, to the PTA, to neighborhoods, to chambers of commerce, to Kiwanis, to Rotary, the hundreds and thousands of private associations that we have. All of them provide small units whereby we assert our differences, but at the same time we never lose sight of our unity. Because, in America, democracy is not about differences, it is not about atomism, but is about a fabric of ties that tie us historically, tie us politically, tie us economically, tie us culturally, tie us morally, and tie us spiritually.

Because, like other nineteenth-century Englishmen and Frenchmen who visited America, Tocqueville did not have much of a high regard for American higher education at that time, he did not stress the role of higher education in shaping American culture. But since the seventeenth century, American higher education has become a new fabric that ties us together, our nation, its past, its present, and its future. We need to add a new element to Tocqueville's analysis. American higher education must prosper, for it must give us not only training, but education too;

and not only education, but culture as well. We must not consider education as credentialism, saying, "You have been graduated in four years, congratulations!" but rather to say, "You have been initiated to the great and awesome task of educating yourself throughout the rest of your life." Because, ladies and gentlemen, we cannot educate people in four years anymore. There is no such thing as four-year education. In the seventeenth century we were giving the bachelor of arts, copied from Oxford, which started giving the degree in the thirteenth century. Much has been accumulated in formal knowledge. We know more about outer space, we know more about Mayan civilization, we know more about Egyptian civilization, Chinese civilization, American civilization, European civilization, African civilization. We know more about the oceans and all the rest of the physical world. But we still insist that it is possible for us to do the same thing in higher education. You come as freshmen, by senior year we give a diploma, which credentials you as an educated person, as a cultured person, as a trained person, as a professional. Instead we should be saying that we have given you an introduction to knowledge, we have initiated you for continuous learning. Learning is a lifelong challenge, rather than merely four years of initiation.

And its aim should be moral as well as material. We must not teach you to say, as the French would put it, *après moi le déluge*, after me too bad, whatever may happen will happen. I can ruin the whole United States and immigrate to Switzerland and live well. Because we are each other's keepers, our future's keeper, but also our country's keepers, our planet's keepers, we have to think not only parochially, but also to think of ourselves as members of the human species, members of the American nation, members of the State of Oklahoma, members of the Southwest, members of this hemisphere. That time of parochialism, of spiritual and social isolation, won't do anymore, if we do want to cherish our equality and our freedom, if we do relish our dignity as human beings.

Today I want to discuss the role of arts, humanities, and sciences. First of all, let me tell you one thing that concerns me most. When I became president of the New York Public Library I was told that all available information doubles every five years. Yet we are unable to touch, to capture more than five percent of that available information now. Ninety-five percent of all information is untapped. Now, some of that information supply is inflation rather than explosion. Some of it is obsolete, but we don't know what is true obsolescence or ultimate obsolescence. When I arrived at the New York Public Library I laughed at the librarians who were receiving four thousand telephone directories from all over the world. I said, "I can understand modern telephone directories for information but why do we have the 1939 Warsaw telephone directory? Why can't we get rid of it?" I was immediately chastised by the fact that the 1939 Warsaw telephone directory was one of the most heavily used books in the postwar period, as a legal document, as a social document, as a historical document to base all of the claims of Jews, Poles, Slavs, gypsies, and others who were wiped out by the Nazis during World War II. That was a historical document, that was no longer obsolete. So what on paper may appear obsolete in reality may not be.

Second, while all available information doubles every five years, unfortunately knowledge does not double every five years. The greatest challenge facing humanities, sciences, and social sciences, our entire educational system, is how to bring distillation of information, transform it into structured knowledge. Now that is very important because unless we do that, we will be inundated with trivia. If Orwell was writing *1984* now, he would not say deny information, he would say inundate people with information, because undigested information is equal in many ways to unavailability of true information. When you come to the University of Oklahoma, if your professor gave you 850,000 articles written in the field of chemistry in one year and said, "Here it is, it's all available, go and read," it would be tantamount to paralyzing your choices. Therefore, unless you develop at school a critical mind, a critical eye, a critical capacity to cope with this information, to distinguish between the chaff and the wheat, between propaganda and knowledge, between fact and opinion, you will not be able to consider yourself a truly educated person, and you will be subject always to manipulation, to advertising, to political sloganeering, or the easiest way out, to "let somebody do my thinking—we have experts for that."

Another problem that worries me is the fragmentation of knowledge. We have an explosion of knowledge and information, and at the same time we have fragmentation of knowledge. We have now, subdisciplines of disciplines so that the unity of culture has been fragmented. The unity of knowledge has been fragmented. The concept of literacy itself has been fragmented or diminished. In the nineteenth century if you said we have a literate, cultured person, it meant they were cultured, according to some definition of what a cultured person was. Now, we have fragmented the very notion of literacy. We say he is functionally illiterate—that means he cannot read and write. Then we say he is mathematically illiterate, he can't add and subtract. Now there are numerous illiteracies: cultural illiteracy, scientific illiteracy, technological illiteracy, historical illiteracy, geographical illiteracy. I just read a few days ago about theological illiteracy. We are using the term illiteracy as a euphemism for ignorance. What has happened is that our knowledge base has fragmented. A major challenge for higher education is the problem of the integration of knowledge. Otherwise, as I have quoted often, there will appear what T. S. Eliot commented in 1922 in his commentary on Dante's *Inferno*, that "hell is a place where nothing connects with nothing," and that is what we will be facing. One student will say, "Excuse me, my major was pre–Civil War, antebellum U.S. history. Don't ask me about anything else." Another will say, "Excuse me, my major is post–World War I, don't ask me about the French or Russian Revolution." More will say, excuse me, I am this and that and etcetera. We cannot fragment knowledge that way. So the greatest task facing us in the humanities, social sciences, and sciences is just that: How to bring a modicum of integration of knowledge. Otherwise, as Ortega y Gasset said in the 1930s, "We will be facing the barbarism of specialism." There are many more educated people, he said, many more cultured people, many more people who have degrees—law, business, Ph.D., and so on—yet they are ignorant because they are not thoroughly cultured. That kind of integration is necessary to give coherence to our world view, to give meaning to our lives, but

THE MATTER OF CULTURE   151

also to hold our society together. Surveys won't do it. We cannot bank upon surveys, world history in ten minutes, or fifty great moments in music. We learn the opening lines of Beethoven's Fifth Symphony, wonderful. But how does it continue? Knowing the opening line is not enough. Nor am I impressed with Hirsch's *Cultural Literacy*, that if you know who Cervantes was, that he was an author, and you know he wrote *Don Quixote*, fine, but you don't know when he lived, which period, what it was all about. We cannot treat great literature along the lines of Evelyn Wood's Reading Dynamics. We cannot have a superfluous summary of *War and Peace*, written by Tolstoy—what was it about? It is about war and peace. Where did it happen? It happened in Russia. But that is not what knowledge is about. Knowledge is about process, digestion, critical view, as well as to give coherence and to take apart and to put together.

Specialization is a necessity for scholarship. The answer is not to end specialization; the answer is fusion of particulars in order to give a synthesis, not merely a survey, but a synthesis of knowledge. That is why I am worried about the differences now between sciences and humanities, humanities and art, as well as sciences and technology. We should get rid of the notion that there is and must be an endemic conflict between science and humanities, or between scientists and humanists. To condemn science as purely quantitative while reserving for the humanities the sole jurisdiction of qualitativeness is to indulge in uncalled for snobbishness. It reminds me of the Anglican bishop who told the Episcopal bishop,"Brother, we both serve the Lord, you in your way and I in His." That kind of attitude has to end. The scientific passion of verifiability, the habit of testing the concept by its consequences in experience, I think, is just as permanently rooted in the humanities as in the sciences. We must remember that without scientific knowledge choice and freedom would be woefully restricted.

The question of the integration of knowledge, therefore, once again highlights the importance of liberal learning and the unity of the arts and sciences. Justice Felix Frankfurter once remarked that "the mark of a truly civilized man is confidence in the strength and security to be derived from an inquiring mind." That is why

I believe in the importance of liberal arts education. A liberal education must do more than acquaint students with the past or prepare them for the future. It gives them, and must give you, a perspective for reflection upon the nature and texture of your lives. It must provide you with standards by which to measure human achievement and to recognize and respect the moral courage required to endure human anxiety and human suffering. In both high school and higher education in America we teach all of you how to cope with success, but we never teach you how to cope with adversity, failure, and suffering. Life is not a succession of successes. Life is also a journey full of mishap, tragedy, failure, setbacks which test, in many ways, the fiber of our humanity and our character as educated and cultured and moral beings.

Related to the debate currently about the role of higher education in general and liberal arts education in particular is also the quest of the United States higher education to find a golden mean between narrow professional training and broad humanistic education. There are serious dangers in the renewed and unilateral emphasis on narrow, one-dimensional, vocational, and preprofessional college education, even though we recognize, I certainly do, the harsh economic realities that press upon students, upon you. Nevertheless, as Professor Roland Hoffman, the 1981 Nobel Prize winner in chemistry, stated so eloquently to the students about excessive professionalism, and I quote, "Don't let the future constrain you. You will determine it. Be intellectually adventurous. The world will wait for you to choose a profession. By grasping the richness and the diversity that is offered to you, you stand to gain a depth of understanding of our culture and that of others that will give you a firm and rich foundation for living in our complex world and for improving it." For if ever the world, ladies and gentlemen, cried out for breadth of view, and length of perspective, surely it is now. If ever there was a danger that a narrow professional view would make people insensitive to the needs of all outside their particular professional enclosures, there is such a danger now. We are becoming, once again, oversupplied with careerists and technocrats of one kind or another. Of course specialized skills are important, of course there is little good in learning that there is much that needs mending in the world without acquiring any notion of how to go about the practical tasks of repair. But there is also not much point in becoming a highly skilled "fixer" who is wholly without ideas or convictions as to what needs fixing or why. We ought to realize that a lopsided education is both deficient and dangerous; that we need a proper balance between preparation of careers and the cultivation of values; that general and liberal education must be the thread that ought to weave a pattern of meaning into the total learning experience because, unless such a balance is restored, career training will be ephemeral in applicability and delusive in worth and value. Education will be casual, shifting, and relativistic. Proper and balanced education is not to be conceived as a passive act, an end unto itself. It is a means to action. It is not all that good, as I mentioned last night, to be cool. It is important not only to be able to engage in new ideas but to be willing to make a public declaration of one's convictions, one's commitments, and to translate them into action and deeds. That is why last night I quoted Oliver Wendell Holmes who said so eloquently that "a life is action and passion. It is required of a man that he should share the passion and action of his time at the peril of being judged not to have lived at all." If we want to be powerful alone, if we want to have comfort alone, if we want to have money alone, we are shackled, we cannot express our views, and power becomes an end rather than a means to liberate, to enhance. Then, we have exchanged a different form of a cage for a golden cage. Just to brag about the quality of our prison, the quality of the fabric, quality of the goal that our prison is made of, is not going to be a liberating experience. That is why it is important not to confuse between means and ends, everything you have is to enhance you, to improve you, rather than constrain and diminish you. That is why one of the wonderful lines in the Bible was to warn that you may have conquered the world, but you have lost your soul in the process.

The value of education, therefore, lies in enhancing men's and women's powers of rational analysis, intellectual precision, and independent judgment, and in particular, to encourage mental adaptability. That is why we need the humanities, to encourage us to develop a mental adaptability, a characteristic that men and women sorely need, especially now, in an era of rapid change easily drifting toward homogeneity, leveling, and mediocrity. We must remember that what liberalizes a fact is the quality of the mind that deals with it, and if education cannot train the mind to apprehend relations between facts and problems of the past and those of the present then there is no such thing as liberal education. Education is the use of the mind, to develop the critical capacity for the mind, to give you an intellectual independence in order to be able to invest in your head. Since I am in Oklahoma I can tell you there is no "depletion allowance" for the mind. There may be for the oil wells, but there is no depletion allowance for the mind.

A proper education must teach us the best our culture has taught, said, and done, as well as about the dead aberrations that clutter our history. It must help us understand the sweep of our culture, the achievements, the problems, the solutions, and the failures that mark our history. This kind of knowledge is critical to our understanding who and what we are because of our past. For if we care where we are, if we care where we are going, we have to understand our past. It must allow us to understand the nature of the American polity, a pluralistic and multicultural society, in which the unique can participate in the universal, without dissolving in it. It must serve as a tool of enlightenment, and as an instrument for individual, as well as collective and continued self-determination and liberation from political, economic, and social ills. Education must serve as a vehicle of the American democracy and its unfinished and continued agenda, by allowing means to those who on the basis of sex, age, race have not been able to partake in the social and economic and cultural benefits of the American society.

At the heart of a liberal education is the act of teaching and that is why teaching is so important. I consider teaching the most noble profession of all, because teaching and teachers are the link between the past and the future in creating the future. Teaching is a continuous process, with scholarship informed by it and in turn stimulating its pursuit. Good teaching is not only compatible with scholarship but like it, it prepares men and women for the future. Teaching is an act of convening for the purpose of the making of a covenant. I agree with Erik Erikson when he speaks of human beings as "the teaching species," for facts are kept alive by being told, logic by being demonstrated, and the truth by being professed.

Last, I want to discuss values. Along with the fragmentation of knowledge and the loss of sense of totality, we face another major challenge. There is a tendency nowadays in our educational system to treat matters of judgment, taste, and value as either irrelevant or ancillary. As a result, we have a situation in which judgment gives away to opinion, taste to preference, and value to that effusive thing called "feeling." Whether confronting hard ethical choices in public policy, or issues of personal identity as in psychology, or questions about beauty in art or literature, or problems of environmental consequences, we need to admit questions of values into the arena of discussion and debate. The moral argument of a poem, the social implications of a political system, the ethical consequences of a scientific technique, and the human significance of our responsibilities should have a place in the classroom and the dormitory rooms as well. To deny that place is to relinquish any claim or any attempt to link thought and action, knowing and doing. And that is why I concluded last night saying that we cannot privatize public morality, nor relegate it to the realm of private choice or so called life-styles. Tension between morality and politics is real and we must confront it. We cannot retreat from big issues of our society in our times, we cannot be social, political, and moral isolationists, nor can we reduce and treat ourselves as entertainment units, consumer units, and economic units. We are more than that, more than even the sum of them. Education properly perceived, therefore, must be a liberating force, a means toward freedom, affirmation of life, freedom of individuals from limitations of ignorance, prejudice, place and time.

That is why I want you in this centennial year, to demand more of yourself, more of your teachers, more of our times. Nobody asked you to be born in these difficult times. In the last several months alone, we have witnessed more historical developments than in the past fifty years. We face in Europe now the unity of Europe, in Asia the unity of the Pacific Basin, and America cannot now merely be complacent and take everything it has for granted. We must especially not take for granted our youth, our talent. We cannot allow one-third of our nation to become an underclass. Every ounce of talent we have in America, from every region, every race, every religion, must be tapped, not because it is economically good or it will allow us to remain a super power, but as the United Negro College ad puts it so much more dramatically, "A mind is a terrible thing to waste." In the year 1990, in the twenty-first century, when we have so much to learn, so many ways to tap knowledge, so many ways to reassert our dignity, for us to cash it in, to forsake the tomorrow, and to neglect our future, and to mortgage our nation's entire wealth, its youth, would be a criminal act. That is why there is so much more responsibility for you, on you, to become educated, to develop your mind, and to develop yourselves as enlightened, caring, critical beings. As John Gardner once said, "You have to be a critical lover, or loving critic, but never be indifferent." And when it comes to American democracy that is what you should be, a critical lover and loving critic. God knows we have many imperfections, many problems. You should neither praise or condemn, you should understand that it is in your hands to shape this nation's future and that is why you are leaders, potential leaders. So don't give up your leadership role, don't choose the fast track over the long track, the easy over the arduous task because, as I said at the outset, in the entire history of this universe no one like you is going to come back again. So do justice to yourselves, justice to the society, and do justice to America and humanity.

Vartan Gregorian believes that there must be a common meeting ground of American culture, and that common ground must be cultivated by a liberal education. A liberal education integrates knowledge, brings persons of divergent backgrounds together, and calls each to serve the welfare of all. It brings assimilation without disintegration, a sense of community without loss of individuality. Each unique person will, in doing justice to society, also do justice to himself. This is vintage liberalism. A curriculum predicated upon it would forge a common bond among students who are unique as individuals and yet distinguishable in groups. At Brown University, 27 percent of the student body is composed of minorities (African Americans, Asian Americans, and Hispanic Americans). Brown's academic ranking is among the best in the country, and its president aims to bring students from various backgrounds together in a shared appreciation of Tolstoy and Cervantes. Brown is also the birthplace of the cartoon character "Politically Correct Man," and its campus is stirred by controversy over issues of race, ethnicity, and culture.

Like other institutions of higher education, however, Brown has to fight the isolating tendencies of modern knowledge. Students who might want to share in a community of scholarship find the university divided into departments and the departments divided into subdisciplinary specializations. The faculty do not know, much less talk to, one another. How can the students be expected to bridge disciplines when the university cannot? Gregorian's solution is a series of interdisciplinary courses bringing together several instructors who can address a common topic from their own disciplinary perspectives. One example that he cited is a course on the cosmos, taught by scholars from various fields. He is specifically critical of the debate over the proposed course "Culture, Ideas, and Values" that his alma mater, Stanford, has put in place of a required course in Western civilization. Instead, he thinks that universities must seek to integrate knowledge by new approaches.

The University of Oklahoma has, in recent years, sought to address Gregorian's concern. In its new general education curriculum (the product of four years of committee work), students are required to enroll in forty hours of general education coursework across four curricular areas, including symbolic and oral communication, natural science, social science, and the humanities. In implementing the new curriculum, the university aims to produce the kind of educated person that

Gregorian wants Brown University to produce. The university
task force responsible for preparing the curricular recommendations identified the problem as overspecialization.

The general education component of undergraduate education
has been deemphasized in recent years in the wake of demands
for increased preparation for the major. The result too frequently
has been the graduation of narrowly-educated students who are
ill-prepared to function as the enlightened citizens upon whom
our nation depends and who, indeed, are often unprepared to
adapt to the rapid changes with which our modern world confronts them.[9]

The goal of the general education curriculum, in the words of
an earlier task force report, is to "promote an understanding
and appreciation of universally shared human experiences."
To accomplish this goal, the university has created an approved list of general education courses, mostly at the freshman and sophomore level, from which students must select
a menu that will satisfy distribution requirements across the
four designated areas.

In addition to designating existing courses that qualify for
general education credit, the university also intends to develop some new courses specifically intended to serve general
education needs. Students are required to take one course in
non-Western cultures, and the university is promoting the
development of new courses to meet the demand. Among
the new courses are "Science and Civilization in Islam," and
"Chinese Drama."[10] In addition to new courses such as these,
the university is underwriting the cost of a new two-semester
course entitled "World Cultures and Traditions." This course
is intended to take the broad view of world cultures. Even
though the University is not proposing to have the course
team taught, it intends to hire several new instructors who
will teach individual sections of the course, and will seek
to emulate the kind of intellectual diversity that Gregorian's

instructional teams would bring to Brown. The course might, for example, explore the experiences of birth or death in different cultural settings, study the role of the family in various social contexts, examine the influence of religion on society as viewed in the Occidental and Oriental worlds, or contrast the Japanese concept of honor with that of medieval Europe.

The difference in the number of instructors is not the only or the most significant difference between what will happen at Brown and what will happen at the University of Oklahoma. Brown, a smaller institution, has a more diverse student body than does the University of Oklahoma; but Gregorian wants Brown students to be educated in a common intellectual heritage, one that will make Brown a community. At the University of Oklahoma, students will shop among a large number of courses that include introductory offerings in most disciplines in the College of Arts and Sciences, plus a few more-advanced courses that seem to fit the bill. The new multicultural courses will fill an apparent void in a curriculum that has in the past been shaped by disciplinary rather than cultural values. In the new course in world cultures, students will learn that the meaning of most human experiences, even universal ones like death, is always subject to cultural interpretation. Western civilization in general, and American culture in particular, will appear naturally among the available perspectives.

There is, of course, nothing inherently wrong with courses in Chinese art or world cultures. When the Oklahoma State Regents for Higher Education complete their announced task of rank-ordering all courses offered by higher education institutions in Oklahoma, courses such as these will no doubt be high on the list. The university needs to ensure, however, that in the emphasis on culture the meaning of the concept of culture is not itself lost from view. That concept is the product of Western civilization. It may be that multiculturalism itself presupposes the transformation from the older conception of culture as taste, intellectual capacity, and moral values (which

clearly guides Gregorian's thinking) to the new conception of
culture as the different ways that things are interpreted in
different places. A serious discussion of the meaning of culture
would require a consideration of the possibility that some
cultures are better than others when measured by an absolute
standard of human progress. Just what such a standard might
be would require a consideration of claims made about culture.
The inquiring mind would be led back to Kant, there to confront the substance of his argument.

All of this, of course, should have more to do with students
than with philosophers, professors, and presidents. Vartan
Gregorian asked the students to reexamine their commitments
in life, and he struck a responsive cord among many students.
Sophomore Katherine Bailey's eyes were opened by Gregorian.

Dr. Gregorian heavily stresses the role of arts, humanities, and
sciences. He tells us we need humanities to encourage us to
develop a mental adaptability. According to Gregorian, liberal
education gives students "perspective for reflection on the nature
of our lives." As members of society, we need to recognize human
courage and learn how to cope with success. He compliments
society for teaching our children to cope with success, but calls
society down for not teaching them to cope with adversity. Gregorian advises us "to find the golden mean between broad training and education." In my view, he wants us to determine a fixed
point for education to include the former and the latter in order
to reach the highest potential for learning. He also stresses the
role of humanities when he says, "If we care where we are going,
we must understand our past." His views on the importance of
the arts and humanities caught my attention. Before listening to
Dr. Gregorian's lecture, I hardly knew what humanities was, let
alone the importance of it.

The humanities' tug on Bailey is related to her conviction that
Gregorian is right when he says that people today are too self-
centered.

Most important to me in establishing stronger leadership is the need for a balance between individualism and community. People are overly preoccupied with themselves, their family, and their own condition of life. This constitutes self-centered materialism where a higher public and community interest is needed. This point was just one of many valuable ideas discussed in the leadership symposia. This symposia awakened me to many problems but also many potentials for our country and I am anxious to use my new knowledge.

Grover Compton shares this view.

Individualism has to be balanced with a sense of community identity. People's private lives need to be sacrificed in favor of the public needs. This is especially true concerning the young people of this nation who are gifted in some talent, leadership skills being one of these talents. America needs its "best and brightest" at the helm guiding the way, not quietly accumulating a fortune. This is not to say that a man should not strive to improve the quality of his private life, but that an equilibrium is the ideal situation.

What does community mean? Gregorian believes that a sense of community can only exist when persons from divergent backgrounds share in a common intellectual and moral heritage. The conflicting claims of community and group pull modern individuals in two different directions. Carrie Newton, a junior political science major, reflected the contemporary conception of culture as she stressed the need for multicultural awareness.

I use the term *intercultural* rather than *international* because *cultural* encompasses groups within nations and the issues they face, rather than simply being concerned with nations and their issues. In my international relations class we learned (at least I learned, I can't speak for the rest of the class) that there are nations and states. States consist of the territory and the government, while nations are the people, the language, and the culture. Essentially the life of the state is the nation or nations within it. That's what makes *intercultural* a much broader term than *international*. . . . I feel that the nature of most politicians and people in general is to overlook intercultural issues. They do not seem to realize that culture, more than government, shapes people's opinions, socializes people, and gives them their identity. What truly amazes me is why politicians and other leaders are not more interested in intercultural issues. It is generally accepted that we are living in a world that is growing smaller (not literally smaller). Buzzwords such as *global village* are prevalent in much of today's literature. Yet most leaders do not seem to have jumped onto this bandwagon. They have not realized that in the future they will have to answer to and lead a more diverse group of people. Perhaps Mikhail Gorbachev is one of the few persons who do realize this. . . . He knows what it is like to try to lead many different cultures with many different needs. American political leaders have been fortunate in that they have only had to concentrate on the white cultural group in America. . . . However, other nations within the United States are gaining numbers and power, and leaders will need to know how to interact with these groups. For the next generation of leaders to be successful, intercultural awareness must occur.

Notice that her international relations class stressed the distinction between states and nations. The state is the regime, an ephemeral political construct; the nation is the people, an enduring entity. Because the concept of the nation is rooted in the "people, the language, and the culture" of a society, it is a broader concept than that of the state. We must become educated, in Newton's view, about other nations (i.e., other peoples) and not just focus on the relations among states. By bridging the gulf between peoples through multicultural awareness, we can forge a better world.

Carrie Newton learned a lot in her international relations class. She makes the case for multicultural education as succinctly as any faculty committee could. The concept, as she invokes it, raises interesting questions, though. To take the example she cites, the Union of Soviet Socialist Republics came apart in 1991 precisely because the nations which it comprised (one of which is Vartan Gregorian's homeland) wanted to become states themselves. Multicultural awareness in the former Soviet Union meant that the union could no longer survive. There is a danger in multicultural consciousness; people may conclude that they like their own culture, do not like another culture to which they are politically attached, and want to separate. Balkanization is the likely result.[11] What could have prevented it? Perhaps the Soviet Union could have remained together if the various nations of which it was comprised had shared in a common conception of justice instead of having been corralled by the power of a totalitarian state. But in order for the various nations in the Soviet Union to have shared in a conception of justice, they would first have had to have a dialogue about the meaning of justice. That would have required freedom of thought and expression, and the sort of intellectual preparation that enables people to consider issues such as justice. They would have needed free universities that called students to inquire about the meaning of justice. If those universities had instead emphasized the relativity of all conceptions of justice, then upon what basis could a unified state have stood? It is perhaps for this reason that Aristotle held that what Carrie Newton calls the state (what he called the politeia or regime) was in fact more fundamental than the nation. Aristotle leads us to a conception of a just political community (polis) rooted in a shared understanding of the good. The sense of community and the sense of morality are inextricably linked.

Aristotle, of course, often has been studied in traditional liberal arts curricula. Perhaps there is a connection between that tradition and the sense of community for which Vartan Gregorian wants these students to search. Communications

major Johnny E. Pate, a senior, argued for the connection
between the sense of community and the liberal arts.

It is essential that we become reacquainted with humanities
and arts, for they are of vital importance to our cultural awareness. The humanities create a foundation, upon which a perception of ourselves is built. They give us an understanding of who
we are and where we came from. But most importantly, the
humanities allow us to identify ourselves as a community.

What is the difference between Pate's community and Newton's nation? In Vartan Gregorian's view a community is based
upon a shared commitment to certain ideals, whereas a nation
is a group of people sharing common language and culture.
The question, then, is whether ideals are capable of tran-
scending culture, or are merely products of culture. We are
brought full circle to the distinction between Kant's conception
of culture and that which is in vogue today. Proponents of
multiculturalism are correct in supposing that an appreciation
for cultural diversity is an inherent component of a liberal
regime. But if liberalism is itself simply a cultural product of
modern Western civilization, then what justifies our attachment to it?

Gregorian succeeded in convincing many students that the
kind of moral transformation required to salvage contemporary American culture requires education in the liberal arts.
Law student Sharon W. Doty put it this way.

The education system is also a place for encouraging rethinking
of value systems and reassessing what we see as right and wrong.
In one of the sessions, Dr. Sharp asked the question, What role
will the arts and humanities play in leadership for the future? It
seems to me that the arts and humanities are the very tools for
challenging values and exposing us to new ideas and new ways
of thinking. The really successfull artist is often the one who
reaches outside the boundaries of what is known or usual and

. . . tries to make a statement through words, sculpture, music, painting, performance art, or any other medium.

If that is true, and I believe that it is, then a study of the arts and humanities is critical to the formation of the values and thought processes of the future leaders. Leaders must know about the people they want to lead. It is not possible to know people by reading polls. Leaders must discover what is inside people . . . their views, their opinions, their hopes and dreams. The truly effective leader of tomorrow, whether in business, community, education, or government, will be the one who has taken the time to listen, read, and understand her fellow human beings.

But if the students accepted the proposition that their university owed them a liberal education, there was some doubt about whether it could deliver it. One student discussion group approached the subject by developing a conception of a liberally educated person and then examining the OU curriculum to see if it could produce one. Marla Gornetski spoke for the Crowe's Nest discussion group.

The consensus opinion of the group was that the University of Oklahoma did not contain the necessary programs to "turn out" well-rounded individuals upon graduation. We looked at the general education classes that are currently required by the university. Some of the colleges within the University of Oklahoma only require beginning English 1113 and 1213, Political Science 1113, and either History 1483 or 1493. This requirement is supplemented by an average of six more courses in some colleges. We felt this was insufficient to mold a well-rounded person. The university's attempt to produce highly skilled workers and technically trained managers has squeezed the arts and humanities out of the typical four-year curriculum. We felt that all students should be exposed to nearly every department within the university during the first two years of attendance, even if the student has already chosen a major field of study. . . . The University of Oklahoma does offer some opportunities to explore the arts and humanities, yet many students are not made aware of them. The

Honors Program at the University of Oklahoma offers a course entitled "The Academic Habit." This class requires students to attend a wide variety of cultural events both on and off campus and summarize their findings in eight short papers. This program is a step in the right direction and should be expanded to include the entire university. Everyone, not just the intellectually gifted, could benefit from this type of class atmosphere. Another area of curriculum my group felt should be emphasized was foreign language. In our world of increased international interaction, familiarity with another culture is of the utmost importance.

The Crowe's Nest group targeted the general education curriculum like a Tomahawk cruise missile. The general education requirements, even the new ones, require too few courses, and most of the available courses are at the freshman or sophomore level. The curricula in the Colleges of Engineering and Business Administration leave little opportunity for students to sample courses in the College of Arts and Sciences. Students in Arts and Sciences are freer to explore, but are not required to get a broad exposure in their first two years. The reimposition of general education requirements represents a return toward a more structured curriculum from the cafeteria-style approach popular in the 1970s, but it lacks the teeth to ensure that most OU students are as enriched as Vartan Gregorian thinks they should be.

The Crowe's Nest came to a logical conclusion, but it is unlikely to reflect the prevailing opinion of the student body if Vartan Gregorian is correct in describing what modern individualists are like. Most students do not want more requirements, they simply want better courses from which to choose. Timothy R. Ford, a sophomore letters major, put it bluntly. "As an undergraduate, I was not forced to declare a major; instead, I was invited to shop intellectually. The University of Oklahoma has distribution requirements designed to encourage this kind of exploration. Unfortunately, the typical undergraduate views the requirements as obstacles, not opportunities. For many at OU, diversity means going to both football and basketball games." The ultimate solution to the problem of modern individualism is not to coerce individuals to do things in groups (like taking required classes) but instead to convince them that it is in their own interest to choose to do so. Americans are indeed guided by the principle of self-interest rightly understood. In appealing to it, however, it makes a difference if the appeal is made on the basis of narrow economic interest, as so much of the education reform movement in Oklahoma is, or on the basis of a fuller and better conception of self, as Vartan Gregorian proposes. In considering these alternatives, the students are confronted with the question of who they are and the decision of who they want to become. The choice is as interesting as they make it.

CHAPTER 4

THE ECONOMIC CHALLENGE

IN THE TWO DECADES FOLLOWING World War II America prospered, giving rise to a political consensus based upon what the historian Godfrey Hodgson has called the assumption of abundance.[1] The American economy dominated all others in world trade and investment, and from the proceeds of the new American abundance a more just and decent society would be forged at home. By the early 1970s, when Hodgson's survey of postwar America ended, the postwar political consensus had been shattered by the civil rights crusade, the Vietnam War, and the Watergate episode. Significantly, the faith in perpetual abundance had also been shaken as the economy fell victim to a rapid increase in inflation and unemployment—stagflation, as it came to be called—and a new generation of politicians came into public life talking about the "limits of growth."

In the 1980s the American economy was restarted, with the Federal Reserve Board holding a tight grip on the money supply in order to restrain inflation, and the Reagan administration administering massive doses of Keynesian deficit spending under the guise of "supply-side" economic theory. From 1983 through the end of the decade, the economy experienced uninterrupted economic growth in the midst of which the oil industry crashed, revived, and crashed again, the stock market soared, crashed, and then soared again, real-estate

169

magnates boomed and busted, the savings and loan industry squandered billions of dollars in secured savings at the taxpayers' expense, and Wall Street predators engaged in an orgy of leveraged buyouts and hostile takeovers. The shattered liberal consensus of which Hodgson had written was not reborn, but instead the search for a guiding ideal gave way to the untrammeled pursuit of wealth. The novelist Tom Wolfe, chronicler of the Me Decade of the 1970s, saw in the American culture of the 1980s a return to the excesses of the 1920s without the saving grace of the hope that had infused that earlier golden era. His book, *The Bonfire of the Vanities*, is a parody of *The Great Gatsby* in which there is lacking both the naive optimism of Jimmy Gatz and the engaging sentimentality of the predator Meyer Wolfsheim.

While the American economy lurched, those of its major economic competitors surged ahead. That West Germany and Japan would experience faster growth than the United States (thus causing America to be in "relative decline" with respect to them) was preordained by the devastation of war. But the economic engines that were created in the two Axis powers (neither of which was permitted by their war-time conquerors to invest much in defense) came by the 1980s to threaten America's global competitiveness. The result was to heighten American awareness of its relative position in the world economy, the threats to it posed by the growing economies of Europe and the Pacific Rim, and the necessity of new policy responses in the United States in both the public and private sectors.

The Centennial Leadership Symposium in Business and Technology focused on this broad problem. The keynote speakers were John Naisbitt, futurologist and evangelist of free enterprise, and John S. Foster, Jr., whose career has encompassed high-level positions in both business and government, including vice president for TRW Energy Systems Group, director of research for the U.S. Department of Defense, and a host of science- and defense-related commissions.

Foster currently chairs the Defense Science Board. Other participants included business leaders from a variety of fields including banking, the savings and loan industry, retailing, and oil and gas production. The students who participated reflected a broad range of disciplinary majors. From among these participants four major perspectives emerged on the challenges to the American economy in the 1990s. They were those of the free marketeer, the industrial strategist, the business leader, and the student in search of a career. These perspectives gave rise to an interesting mix of shared and contradictory opinions. John Foster's keynote address provided an outline of the challenges facing the American economy in the years ahead.

The Next New Frontier

John S. Foster, Jr.

A century ago Oklahoma was on the geographical frontier of the United States. This gathering shows that Oklahoma is still on the frontier. This time it is the frontier of thought and education. Our world has become a lot more complex since the days of the Indian Territory and early Sooners who are the roots of this great institution. Today science and technology, not the covered wagon and the plow, are the basic tools of national progress. Today, technology creates new opportunities for our people. New opportunities are jobs. And jobs are the core of a nation's economic and international power. Think of the new technological industries that have appeared in the lifetimes of most of us here today. Computers, television, jet airplanes, microelectronics, satellites for intelligence and for communications. Those are just a few. But just those few employed millions of people around the world in jobs that just did not exist a few decades ago.

Both in the material things which make our lives better, and the jobs at which most Oklahomans work, the Oklahoma of 1990 is far different from the Oklahoma that Bill Crowe left in the 1940s to become a midshipman at Annapolis. The entire process creates national wealth, high standards of living, a growing economy, and greater opportunities for all. The physical frontier might be gone, but the technological frontier and the promise it holds are truly endless. But in today's competitive world the achievement of national wealth with the better life it brings depends on more than just scientific and technological achievement. It depends on American leadership in science and technology. And that is where I believe we should return: to American leadership in science and technology, the byword of earlier times.

I believe there is a golden rule of interdependence between those who invent new technology in our research communities and those who apply it in industry to create jobs and wealth: the branches of our national government that encourage and support technological effort, the departments and agencies that administer policies that impact science and technology, and last but not least, the educational institutions that must cultivate curiosity and pass on knowledge to the next generation.

Our future as a world leader requires that all of these communities do unto others as each would have them do unto themselves. In this modern context, interdependence is the key concept of the golden rule. The United States government must create laws and regulations which recognize, if not support, the economic needs of the state of Oklahoma. The state of Oklahoma must provide adequate funding for the educational institutions that shape its future leaders. The University of Oklahoma must teach courses which prepare its students for the jobs that the business community needs to fill.

How are we doing in this world of interdependent necessity? Well, frankly, not too well. We are seeing some truly disturbing and potentially serious trends. Our educational system is under stress at all levels. Scientific and technical teaching has collapsed in most of our secondary schools, and even in some colleges and universities. And our skilled engineering and technical work force is shrinking. There is a growing disenchantment with the performance of our government. Federal lawmakers often do not perceive the needs of state and local governments, and rarely take into account the competitive issues facing American business. At the same time, it is increasingly difficult to attract talented and experienced people to public service to manage the responsibilities of government because the government itself has placed so many barriers in the way of the flow of the people into the government and out of the government. Reversing these trends will require an informed nation and a consensus for change as well as a lot of hard work and above all, leadership. Which, of course, is why we're here tonight.

There are a few hopeful signs. One of the most impressive is a development in the crucial field of education that comes out of Oklahoma itself. I am enormously impressed by the legislation that was passed just this year to implement the recommendations of your Task Force 2000. It is a major accomplishment. And at the risk of telling you what you already know, I cannot resist enumerating some of its outstanding provisions.

It institutes a salary increase for teachers with incentive pay. And it raises a beginning teacher's salary to $17,000 a year in 1991. It encourages greater use of technology and innovation in the classroom. It makes high school graduation dependent upon attaining a certain level of competency. It implements strong school accreditation standards. It replaces the current teacher tenure system with a streamlined due process system. It requires study to make sure teachers of the future are prepared for the new challenges facing education. It establishes an alternative certification process for schools to employ professionals with expertise in math and science to teach in secondary schools. And finally it puts real muscle into these provisions by earmarking revenue from new taxes for mandated education reforms.

I congratulate you on this forward-looking legislation. I am particularly heartened by the provisions it contains to raise teacher salaries with incentives. This is an absolute must. If we want leadership in the classroom or anywhere else, we must provide the rewards and the respect that will attract the most talented people. You have taken a major step forward and I urge others across the country to emulate your example.

Task Force 2000 also clearly follows the golden rule of interdependence in a modern society. It links schools of Oklahoma to the needs of business and industry, and to the needs of the nation. And it seeks to compete in a world that is no longer awed by American technology and productivity. Now business, government, and our research institutions must follow Oklahoma's lead. The need is urgent because America has, for example, fallen behind in a number of cutting-edge technologies that could mean jobs and growth for our people. Here are a few: high-temperature superconductors, advanced materials, thin diamond coatings, semi-conductors, high-density data storage, high-resolution television. Even this short list is sobering. But the total list gets longer every day. Ironically some of these are technologies that we invented in the first place. In these, as with others in recent decades, we have failed to sustain our entry into the marketplace. Too often, the bridges are out between the laboratory and the customer, and between engineering and the factory floor. Too often we tend to go for what the technologists want to develop rather than what the customer needs. Too often we fail to invest in the high-value manufacturing processes required to produce high-quality, reliable, low-cost products.

We have violated the golden rule. We have forgotten about the interdependence of all elements of the system. The result is that we have lost our lead in the marketplace, and our reputation for quality. To see how severe the consequences have been, we need only to look at our trade balance. You know, it is particularly ironic, because there was a time when "Made in the U.S.A." meant top of the line. Yes, there are some moves afoot to mend the situation. Total quality management programs are appearing in a number of companies as Professor Deming's ideas come home to his native land. They are urgently needed. We need to drive home the concept of total quality in every step of the design, the development, the manufacturing, and the marketing processes. The future heroes of industry will be the technologists and the managers who are dedicated to a continuous product and process improvement in all aspects of the jobs, and who understand the interrelationship between all of the steps involved in bringing a product to market. That, however, means reversing the habits of the last two or three decades. It will require tough, determined leadership in government, and in industry.

Perhaps a good place to start practicing the golden rule would be in the scientific community. Over the next decade, giant projects now in their initial stages will cost this country some $160 billion. And that does not count inflation, developmental delays, and the inevitable upward revision in costs. Examples include the Superconducting Super Collider, the national aerospace plane (commonly known as the "Orient Express"), the program to map the human gene, the space station, and a possible manned mission to Mars.

The press has come to call most of these "big science." And they are indeed the Olympics of science and technology. The United States needs to pursue both big science and small science. These are the interdependent legs of our scientific stool. We must maintain a balance between these huge technologically exciting projects and the smaller ones that, while not as dramatic, are every bit as important. But it seems to me that we are currently out of balance. I believe that during the 1980s the technical community proposed and the administration and Congress approved too many large projects in too short a time. These megaprojects now threaten a wide spectrum of small science. And these small science endeavors are the seedbed of our technological progress. Investigator-initiated research has given us such scientific breakthroughs as the transistor, the laser, and antibiotics. It has produced six out of the last ten Nobel Prizes in physics awarded during the 1980s.

Furthermore, small science is a true bargain. A single billion dollars could reinvigorate the entire field. Yet the trend is in the opposite direction. In fiscal 1991, for the first time, the administration's budget request for the largest big science project of all, the space station, involved more money than they requested for the entire National Science Foundation. Some of these huge projects are already showing signs of trouble. The space station is wrestling with problems that have caused some to question whether it is even buildable. The Superconducting Super Collider's costs are escalating well beyond the original estimates. The perception is emerging that the scientific and technical communities have pushed for programs that exceed their ability to manage effectively. The result is a growing concern that these communities are feathering their own nests at the expense of the larger national interests. Such a perception can only diminish the scientific community's stature with the American public. I don't believe that we can afford that. If we are to avoid it, scientific leaders must find a way to focus on the nation's priorities and place those broad priorities above narrower individual and institutional interests.

As ineffective as they often are, perhaps it is time for a blue ribbon commission to review the situation and, if not apply the golden rule of interdependence, at least provide recommendations for a more balanced application of our precious national assets on science. My vote is for a national science and technology strategy.

Perhaps in no area of our whole complex society is there more room for the golden rule than the relationship between government and industry. At present distrust and acrimony reign supreme. One result has been a burden of legislation, regulation, and congressional oversight that has brought the government procurement system near paralysis, radically slowed the introduction of new technology into defense and other government-supported systems, and discouraged a growing number of companies from even doing business with the government.

A number of blue ribbon studies on this problem have been made without making much of a dent in it. So, as I said a few moments ago, that is not always the best way to solve the problem. But at the core of this problem are years of mounting distrust between the government and industry. So long as that distrust is allowed to deepen and fester, the problem will only get worse. It must be changed, and doing so will be a leadership challenge of the first order. One example is the interrelationship of our financial markets and our tax laws to long-term research and development. We have allowed these to be skewed too much in favor of short-term profit and quick gains—in short, in favor of today's profit at the expense of tomorrow's national best interests. As current tax and investment laws are structured, the corporation that sacrifices some short-term quarterly profit in order to invest in long-term growth is actually penalized for its foresight. Its stock price is likely to be pushed down, and it will be taxed on its R&D investment in its own and the nation's future.

The Japanese say that we have the "English disease," because that is how England slid from being the world's greatest industrial power a century ago to its present second- or third-rate status. This problem is deeply embedded both in legislation and in the economy as a whole. Changing it will be a matter of major leadership for legislators and industry alike. But it must be done. I believe that a major reason why we have not done a better job in developing more equitable tax and research and development policies is the gulf of mistrust and misunderstanding between government and business leaders, and what it takes to compete in the current business world. Too few government people, especially in the established bureaucracy, have ever had to meet a payroll. While being able and dedicated Americans they have never faced the threat of Japanese or German or other national firms at their customer's doorstep.

They are unlikely to ever understand it unless we make it more attractive for our most capable, experienced people from business, industry, and academic worlds to enter public service without suffering severe damage to their careers and to their finances. We must respect the integrity of Americans who wish to give some of their time and abilities to the responsibilities of government service. Think about those responsibilities for a moment in terms of science and technology and their role in enhancing national economic growth and competitiveness—the development of national science and technology policies, exploring space, cleaning up and protecting the environment, managing the national laboratories, providing leading-edge technology for a national defense, and a long list of others.

This is no job for amateurs. Unhappily though, it has become increasingly difficult to attract experienced people to public service because of the so-called ethics legislation. This is legislation that Congress has enacted over the past few years. The public-spirited business executive who agrees to put his or her expertise and understanding of the interrelationship between public and private sectors at the service of the country is now required to give up pension benefits and stock holdings and submit to an intense review of his or her finances, tax returns, and family relationships. On top of all of that, he or she must take a cut in pay, as much as 90 percent for a position in the upper reaches of government. And after leaving government service, our executive

is, in effect, forbidden to work in his or her field for as much as
three years, and in some instances the prohibition is lifelong. The
Congress recently suspended implementation of the latest round
of ethics restrictions, so maybe they finally realized that things
had gone too far. But that is only a stopgap. These laws, I believe,
must be radically modified and, furthermore, they should be
made to apply to all branches of government.

The move of business people in and out of government service
is one part of the issue. Career government service is the other.
I have been encouraged by President Bush's support of the civil
service. He has proposed a federal pay raise plan and he has
made speeches praising the nation's civil servants. It is high time.
Talented people will look for careers only where they are well
respected and rewarded. In fact, I urge those of you starting out
on your careers in the near future to consider spending at least
some time in government service. I can tell you from my own
experience in government that working for the government can
provide you with the deepest sense of career satisfaction, a sense
that you've had a discernible positive impact on the events of the
day. Most important of all, you will learn the workings of the
political system, and those are the skills of leadership. This is
invaluable knowledge.

Scientific and technological expertise alone is not enough. It
won't navigate you through Washington's political shoals. Political skills are absolutely essential. You must learn to identify who
the political players are, whose support you need, how to weld
them together in a political coalition strong enough to get the
kinds of policies that are required and the funding support that
you need. The best and quite possibly the only place to learn
these skills is inside the government. And perhaps you may leave
government service with the golden rule in mind, at least with a
keener understanding of the interdependence of government,
business, and even education.

Yes, education. There are leadership challenges galore in technology, industry, science, and government, but possibly the most
urgent one that we face is now in education. Education is a critical
foundation for our nation, and that foundation is turning to
rubble because our educational system is in decline. The recent

report of the National Commission on Excellence in Education stated that, and I quote, "If an unfriendly foreign power had attempted to impose on America the mediocre educational performance that existed today, we might well have viewed it as an act of war."

National technological prowess begins or fails in the schools. That is where young people are introduced to science and technology, taught their principles, provided with the necessary skills, and motivated to pursue careers in engineering and technology. That isn't happening. You have already heard the appalling statistics of our children's dismal performance in standard mathematics tests, only barely ahead of Third World countries; the sobering prediction of massive shortfalls in numbers of trained scientists and engineers by the century's end; the dwindling number of American students going for Ph.D.s; the woeful lack of scientific or mathematical qualifications among our teachers. To quote Harvard President Derek Bok, "If you think education is expensive, try ignorance."

We all know what the problem is. The question is how do we change it. The answer involves far more than altering the habits and structures of our colleges and universities. It must reach back all the way to the beginning, to the attitudes we inculcate in children from kindergarten on up. We must insist that school curriculums from the earliest years include strong exposure to math and science. We must ensure that teachers at all levels are fully qualified to teach them, and that they have up-to-date textbooks, computers, and laboratory equipment to make the subjects exciting and interesting and relevant. In particular, we must also ensure that young girls and black, Hispanic, and other minority students are encouraged to study math and science. This will require our most innovative leadership simply because these are historically the very groups that are most alienated from science and math.

Add them up, though, and they are far from being a minority. They constitute the majority. They constitute the majority of the country. They will be the new American leadership. So if we want trained scientists and engineers in the years to come, we need to start cultivating these young people now. These are all problems to be addressed in the early school years through high school. But even our institutions of higher learning have not escaped the troubles afflicting our educational system. At too many of our colleges and universities we are grappling with a particularly troublesome problem—the catastrophic decline in teaching and its relative eclipse by research.

Too often faculty members simply are not rewarded for spending time with undergraduates. It seems to me that both teaching and research are important; and, in particular, that the combination of teaching and research by college professors enhances both their teaching and their research. But the research must not be emphasized to the detriment of teaching of undergraduates. To do so is to mortgage the nation's scientific future and its economic competitiveness.

Once again, it comes down to leadership and interdependence. It is understandable that colleges and universities should seek to accommodate those who receive federal grants. It is understandable that faculty members should choose to expand their careers along paths promising the most rewards. But we all need to step back and look at what the country needs, and then work to improve the system so it rewards the people who contribute to those needs.

What the country needs now is more young people entering scientific and engineering fields. University administrators and faculty also need to revisit their attitude toward introductory science courses. Too often, introductory math and science courses seem to be designed to weed out students rather than gather them in. The ones that make it through are very good indeed; but the ones that do not make it emerge discouraged and alienated. Given the proper encouragement and help, some of them might have turned into very competent scientists and engineers. And remember the demographics I mentioned earlier. The scientists and engineers of the future are going to have to come increasingly from among women, blacks, Hispanics and other minorities, groups that are most likely to be discouraged by a hostile classroom environment.

We can't afford to let them stay that way. Those introductory courses have got to be user friendly. If we are to redress the situation that I have outlined this evening, we all have to play our part in this interdependent world. College and university faculty must refocus on their relationships between teaching and research. More and more, teaching must become a primary mission. We must encourage young minds and talents, especially in the coming decades as we work to undo the damage our long neglect has caused. Teaching must become cultivated, respected, and rewarded. Students must turn their attention, talents, and their intelligence to the scientific and technical fields because they are our future. They bring us intellectual and economic growth and the world leadership. Without them the United States and our lives as Americans will inexorably decline.

Students who go on to enter university careers must place teaching at the center of their responsibilities. Teaching is among the greatest of the arts, and the young people whose lives leaders change and redirect will remember them for a lifetime. Those who go into industry, especially in the engineering disciplines, must understand the entire process of bringing a product to market. They must certainly understand the importance of the manufacturing step. That is where the money is made. And, in the future, profits will depend directly on the caliber of our product and the production process, the manufacturing technology, and our quality consciousness.

Therefore, our engineering schools must broaden their curricula to include a stronger focus in manufacturing and production engineering, and a no-rejects approach to designing-in quality. I would like to see more schools create endowed professorships for manufacturing. Industry must step up to the job of helping the universities develop such courses. They must donate their own expertise and help make equipment, financial support, and human resources available. State governments and local industries need to establish more regional consortia for science and technical education.

Oklahoma has already shown it is determined to improve education within its borders. It might take the lead in such a regional endeavor. If you younger people follow my urging and devote part of your career to government service, then focus your attention and efforts on the politics of science and technology. Learn the important questions and issues, what should be the objectives, what strategies are viable. Learn how to assign responsibility and authority to others to design and implement plans and programs.

At the public level, Congress must face the need to put the country first, ahead of individual gain and party politics. The political tug of war between Congress and the executive branch is built into our Constitution, and we should neither expect nor wish it to go away. But we have passed the limit if this country is to remain a great power in the coming century. For Congress to assert its authority is right and natural. For Congress to paralyze the executive branch and to provide language on just how the executive branch should manage its programs and unduly restrict those who should and would serve is improper and destructive.

It boils down to one thing: leadership—leadership in every area and at every level. It seems to me that what we have to do is rethink the habits of narrow self-interest that have characterized our public and our private lives in recent years. We must adhere to the golden rule as it applies to science and technology in our society. We need to remember that we all belong to a great nation and that its future is in our hands. In the long run the good of the nation is the good of each of us. If some of us fail, we all do. If any of us succeed, we must all succeed. Or as Ben Franklin observed on another occasion, "We must all hang together, or assuredly we shall all hang separately."

The United States has been singularly favored by history. Every other nation in human history has been molded by scarcity. The United States has been molded by abundance. Now, however, the era of ease and affluence has passed. Henceforth in the face of ever-more-challenging foreign competition, abundance will be the result of hard work, sustained work, generous cooperation, and clear-sighted leadership in education, manufacturing, technology, science and government. Central to all of these areas are science and technology.

More is at stake here than our wealth, our comfort, and our world leadership. The great ideals of democracy and personal freedom are on the line. Human beings believe in political ideals and institutions only so long as they think those ideals and institutions bring strength, security, and success. Americans have enjoyed unparalleled material success, and our resulting wealth and power helped to make our ideals and institutions glamorous to the rest of the world. But we sometimes forget that our success rested on our technological accomplishments. If we carelessly allow the technological preeminence to decay, then outside observers will come inevitably to the conclusion that the validity of our political ideals may be in question.

Freedom has brought us strength and success. It is up to us to reciprocate.

In calling for a national economic strategy based upon the golden rule of economic interdependence, Foster confessed his faith in the mediating role of public institutions in private business, and the need for a synergistic relationship between the two. In the debate between big science and small science, he wants *public* support of both. In refashioning America's human capital, he wants to refurbish the country's *public* educational institutions. He praised Oklahoma's recently enacted educational reform bill that is designed to infuse the state's school systems with more *public* resources. In forging links among private-sector initiatives and between the public and private sectors, he favors a *public* national commission to set a science and technology strategy for the nation. And in leading America into the next century he believes that *public* service by private businessmen is essential, and that careers in *public* service must be made more rewarding.

This is the language of a person whose experiences have been at the nexus of public and private service. The individual entrepreneur sees the world from the narrow perspective of the small business firm. The head of the giant corporation has a perspective that is substantially broader but no different in kind. The political executive's point of view is even more comprehensive, but channeled by the ephemeral demands of politics. The first responds to markets, the second to boards and stockholders, and the third to voters. It is only by grasping the interconnections between the worlds according to each that one can grasp the underlying complexity of the situation that confronts all. The nonelected public servant, career or noncareer, comes to have an understanding of the whole that is less prejudiced by constituencies than the elected official's and more comprehensive than is available in the private sector.

The proposal to establish a blue ribbon commission to develop a national science and technology strategy is technocratic. Foster is drawn to it despite a learned skepticism. It embodies a belief in planning by those best qualified to plan. These will be persons whose life experience is rooted in private-sector management but leavened with public-sector participation. Coming together under public auspices, a distinguished group of such persons can take the system from cradle to grave and design a program for national renewal. Such a program would involve addressing the foundations—America's eroding system of education—as well as the marginal policy choices in national planning and investment in research and development. The proposal faces two evident obstacles. Can such a plan actually be designed, given limitations on human knowledge? And if it can, will the political system demonstrate the will to implement it? Foster is aware of both problems, and is especially concerned about the latter. The leaders of tomorrow who traverse the ground between public and private management must possess the political acumen to win acceptance for their plans among the political actors upon whom the implementation must ultimately depend.

Foster's policy prescriptions require substantial public investment. While he emphasizes the value of small science and points out that it is relatively cheap in comparison with big science, he wants to see both funded. The practical implications of his recommendations with respect to reform of public education make the Oklahoma reform bill seem like a useful first step down a long and expensive road. The revitalization of career civil service will require significantly higher salaries and hence greater governmental cost. Under the Foster regime, taxes or deficits will go up, not down. He favors the Oklahoma school reform and funding bill, which raised taxes $230 million. It is significant that he does not choose to emphasize the federal deficit or the general level of taxation among the problems plaguing the economy, and the reason is obvious: his solutions will require either taxes or the deficit to grow absent a full-scale attack on defense or welfare spending, which he does not recommend.

It is not surprising, then, that Foster's prescriptions are in a different direction from those raised by the business executives composing the symposium's distinguished panel. From where they sit, the problem is too much government rather than not enough. Three main issues raised by panelists illustrate the corporate perspective: the national debt, government regulation, and national energy policy. The issue of the national debt was raised by the CEO of J. C. Penney, William R. Howell.

I feel that one of the greatest threats to improved productivity and private investment in our great country is the federal deficit and the mounting national debt. In 1980, the U.S. federal deficit was $73.8 billion, 2.9 percent of the nominal GNP. Last month, the White House estimated that fiscal year 1991 deficit will reach $232 billion, 4 percent of nominal GNP. Our ability to improve productivity with new investment is reduced by the federal deficit. As control of resources is transferred from the private sector to the government, the cost of funds increases through higher interest rates, which we are experiencing right now in 1990, and private investment declines, which we are also experiencing right here in 1990. Over the long term, reduced investment and productivity lowers your standard of living and my standard of living. I am concerned about that as I look to the future.

During the last decade, our government has not made progress in reducing the deficit. Failure to adequately address the deficit issue has resulted in a mounting national debt at proportions that no one, not even Naisbitt, forecasted in 1980. In 1980, our national debt was $1 trillion. I don't know how many of you have even seen $1 million in currency. I've never seen that much currency on a table, let alone $1 trillion. A lot of good things happened in the eighties but we ended up with a national debt of $3.5 trillion in a period of ten years. Now it's forecasted by 1995 (and this is probably entirely too conservative) that our national debt will be $4.5 trillion. This is totally unacceptable, in my opinion. The interest payment alone is $160 billion a year and it will soon be the largest single item in our national budget.

In New York City on the corner of Sixth Avenue and Forty-second Street, an electronic sign, the marvel of today's communication, records for all of us the national debt. On the right-hand column where the dollars are recorded—and a dollar is still a dollar to me today—the numbers are moving so fast that the human eye cannot even discern what the numbers are. You've got to get over to the thousand dollar column to determine what's going on in terms of our national debt as a society.

Deficit reduction must come, but not in the form of higher taxes because we need to stimulate our economy, not retract it. Historically, Congress has not exercised restraint in spending. The record demonstrates that Congress is a spending agent. They have always spent more than our revenues have contributed to the well-being of this nation. Specifically, we collect about 20 percent and spend about 23 percent of the gross national product. That is out of balance. No company represented in this room could survive or exist long term while spending more than they take in.

The pain, I think, will be difficult. A lot of people like to campaign on the issue of reducing the deficit but no one has been able to accomplish it once in office. It's time to face up to the pain. The pain of spending cuts is preferable today to the pain of a complete financial and economic collapse. I sincerely believe that most of us today want to turn a better world over to you than we received. Unless, however, we do something about deficit spending and start reducing this national debt, the world will not, in fact, be a better place than it was when we inherited it.

Like John Foster, who faults the Congress for shackling executive leadership, William Howell lays the blame for the federal deficit squarely on the shoulders of the Congress members who voted for it. Defenders of the Congress might point out that during the 1980s neither President Reagan nor President Bush submitted a single balanced budget to the Congress, and that the two Republican presidents signed every federally appropriated dollar into law. In fact, due to differing economic assumptions, it is not possible to demonstrate that the Congress appropriated more than the presidents requested. The real debate between the White House and the Congress has been over the distribution rather than the level of federal expenditures.

A policy failure as large as the federal deficit is big enough to spread its blame to all involved parties. The real question lies in the search for a solution. Howell rules out increased taxes, implying significant spending reduction. As a corporate CEO, Phillips Petroleum Chairman C. J. ("Pete") Silas would proceed just as he would in managing his own company.

I quite frankly do not have it within my prerogative to tell the president or Congress how to go about addressing it [the deficit]. But I can tell you that I would address it like every other issue at Phillips Petroleum or J. C. Penney or a bank, or wherever. In an operating enterprise, you put everything on the table. Nothing is left off. Until such time as the leadership in the White House and in Congress are willing to put everything on the table, and suffer the consequences at election time for their decisions, then we are going to have the deficit as a national issue.

Leaving everything on the table would, presumably, include increased taxation. Still, when Phillips Petroleum was faced with the threat of a hostile takeover in the 1980s in the face of a declining oil market, the company's response was to retrench. Pete Silas told the story.

One great experience certainly has affected my life and our corporate life since 1985. Many of you were in high school in 1985 when we had two successive takeover attempts of our corporation. At that time people felt that if you had too much equity, you ought to pass it out to the shareholders. They were looking for short-term gain and were not worried too much about the long term.

During this period of time, the stock market appeared more anxious to get equity out to the shareholders, and we took on a $9 billion debt and bought back half our stock. The price of oil was $26 a barrel. In so doing, we had to find some way to get our debt down. We were forced to sell some $2 billion of assets to buy down some of that debt and to restructure the corporation. One of the biggest reasons why the pyramid is coming out of corporations today is because of survival. You've got to cut your costs to be competitive with other companies as well as other countries.

We proceeded to reduce our work force by nine thousand people through early retirements and layoffs. Today our debt is down to $4 billion and we are doing very well. But in the meantime, the price of oil went from $26 a barrel to $9 a barrel, which was certainly very tragic, not only for our corporation, but for the whole Southwest. There were six oil companies that did not survive prior to this . . . we were the first one to survive.

Why did we survive and what did we learn from the experience of the 1980s that can affect our view of the 1990s? We've learned that we must be able to handle change and recognize the world is changing. The financial community was changing, our industry was changing, and we had to adapt to change or we would not survive.

Silas saved Phillips by cutting his payroll by nine thousand employees, reducing the scope of his company's activities, and reducing its debt. Why can't the federal government do the same? Why can't it be run like a business? The answer, of course, lies in politics. The conflicts between the Republicans and the Democrats, the presidency and the Congress, the military-industrial complex and the welfare state—in short, between and among Americans—is the stuff of which democratic politics is made. Public managers cannot act like private managers because of the constraints imposed upon them by the ordinary operation of a democratic political system.[2] Citizens in democracies are like stockholders in corporations—they want immediate dividends. Unlike corporate managers, however, democratic politicians cannot simply cut programs and payroll for the very good reason that the public wants them to continue, and will hold the politicians to account if they are cut. If the nine thousand employees who were riffed by Phillips had had the right to vote on the retention of top management, management would have had a strong incentive to keep them on the payroll.

Corporate frustration with the intransigencies of democratic politics is understandable, and understandably matched by a resistance to federal regulation. High on the list of salient issues for the 1990s propounded by the business executives was the overregulation of industry. Interestingly, the subject of government regulation of business was put on the symposium agenda by savings and loan executive George Jeffrey Records, CEO of the Midland Group. Responding to John Naisbitt's prediction that government's role in regulating business would decline in the future, Records found no basis for the prediction.

My experience has been exactly the opposite for the last two or three years. I've been running a savings and loan association and we have had a lot of problems in our industry. Those problems have been supposedly solved by some legislation. Now, instead of two regulators who supervise our business, we have overlaid two more regulatory apparatuses. Those regulatory apparatuses respond more out of fear of what the press is going to say about any actions that they take, rather than to what makes either economic or business sense. That is a terrible way to solve a problem which we do have in the financial industry in this country. That is a terrible way to induce more people to expose capital to risk in a business that clearly needs more capital to support financing homes and industry in this country. The leaders in the financial markets face a terrific problem in the next several years in overcoming the damage that has been done in the last two or three years to the regulatory system.

These problems didn't come about because we had a great number of bad people running financial institutions. These problems came about because we had watershed change in the economic conditions in which financial institutions operate and because we had some people who were breaking the law. We can take care of the people who were breaking the law. We have a court system to do that. To impose additional regulation on top of an industry that needs help is the wrong way to go about it.

There are all sorts of other businesses where government has become very intrusive in the last five or six years, and I don't see it getting any better. The oil business faces the same kind of problem with the Clean Air Act. Each one of these bills, like the Clean Air Act or FIRA (the Financial Institutions Recovery Act), takes on a life of its own. It builds up its own bureaucracy, they get their constituents, and they get their lobbyists and their newsletters. The next thing you know, there is an industry just to perpetuate that particular solution to the problem.

The savings and loan fiasco to which Records referred had its roots in the early 1980s, when industry representatives convinced the Reagan administration and the Congress that the regulations under which the industry labored were too restrictive to enable it to remain competitive in an increasingly competitive capital market. The government responded by relaxing restrictions, thus permitting savings and loan institutions to put depositors' money into more risky (and potentially more profitable) investments. The economy of the 1980s created pockets of investment dollars that were channeled through savings and loans into a variety of higher-risk real estate ventures. With the collapse of the oil industry (especially in the Southwest) came a corresponding collapse in real estate values, leading to a very high rate of loan defaults. The problem was compounded, as Records notes, by the unscrupulous and sometimes illegal practices of some savings and loan institutions. In responding to the crisis, the Congress took what is for it the natural path of more rather than less regulation, believing that, on the one hand, the industry had earned it, and on the other hand, the public expected it. The honest savings and loan operator who came through the crisis with a financially solvent institution had to pay the price in increased regulation for the misfortunes and transgressions of others. The new regulations, designed in part to bolster consumer confidence in the industry, hampered investment activity and discouraged larger capital investors.[3]

Records's concern about the manner in which government regulation has affected his business is reasonable, although some might say that the savings and loan scandals prove the necessity of governmental involvement. Records's larger point, however, is that government regulation of business is increasing, at a cost in productivity and competitiveness. This concern is related to Bill Howell's. The main reason why government regulation of business is likely to increase in the 1990s is because governments have no money to spend. Finding it difficult, if not impossible, to develop new spending programs, politicians have no alternative but to try and influence private business through the long arm of the law. Consider, for a moment, the likely outcome of John Foster's proposed blue ribbon commission on science and technology. He wants it to advocate more federal funding for small science, which it might do. But surely it would also explore ways in which to affect research and development investments in private business, in think tanks and private research organizations, and public research universities. Its proposals would include tax incentives and regulations.

The subject of government regulation of business is large and complex. Since all regulation adds to the cost of business,

business has a natural incentive to resist regulation and to find a partial cure for what ails it in reducing regulation. In some areas, however, where government's main purpose is to ensure a level business playing field, business has an incentive to support government regulation in order to make sure that everyone is playing by the same rules. When the government tries to create the playing field instead of merely leveling it, business will protest. Joseph H. Williams, CEO of the Williams Companies, echoed George Records's concern with regulation as it applies to the energy game.

In the energy industry the regulatory forces have tried to simulate a free market by adding more regulation to try to create it. You have to stop and say, "Wait a minute. What is going on here?" This is what centrally planned economies do. . . . I'm not so sure that Mr. Naisbitt has been in touch with all of the forces in society that are supposed to be dissipating, because I haven't seen them dissipate that fast.

Williams here touches upon a topic that is near and dear to the hearts of Oklahomans and illustrative of the complexities of the business-government relationship. It is natural that in Oklahoma business leaders would share a concern for the health of the oil and gas industry and a skepticism about federal energy policy. Phillips Petroleum Chairman Pete Silas spoke to this concern.

It would probably take all day to talk about the energy crisis and where we are today. As we are speaking today [in October 1990], at least 4.3 million barrels a day have been taken off the market out of Kuwait and Iraq. There is certainly a perceived shortage caused by a free market conviction that there is going to be an armed conflict in the Middle East. The result is a bid-up in the price of oil. At the same time, there has been an increase in production by the non-OPEC countries as well as the other OPEC countries not involved with Iraq and Kuwait. There is a chance to replace most of the oil that has been taken off the market, but maybe not all.

Energy has been brought back to the top of the agenda in this country. It cycles about every four, five, or six years up and down. We have, in a way, caused our problem. We have had policies in place since the late 1970s and early 1980s to import more oil. We are reluctant to build nuclear power plants, reluctant to have coal-fired power plants. We cannot burn gas for power generation and we have restricted off-shore exploration and exploration in Alaska. So we have put ourselves in this position of importing over half of our oil.

It is very important that we learn this lesson: We need an energy strategy to develop all of our energy resources. I hope we will get back to a basic understanding that we need nuclear power, we need coal, we need gas, we need oil. These energy developments can be done in an environmentally sound way. What really concerns me is that when we talk about alternate energies we are tempted to anticipate fusion, solar energy, and wind power. People say these new technologies are just around the corner; therefore, we don't have to make tough decisions about nuclear, coal, and oil. When you let a politician off the hook, when he does not have to make the tough decisions, he loves it.

But I can tell you, alternate energies are not going to take care of this country's economic strength. You need nuclear, you need oil, you need gas, you need it all, but we have to make some tough decisions. We are the world's largest consumer of energy and we have the cheapest energy. We are going to have to pay more or find ourselves right back where we are today for the third time around. I hope that as a result of the current crisis, not only the media but also the American public and Congress will recognize we have to make some tough decisions to solve our energy problem for the economic security of our country.

Silas recognizes that American reliance on imported oil is due to domestic political pressures. Environmental concerns limit the capacity to develop some alternative energy sources, and it is cheaper to buy oil abroad than to provide the kind of incentives that would make domestic extraction profitable. He might have added that Americans have not been eager to undertake conservation measures that would reduce the amount of energy consumed here. As Joe Williams noted, the federal government seems to want to have it two ways with the energy industry. It shackles the industry, on the one hand, with regulations to protect the environment and the consumer and, on the other hand, with more regulations designed to foster competition.

What does the domestic oil and gas industry want? Silas pointed to two ways to address the energy situation in order to avoid future crises. The first is the development of alternative energy sources. This proposal makes excellent sense from a public policy point of view, but may run counter to the interests of independent oil and gas operators who are unable to move as easily from one sector of the energy industry to another as are corporate giants like Phillips 66. The second proposal—to expand domestic production of oil and gas—also makes excellent sense if one's goal is to avoid dependence on foreign oil in the near-term future. (It might carry a different implication when viewed from the perspective of, say, the year 2200.) But what will it require? The oil and gas industry will need incentives to invest in exploration and extraction, and protection against being undersold in the domestic marketplace by foreign competitors. Oklahoma's representatives have often favored an oil import fee to stabilize the price of oil at a level at which a profit can be made. An oil import fee is, clearly, an act of the government.

Big business cannot, in fact, get along without government because government erects the framework required for corporate stability. If the government did not regulate the savings and loan industry and the stock market, who would invest in either? Big business does not object to regulation; it objects to "overregulation." The historic association between business and government that has characterized the American economy sets the representatives of the corporate mainstream apart from the new ideologists of the economic right who stress entrepreneurship, small business development, and low marginal tax rates. Their faith is in supply-side economics. In *Wealth and Poverty*, a book that received considerable attention in the early 1980s, supply-sider George Gilder argues that economic growth must come from the creative instincts of the entrepreneur who sees the potential for a market where one has never existed.[4] To the contrary, Pete Silas prefers the Japanese corporatist approach:

What I have tried to do with our research and development people is to make something the market wants. That is what the Japanese do. The Japanese are market-oriented. They find out what the market wants, and then go back and find what fits the market. In many cases, research and development has been done in this country for research and development's sake. You discover something, and then say, where can we sell this? With research and development focus, you have to go out and look for a market and then develop it, which may take twelve years. I have tried to convince our people in research and development to find out what the customer wants. Then you can shorten your time to the marketplace.

It is not surprising, then, that Silas finds himself ill at ease with the editorial pages of the *Wall Street Journal*, the traditional voice of American business, which succumbed in the late 1970s to the ideology of the supply-side right: "The *Wall Street Journal* does some wild things to business in its business reporting, even though they happen to have given a very favorable article to our company recently. But when the *Wall Street Journal* comes around, we all hold our breath."

This brings us back to John Naisbitt, like Gilder, a believer in the future, a future in which small businesses and creative entrepreneurs will lead America and the world to a better, more peaceful existence. Just as Gilder drew his examples of

the supply-side credo from among his neighbors in Massachusetts's Berkshire Mountains, Naisbitt also finds evidence of
the future surrounding him among the higher peaks of the
Colorado Rockies. Telluride, Colorado, an old mining town
that has become a posh resort area is, according to Naisbitt,
full of "small businessmen" who are able to manage regional
and national businesses from the mountain retreat by using
modern means of communications. It is, of course, easier to
buy into the Telluride real estate market if you have the benefit
of income from selling millions of books and handsome speaking fees to boot. The world of the entrepreneur whose main
product is himself—Michael Jordan, Michael Jackson, John
Naisbitt—is quite different from that of the company that has
to produce and distribute a product or service in a regional,
national, or international marketplace. The economics of ce-
lebrity are different from those of production and distribution.

To the hard-nosed business executives on the panel the
Pollyanaish view of the economic world that Naisbitt represents seems a bit farfetched. As their businesses struggle to
survive in a competitive, sometimes hostile, always difficult
environment, they find it hard to believe that war will end,
that deficits don't matter, and that free markets are always
preferable to protectionist policies. Similarly, it is easy to see
why an apostle of growth like Naisbitt would say that governmental control of business is withering away, that the national
and trade deficits are not a significant problem, and that new
management techniques will permit corporate America to regain the competitive edge.

And what do the students make of all this? Among the
questions and issues elicited from the student discussion
groups and the papers that each student wrote were a number
addressed to particular issues raised by speakers and panelists, such as economic competitiveness, privatization of
schools (to be discussed in chapter 5), the federal deficit, and
so forth. But among the papers written by the students three
issues surfaced more frequently than others: women in leader-

ship, ethics in business, and the cultural dimension of the international economy. The students, unlike their adult role models, by and large eschewed national strategy, the value of free markets, and the vices of excessive regulation in favor of issues that seemed to touch them in a more personal way.

John Naisbitt introduced the subject of women in leadership by claiming that the next generation would witness the emergence of women in leadership roles in all walks of life. He emphasized the contributions that women would make in the business world by altering management styles. Naisbitt offered his audience the following facts.

Women have been starting new businesses in the United States at twice the rate of men. And today just about 50 percent of the accountants are women. A third of all computer scientists are women. We are moving into critical mass. A third of the managers in advertising, public relations, and marketing are women. Overall 40 percent of the managers in business today are women. A third of the M.D. degrees granted today are granted to women, 40 percent of law degrees. The freshman classes and in law or medicine are more or less 50-50. In the year 1970, women were awarded fewer than 10 percent of the M.B.A.s in the United States. Now that figure is up to about a third, and increasing each year.

Along with this increased role for women has come an alteration in management. Women, Naisbitt claims, are by nature suited to the needs of the new business workplace, with its emphasis on communication and information. Naisbitt again:

I think, too, that the managerial styles, as a result of how women are acculturated, are more suitable to the information workplace. In the industrial workplace, people got paid for doing what they were told to do, and the managers were order-givers. But in the new information workplace, we have to have managers who can create nourishing environments for personal growth.

Women are much more acculturated to creating and nourishing individual growth and individual creativity. That is what is called for and what is needed in the new workplace.

The notion that women will succeed in business management by transferring their nurturing roles from home to office makes some women cringe. Freshman Marcy L. Phillips, in an essay entitled "Could Oklahoma Be Trendy?" had this reaction to Naisbitt's remarks:

In a state that is so economically depressed, the increasing role of women in the workplace is welcome. As more women work and attain better positions, their family income will increase. From history, it is known that when income increases, families spend more money, and thus the economy improves. Once women are taken more seriously in significant job roles, our state will reap the benefits from a desperately needed improved economy.

An additional benefit of women flooding the business field . . . is a more comfortable homelike atmosphere in the workplace. Although Oklahoma is a very competitive state, our people dislike the cold, harsh attitudes that accompany the furiousness of the fast-pace business world. I have often heard my dad and my grandpa recollecting fond memories of working with "good ole boys" who always had time to go fishing on a Saturday morning or catch a Browns game at the corner pub. True, most women aren't likely to chat with their colleagues about that game forty years ago when the great Bob Fenimore ran the winning touchdown against OU. Still, their innate gentleness and compassion can put any man at ease in his office. In a state where men grow up attached to their revered mothers, women coworkers possess the ability to transform stark-white, lonely offices into homey abodes where men as well as other women can work with more ease and comfort.

Junior psychology major Pamela Brandes rejected what she sees as gender bias in Naisbitt's view of women, but nevertheless affirmed his main point.

Generally, I do agree with Mr. Naisbitt's remarks, but I feel his views are lacking some of the actual reasons of the phenomena that he has observed. Naisbitt felt that one of the things that is facilitating woman's entry into the job market is the woman's role of "nourisher and provider" of society. For the most part, I agree with this assumption. Women of the Industrial Era generally had one of two occupations: they were nurses or they were homemakers, both caregiver roles.

Naisbitt feels that women encourage creativity that will be needed in the future. I wish I were able to understand exactly what he meant. Is he saying that men are barbaric and unfeeling compared to women, who are loving and nurturing? Does this mean that men are not creative? If men aren't creative, why were so many of the great inventors male? I feel that his distinction between the sexes in this manner puts psychology back to the years of Freud by painting an unflattering, irrational picture of both men and women. Granted, there are differences between men and women, but basically, we are all humans; creativity isn't gender-specific.

. . . In some of my own reading about female styles of leadership, I sought to answer a question: Do female leadership styles really differ from men's? I feel female strategies of leadership have some advantages over male strategies, but not because women merely "nourish creativity." I feel that *all* workers of the Information Age will need these qualities, but that these qualities are, once again, not gender-specific.

Sophomore Tiffany Laine Feuerborn, who "enjoys competing with men, [and has] chosen business, a male dominated field, for [her] profession," was motivated by John Naisbitt's talk to research the role of women in business. Her inquiry led her to agree with his argument.

Wishing to learn more about the management styles of women, I came across another article in the September issue of *Working Woman* by Tom Peters: "The Best New Managers Will Listen, Motivate, Support. Isn't This Just Like a Woman?" Peters declares the trend for the future is for women to control corporations. Women will concentrate on more interpersonal relationships and work to make all workers partners in creating team-oriented goals. Women place much emphasis on long-term plans and try to make certain that all employees are included in implementing those plans. Females act as if they are interested in their employees' families, which creates a more caring environment.

As I see it, we are going to need more nurturing management executives in the future. As more and more working men and women have elderly parents to care for plus their own children to look after, upper management will need to be more understanding of the problems these people face. Since in our society women still bear the burden of their parents' and children's welfares, women executives should provide deeper understanding of these special circumstances.

Yet Feuerborn noticed something that bothered her.

. . . Looking back on the speakers and experiences of the Leadership Symposium, I have noticed something very important. There was only one woman on the panel for the Business Symposium out of eight people, and there were no women discussion leaders from thirteen people. Granted, Mary Johnston Evans is an extraordinary woman, and I feel privileged to have heard her speak. However, I think it is regrettable that women were not represented better in the business portion of the symposium. To me, this is just another example of how most people generally associate business leaders with being male.

Mary Johnston Evans, whose illustrious business career includes numerous corporate board appointments, was indeed the only female panelist participating in the Business and Technology Symposium, and she agrees with Tiffany Feuerborn that women can and should play an increasingly important leadership role in business. She also believes that society will be the loser if women in business simply try to become like men in gray flannel suits.

In the United States, our corporations in the last twenty years have been pushing very hard to satisfy their consciences and the Equal Employment Opportunity Commission requirements to make some progress in integrating women and minorities into the work force. We have done a lot of good work in that direction. In some places, it has been uneven. But I think that our shrinking labor pool, the trend toward globalization, the demographics in the United States, and the evolution of ethnic diversity are going to give a booster shot to that effort. In the rest of this decade and beyond, the companies that will come out on top are going to be those that attract and keep that rainbow of talent.

It is one thing to open up a factory to a diverse population; it is another thing to open up our executive offices. . . . we are beginning to see that we have got to have diversity in the executive offices also. We need a climate of innovation and management teams that crackle with new ideas. We can't get it if everyone is alike and there is not enough stimulation or conflict. Sometimes we have to have conflict to produce exciting new ideas. I am afraid that we shortchange ourselves as well as our employees if we try to make them all alike. For a long time, the message to young women was, Get an M.B.A., buy a gray suit and a bow tie, talk tough about the bottom line, act like a man, and then you will succeed. Why tell them to be like men? I suspect that in doing so, we twisted some human relationships, led those women to be less than they could be, and stifled some skills that they possess intuitively. I think it is a terrible waste not to encourage the singular quality of each individual.

The tension between the desire for more women in leadership roles, and ambivalence about the kind of role they might play permeates this discussion. Pamela Brandes resists any imputation that women will succeed in business because they are "nourishing"; Tiffany Feurborn thinks that women might well play a different role than men precisely because of the differences between them. Mary Johnston Evans, a leader in business, is convinced that women will be poorly served and serve poorly if they simply emulate the men who surround

202 THE NEXT GENERATION

and have preceded them. Ruth E. Schafer, a freshman nursing major with a grown daughter, has learned that the struggle of women for equality in the workplace is a difficult and sometimes lonely task.

I saw in myself many of the attributes which have been mentioned as necessary for leadership. But I have also seen that they can work against you as well as for you, especially for a woman. Often the drive that gets a woman to the top, can cause problems along the way. Surprisingly the problems are not just with resistant, intimidated males, but also with other women. What is considered assertive in a man can easily be interpreted as aggressive in a woman. Perhaps that is where the loneliness comes in for the woman in leadership.

It is not surprising that the female participants in the Leadership Symposia found this a more vitally interesting topic than did the men; it speaks to their experience uniquely. Yet a greater role for women will have implications for men. Eric C. Schultz, a senior electrical engineering major, supports the aspirations of women and is prepared to accept the responsibilities that this will impose upon men of his generation.

I think that it is high time that women take a shot at solving these and other problems facing us today. Men have been working at it for years; how far have they progressed? Give the women a chance to do what the men haven't had the presence or ability to do. On the flipside, more women in the workforce means fewer full-time mothers by definition. I believe that the large increase in juvenile delinquency and general breakdown of the moral fiber of youth today is directly related to the rise of the "latchkey" child, children without parental influences for a certain number of hours daily while both parents are at work. We cannot allow our children to suffer if both parents are employed. What is the answer? Who knows? I'm willing to admit that the thought of staying home when one could be out in gainful employment is not as enticing as it once used to be, but then the economy is not conducive to surviving on a single income anymore, either. Maybe parents should work for agreements with employers so that one parent can be at home each day of the week. As we enter the Information Age, this prospect is not as farfetched as it once was. And yes, this *does* mean that the male should take an increased role in the raising of children. I think these are changes whose time has come.

Schultz believes that his life will be different if society makes it easier for women to pursue careers. But will it? Even if many men are like Eric Schultz and are willing to shoulder more of the responsibility of child rearing, not all women who want careers will be married or married to men like him. It is not enough to simply say that the doors of the business world should be open to women; it is necessary to make the changes that will permit them to step onto the ladder in the first place. This will cost business money. Freshman psychology major Michelle Rodgers believes in the family and in the right of women to pursue careers. She thinks that a responsible business community will step forward to preserve the one and protect the other.

Corporate America can play a vital role in the push for a stronger and improved society. Instead of working against the family unit and creating such a strong negative stereotype of the work force, they could prove to be a powerful asset. . . . corporations could set up programs creating day care on the job site or allowing parents time off for activities and even the first day of school each fall. This would give the parent an opportunity to spend time with his/her child and also provide a better working relationship with parents and teachers. It is important for a parent to become involved with his/her children's school and their learning experience in general. To show a vested interest makes the child aware of the necessity of a good education and it also helps the child become active in extracurricular activities. Parent participation plays a major role in each stage of education, and corporate America can help to improve the level of participation by adjusting the workplace to supplement the family unit and its relationship with education. Parents should no longer have to choose between their job or their kids; both should work hand in hand.

In fact, business has been slow to respond to the demand for day care. The issue of federally regulated child care has raged in the Congress for several years now. The "ABC" bill promoted by congressional Democrats would have established federal funding and standards for day care centers. It was opposed by business interests. Another bill that would have mandated parental leave for childbirth and other family emergencies was likewise opposed by business. As we have seen, there is a natural tendency for business to oppose government regulations that impose costs. SuAnne Carlson, a senior public affairs and administration major, argued that business must be prepared to bear a share of the burden if the needs of women and their families are to be served.

Our country is faced with a monumental national deficit, a social security system riddled with problems, and most importantly the shameful neglect of our future—our children. One child in five lives in poverty. Every eight seconds of the school day, a student drops out. Every seven seconds, a child is abused or neglected. Every sixty-seven seconds, a teenager has a baby. There is no adequate system of child care and most corporations do not give parental leave.[5]

Even though the U.S. economy requires that most families have two incomes to reach middle-class status, the social programs in operation do not address the needs of working parents. When the family-leave bill was proposed in June 1990 it was vetoed by President Bush on the ground "that it was too burdensome for business." The bill would have allowed a worker to take up to twelve weeks a year of unpaid leave to care for a newborn, an adopted child, or a sick family member. This is far short of what other industrialized nations allow. Salaried women in France can take up to twenty-eight weeks of unpaid maternity leave, up to twenty weeks of adoption leave. Along with Belgium, Italy, and Denmark, France provides at least 75 percent of children ages three to five some form of state-funded preschool programs. In Germany, parents may deduct the cost of child care from their taxes. Congresswoman Pat Schroeder of Colorado observed, "Under our tax laws the deduction for a thoroughbred horse is greater than that for children."

Moral grounds alone should be enough to justify taking better care of children. However, as New York Governor Mario Cuomo stated, "If compassion were not enough to encourage our attention to the plight of our children . . . self-interest should be." Healthy, well-educated children will be the main component to providing future leaders. They will need to provide us with a skilled work force capable of dealing with sophisticated technology. They will also need to be educated away from ethnocentric tendencies which would inhibit effective leadership in the global arena. Unless we remedy the present appalling situation for children, our interest will not be served.

Carlson sees that the goal of increasing women's participation in business and other leadership roles is not just a women's issue but, rather, a children's issue and hence a societal issue. The bottom line for society is not the same as the bottom line for business; it is written on a different tally sheet, on which the final social cost will be measured in the next generation.

Whether women will in fact bring different qualities to the workplace and positions of leadership in it, what they want from American society is the same opportunity as men. Junior letters major Gail M. Puckett put the case squarely on the grounds of equal opportunity:

We cannot remain a risk-free society as far as leadership roles. Men must take the risk of promoting a woman over a man. I am not saying a woman should be given the leadership position over a man to achieve parity. As a woman, I am prepared to sink or swim in the marketplace on my capabilities. However, give me the opportunity to be promoted into the hallowed halls of the men. This means as a student I must attain a superior education. Allow me then to pursue my career choice, without feeling I have to choose a career path that is more receptive to women. We are doing our companies, state, and nation a grave injustice if we continue in the leadership patterns of the past.

Whether women or men lead, what is demanded of leaders in business today? The panelists had much advice on leadership to offer to the students. Oklahoma City banker J. W. McLean is a life member of the Rice University Board of Governors and has written extensively on leadership. He knows the worlds of education, business, and government. He offered to the students twelve myths that inhibit effective leadership, here transcribed from the paper of junior mathematics major Candace Noel Gethoefer:

Myth 1:   Charisma is a necessary leadership quality.
Myth 2:   Leaders can never be wrong.
Myth 3:   Leaders must be consistent.
Myth 4:   Leaders should always know the goals in advance.
Myth 5:   It is usually more difficult to lead than follow.
Myth 6:   Leaders should know how to perform the jobs of the followers.
Myth 7:   A leader in one environment should lead in others.
Myth 8:   Why should I try for a leadership role when there are others with much more support from higher-ups?
Myth 9:   Leadership requires motivating others and people resent being manipulated.
Myth 10: Leadership is often incidental since the success or failure of most group efforts is ultimately determined by outside events.
Myth 11: Leaders are an endangered species.
Myth 12: Leadership is just too complicated for me.

McLean's myths encompass several theses. Those who are to lead must believe that it is possible, must believe that they are capable of it, and must not be dissuaded by a "fear of flying." This is the sort of practical advice that the student leaders came to hear. They believe, or want to believe, in themselves as leaders. They are not lacking in confidence. They want to know how to do it. As McLean suggests, leadership in business requires more than substantive knowledge, more even than interpersonal skill; it demands the will to lead, the commitment to achieve a goal. Many have the ability to lead, but few do so. The reason why some do not fulfill their leadership potential is because they have a false understanding of what it requires.

Joe Williams was especially emphatic on the subject of leadership. The cult of the M.B.A. in the 1970s produced a generation of business leaders who believe that the proper task of leadership is not to lead but to manage.

Leadership is a tricky subject. It is the source of many platitudes and boring discussions; eyes glaze over. It is known as a subject to avoid.

So what do we do in temples of culture and institutions of learning such as we have here? I will tell you: We teach management. We have schools of business management, management journals, management seminars, courses in management. Not in leadership. That is why I think it is so rare and so interesting to have a symposium on leadership right here at OU, and why I am so intrigued with it. These distinguished panelists are all members of boards; I am also on a number of boards. One of the principal responsibilities of board members is to identify, select, nurture and promote people into the upper echelons of their organization, whether private or public. Rarely, if ever, have I heard the question come up, What kind of manager is he or she? Instead, the issue is leadership. People talk in terms of characteristics of leadership rather than the skills of management. . . .

I have a little checklist of characteristics that I think about and have learned to use over the years. When I am on a compensation committee or a nominating committee I keep it in my briefcase. Apart from three basic traits—integrity, which is critical; intelligence, which is important; and the willingness to work hard, which is obvious—let me suggest ten characteristics that all leaders must have to some degree or another if, in fact, they are going to rise to the top. First of all, a leader possesses a sense of urgency, a restlessness with the status quo, a desire to get on with it. Second, a leader causes things to happen. There are plenty of people who are very competent, but they do not cause things to happen. There are others who do indeed cause things to happen, and you can recognize that. It is hard to describe the difference, but it is easy to see.

Third, leaders have an ability to cope with ambiguity. This is a critical attribute of leadership, because the higher you get in the decision-making process, the greater the circumstances that you have to cope with. Yet you are generally called upon to make a black-and-white decision. You may well have to deal with multiple problems that conflict with each other, and the situation is indeed ambiguous. So the ability to cope with ambiguity is extremely important.

Fourth, the ability to conceptualize is extremely important. Fifth, a leader needs to be tough enough, not in the sense of being mean or demanding, but in the sense of being able to withstand doubt or to hold your conviction against attack until the end of whatever the issue is. Sixth, an intuitive vision is very, very important. Mr. Naisbitt talked about that today. Seventh, leaders must learn and develop the ability to listen. Most good leaders, in fact, are good listeners. They learn from the people that they lead. Eighth, the ability to cope with loneliness is a very important factor. It is a trait that can be learned, but it is not easy. The higher you get in the decision-making tree, the lonelier your life becomes; and some people absolutely cannot cope with that.

Ninth, a leader needs the ability to simplify. Some of the most complex people I know come up with the simplest answers. Unfortunately, the converse is true. Some of the simplest people I know come up with the most complex answers and screw everything up. The ability to simplify is really important. The last characteristic, the ability to close, is critical. You can have all the other traits—you can conceptualize and get things started, you can visualize and have a sense of urgency—but if you cannot draw the issue to closure, it doesn't work.

Those are the leadership attributes I look at. I think that the difference between leadership and managership is really what this symposium is all about. All of these panelists are here because they are leaders, not because they are managers. Whether you can teach qualities such as these or whether they are inherent qualities is always a point of tension in academic circles. But I would suggest that it is our obligation in industry and in any other type of organization to develop value systems and to nurture and develop the best qualities of leadership not only in our own organizations, but in our academic institutions and in our schools of management. Indeed, I think that what we are doing today at OU is precisely that. When we are talking about leadership, we are trying to establish what the values of leadership are, so that those values can be perpetuated. If that is the point of this academic celebration, I think that it is well served.

Given the emphasis of the Centennial Symposia on education (which Joe Williams strongly supports), it is interesting that his conception of leadership stresses the difference between the skills of the leader and the role of the manager. Leadership is mostly a matter of character; management can be taught. It is not surprising that the University of Oklahoma offers a degree in business management, but why does it not also offer a degree in leadership? Who has ever heard of a master's degree in business leadership, an M.B.L.? The panelists participating in the Symposium in Business and Technology were all well educated and committed to strengthening our system of education. But when they came at last to talk about leadership, the task of leadership itself, they stressed character more than learning.

The dimension of character they stress is affective rather than intellectual. Having confidence in yourself, being able to

cope with uncertainty, dealing with people, the ability to bring
closure—these are facets of personality. As Joe Williams
noted, academicians can debate whether they are innate or
acquired qualities, but based on his experience they are requisite to effective leadership. Toward what goals should business leaders aim? Williams emphasized that the qualities of
leadership are themselves values to be perpetuated, but he did
not say how they might square with other values important to
society and its leaders. In one of the required readings for the
Business and Technology symposium, businessman J. Irwin
Miller addressed the moral dimension of business in an address to the National Humanities Center on "The Importance
of Humanities to Business."[6] Miller spoke of the moral disintegration of the new generation of business leaders.

Anyone dealing with young people today will recognize this
familiar experience: The young man or woman finally gets the
job she or he has wanted above all else. Does the young person
then plunge in with total commitment to make a glorious success
of the new assignment? Not at all. The new assignment gets
only partial attention as its holder starts worrying all over again,
"Where do I go from here?"

This short-run view of life is learned by the younger generation from their elders. "Business chief executive officers and
their boards succumb to the pressures of the financial markets
and their own fears of takeovers and pour out their energies
to produce quarterly earnings—at the expense of building
their companies for the long term." Both generations of business leaders reflect a general decline in American culture, in
Miller's view.

The decline of manners and the cynical pursuit without shame
or restraint of personal advantage and of money characterize our
times. There are exceptions, of course, but these behaviors occur
more frequently than we ought to be comfortable with. They add

up to a growing dehumanization of a society which is so complex, so interdependent. Only through individual self-restraint, through taking the long view, and through dedication to cooperation can one hope to succeed and lead.

Miller's concern with the ethical foundations of business was reflected in the symposium discussions. Edward N. Brandt, Jr., executive dean of the OU College of Medicine, speaking on behalf of one of the student discussion groups, raised the question of the relationship between business ethics and government regulation.

Our question relates to business ethics. We debated these issues a good bit. If Mr. Naisbitt's views hold true, and government functions are taken over more and more by the private sector, do any of you believe that there will be a corresponding change in business ethics or culture to compensate for a weakening of governmental regulation and control?

George Records, who had previously identified excessive government regulation as one of the main impediments to economic development, responded to this question.

I think that you start off with the assumption that government control is going to dictate ethics, both in setting the environment and in determing what ought to be done. I am very optimistic about the ethics. We have made great progress, as demonstrated by the fact that we are talking about ethics in medical school, law school, in corporations, and in grades K through 12. The fact that we are talking about it means that we are thinking about it.

I still feel that corporate America generally is ethically run. All you hear about are the bad cases, which brings us back to the problems identified with the news media. I think we ought to talk about the positive things that are happening in our country. In spite of what the government says, I feel that corporations can run their businesses ethically. They can be environmentally sound. We do not need a command-control type of society. There is a concern that corporations cannot behave properly without government control. I am on the other side of that fence. I think we can, and I think it has been demonstrated.

SuAnne Carlson also emphasized the ethical responsibilities of business.

Government and educational institutions have an obligation to society. I believe this is also true of the business and technological sector. I am not referring to making greater efforts in technological advances. . . . As we continue to extend our capability to manipulate nature, we are confronted with moral dilemmas. Scientific technology has enabled us to extend life and even help facilitate creation of life. The moral implications of this magnitude of intervention are daunting. Business corporations are also using technology more extensively. The emphasis now needs to be directed toward using that technology in a responsible ethical manner. The energy-related businesses have the ability to extract minerals and oil from remote areas of the earth. We must deliberate the extent of our invasion into pristine areas and our responsibility to the people directly affected. The emphasis must be on using technology and our resources in a prudent way. To do this, we will have to redirect our technological education to include ethical considerations.

But even if most businesses are honest, and conduct themselves in an ethically responsible manner, they will face increasing temptation to violate ethical norms that prevail in the United States in order to compete abroad, according to senior journalism major Robbin Harrison.

I believe one intriguing development of the global marketplace will be a proliferation of ethical debate. American companies will be increasingly involved in foreign investment. They will have offices and workers in other countries, and many will employ natives of other countries in their international divisions. The

United States will be forced to deal more frequently with the question of ethical relativism.

I felt that the business leaders at the Centennial Symposia overlooked this formidable issue which undoubtedly will emerge alongside the global marketplace. In some foreign countries, for example, bribery is an accepted business practice. In short, the company that offers the most attractive bribe will win the contract. Obviously, this is viewed in America as highly unethical, even illegal. And this is but one example of the differences companies will encounter in the international business arena.

What is the solution for American companies operating in countries with alternative ethical standards? The answer remains to be seen. Those that refuse to play by the local rules may be at a striking disadvantage. But, the answer surely is not as simple as "When in Rome, do as the Romans do." On the other side of the coin, foreign-owned companies may try to transplant their ethical standards into facilities in the United States.

This dialogue produces three different versions of the problem. To George Records, ethics is simply a matter of being honest. He believes that much governmental regulation is unnecessary, and even counterproductive, since business can and will conduct itself ethically. SuAnne Carlson sees the problem of business ethics in broader terms. The decisions that businesses make involve the allocation of societal values. Simply being honest is not enough; businesses also need to be socially responsible. Robbin Harrison places the problem of business ethics in a comparative context. In a competitive international economy, adhering to conventional ethical standards may place business at a disadvantage.

Thus, business ethics involve honesty, social responsibility, and competition. How do we ensure that ethical conduct will prevail? Symposium speakers such as Vartan Gregorian and Ernest Boyer, and business leaders such as J. Irwin Miller, find the answer in the same place. It is not the church; it is the school. It is only by teaching children sound values and a

sense of ethical responsibility that society can hope to ensure
that, as adults, they will conduct themselves in an ethically
responsible way. Of course, the family plays the most important role, but the family lies within the domain of private
life, affected but not determined by public policy. From an
increasingly early age, the schools supplant the family as
teachers of values. Public policy should seek to use common
schools as vehicles for shaping the values of children, and
institutions of higher education should assume the responsibility for developing in students a capacity for mature and
rational deliberation over ethical issues. This requires education in the liberal arts and not simply technical training.

As in the other symposia, then, the discussion in the Business and Technology Symposium led inexorably to the issue
of education. Much of the discussion focused on the quality
of basic education and training offered by public school systems like that of Oklahoma. Much of the concern was tied to
the issue of economic development. There was an extended
discussion of privatization of the schools, a consideration of
the role of the university, and a general emphasis upon the
need to broaden and internationalize curricula at all levels.
The symposium panelists want the citizens of Oklahoma to
become citizens of the world so that Oklahoma can join itself
to the world economy of the twenty-first century. The cultural
dimension of business came to center stage.

Some of the impetus behind the discussion of business and
culture came from John Naisbitt's conception of the global
economy that looms on the horizon. Naisbitt himself is of
two minds on the subject of culture. On the one hand, he is
convinced that the global economy will synthesize culture;
on the other hand, he believes that the unique diversity of
American culture will prove an asset in the global marketplace.

One of the other things I wanted to add is the phenomenon of
global life-styles and cultural nationalism. As the next millennium
approaches, the world is moving in two directions: one direction

is toward an emerging global life-style, and the second, cultural nationalism, is almost a kind of backlash against the homogenization of life-styles. Increased trade, travel, and telecommunications have laid the groundwork now for an unparalleled exchange of cultures. Every year, one billion people fly from one place on the planet to another. That is three million a day. And by the year 2000 that will double. Two billion airline passengers each year.

Life-style messages travel at the speed of light so that young people in São Paulo, in Shanghai, in Prague, can all dress in the same look. Our life-styles are coming together in the developed countries all over the world. What we wear, what we eat, where we travel, what cars we drive—we're borrowing from each other, we're kind of playing in each other's backyards. We're tasting each other's food and cuisine. In Tokyo or, for that matter, anywhere in Japan, I can order a California roll, which, as you probably know, is a sushi containing crab and avocado that was invented in San Francisco. It has spread all over Japan.

There are 11,000 McDonald's outlets worldwide and 600 new ones each year. The star of the McDonald's chain is in Moscow, where on opening day there were 30,000 transactions. And prior to that, the record opening day for a McDonald's was 9,000 transactions about three and one half years ago, interestingly, in Budapest, Hungary. Now in Moscow, they are running at 50,000 transactions a day. So in Moscow, that city of queues, people are lining up for as long as two hours in order to buy fast food.

I recently visited Harrods, the great British department store, and in the produce section I saw French peaches, Dutch radishes, English strawberries, California asparagus, Russian button mushrooms, Israeli tomatoes and East African lemongrass. Harrods, which also operates in Germany and Japan, is owned by Egyptians. It really is. Also undergoing a boom are the international retailers like American Esprit, Swedish IKEA, Italian Benetton. You can buy a Benetton sweater in seventy countries from one of their more than 6,000 outlets.

Retailers are leading today in global pricing through electronics. Today, if you buy a Chanel handbag or suit, it costs the same price whether you purchase it in Avenue Montaigne in Paris or at the Chanel boutique in Hong Kong's Peninsula Hotel or on

Rodeo Drive in Los Angeles. Although there are great discrepancies today, soon cars will cost the same everywhere. Part of the globalization that I was talking about last night is the trend toward global pricing.

The exchange of food and fashion is, for the most part, welcome because it increases our options. It is quite superficial and fun and threatens almost no one. But cultural exchange grows more sensitive in areas of film and television, where the United States is criticized for exporting too aggressively. Here we begin to deal with the deeper areas of language and values. The American television show "Dallas" is seen in ninety-eight countries. In Shanghai, every Wednesday night 70 percent of the television sets are tuned to an American television show called "Hunter." In France, extraordinarily, last year 50 percent of all of the films shown were American. No wonder Jack Lang, the cultural minister of France, speaks of American cultural imperialism.

As American culture tends to dominate, even in developing countries whose sense of identity is rather fragile and vulnerable it has been accompanied by a growing anti-Americanism, and I think this will not diminish. As we move toward the millennium, the great battles will be cultural—language, tradition, religion—rather than strictly political. Salman Rushdie dared to blaspheme the Prophet, and the Ayatollah imposed a death sentence. In the Soviet Union, cultural nationalism first tested the limits of glasnost and perestroika. Indeed, Estonia's first act of defiance was to inform the Central Committee in Moscow that henceforth Estonian would be the official language of Estonia and the Russians would just have to learn it. As Turkey petitions to join the European Common Market, paradoxically the influence of Islam grows. Many university women in Turkey are beginning to wear the Islamic veil again, even though it has been outlawed since Atatürk's secular reforms of the 1920s.

At the dawn of the twenty-first century, the great challenge is how to maintain one's cultural heritage amidst the growing homogenization. And the more homogeneous our life-styles become, the more steadfastly we cling to the deeper values, religion, language, art, and literature. This is where the new renaissance joins cultural nationalism, because it is our artists who articulate our national identity. As Europe moves toward one economy, the Italians are becoming more Italian, the Germans more German, and the French, if you can believe it, more French.

There appear to be two issues here. The first is the economic implication of the spread of consumer goods, the most superficial manifestation of culture. Most of this spread is going from the West to the East, and much of it reflects American taste. From an economic point of view, America does all right in the global consumer economy because we can export our fast food, designer jeans, television programs (although not the televisions)—in sum, our culture. Of course, when the Koreans make clothes that look just like ours much more cheaply, the domestic textile industry is headed for trouble. The second issue is the political implication of the internationalization of the economy. It leads, according to Naisbitt, to a kind of reactionary nativism that is sometimes accompanied by anti-American attitudes. This requires businesspeople to be diplomats, as Sarah Helin, a senior marketing major, has learned.

Many people are rebelling from this cultural blending. For example, Japanese children are interested in knowing traditional Japanese culture. Quebec is requiring people by law to speak and use French at work and commercially for advertising. Some cultures are beginning to protest intervening cultures and emphasizing a distinct society of their own. The ideas and actions of people may be changing in many countries, but this period of cultural integration is just above ground. Below the surface, countries will continue to favor their culture and rely on tradition.

The solution to this problem is a greater appreciation by Americans of foreign cultures gained by studying the language and culture of our economic competitors and of countries representing potential markets. Senior Nancy Belshe, a social work major, emphasized this point.

During the Leadership Symposia, several business leaders pointed out the need for second language skills in the changing marketplace; however, I didn't hear any of the businesspeople place an emphasis on the need to understand the culture of the people of that language. The proper way to show respect to those you seek to do business with is to care enough to educate yourself about that person's world. Children educated from first grade through high school with respect for both the people, their language, and their culture would not be likely in adulthood to make the embarrassing mistakes in conducting business dealings that several large companies have.

Panelist Mary Johnston Evans stressed that knowledge of foreign cultures requires experience as well as education.

I would like to have language required, even if it is unpopular. . . . I would also like to urge you, when you graduate, to accept with alacrity the opportunity to live abroad. A year or so ago I sat next to Joe Williams at a dinner, and he talked to me about living in Iran for several years early in his career. Can you imagine what kind of an opportunity that was and what it means to Joe now in the position where he is? If more Americans had lived in Iran, and in all these other places around the world, our understanding would be so much better. I encourage you to volunteer for these opportunities around the world, try to get stationed abroad somewhere, try to get transferred, try to live somewhere else with other people. There is no substitute. You can read about it, you can study about it, and you can think about it, but being there would be of invaluable importance. Many people, who are at the top of their companies now, lived in Europe in their first two or three years in business, and they are light years ahead.

Leadership, ethics, education, culture—these were the leitmotifs of the Symposium in Business and Technology. It is worth mentioning what was not emphasized. The speakers and panelists did not, by and large, choose to stress technical training, computer skills, management schooling, or economic theory. Their vision of the world of business and technology is much broader than a narrow preoccupation with the skills and techniques that may be essential to it. Instead, they stressed issues of character—leadership, morality, cultural knowledge, and sophistication. The business leaders of the next generation must be guided by a larger view of the world than was required of business leaders in the past. They cannot assume the preeminence of American economic power. Their own success, and that of their businesses, will depend upon their capacity to function in a sophisticated multinational economy that is shaped as much by cultural values as by economic forces. It is the obligation of the university to prepare its graduates to function in that new world.

CHAPTER 5

THE EDUCATION CRISIS

THE SUBJECT OF EDUCATION dominated the Centennial Leadership Symposia. In all four symposia, the speakers and panelists stressed the crucial role that education must play in shaping a better future for Oklahoma and the nation. America's educational system must provide the human capital necessary to economic competitiveness. It must provide the common meeting ground of the various cultures of which American society is composed. It must prepare Americans to bridge the gaps among their own cultures and between American culture and those of other countries. It must provide the foundations for cultural appreciation and achievement. It must prepare students to lead ethically responsible lives. It must train the next generation of scientists, engineers, and businessmen and businesswomen. In all walks of life, it must prepare a new generation of leaders.

And it is failing. By most measures and in almost every report on the subject, American students are falling behind those in other countries in basic educational preparation. America's schools are underfunded, their facilities outmoded, their faculties underpaid, their students unprepared. Entrenched bureaucracies find it difficult to innovate, strong teachers' unions resist management initiatives, and politicians are afraid to run the political risks associated with genuine reform. In many places schools are unequal, and these inequalities are often connected to differences in socioeconomic status and to patterns of racial segregation. In higher education, America's colleges and universities are flooded with students who are asked to pay a higher and higher price for a product that seems to be on the decline. Yet too often they are unprepared for the demands that higher education does place upon them. Teachers are increasingly isolated from students and alienated from administrators. Administrators sometimes seem more concerned with advancing their careers than with nurturing the institutions entrusted to their care. From kindergarten to the doctorate, America's educational system is failing its people.

These problems are American problems, but there is a particular Oklahoma permutation. Like other rural states with a populist tradition, Oklahoma has established more publicly supported institutions of higher education per capita than some more populous states.[1] In common education, Oklahoma operates more school districts per capita than all but five other rural states. At the same time, the conservative tradition in Oklahoma politics has held per capita and per pupil spending for common education near the bottom of national rankings of states.[2] In the 1980s, a severe recession in the state's oil and gas industry added economic privation to the list of challenges facing an already burdened educational system. From this difficult situation there emerged a renewed concern with Oklahoma's educational system that mirrored concern at the national level, but with a greater sense of urgency. As George Kaiser, chairman of the Oklahoma State Regents for Higher Education put it, "I guess one good thing that could be said about the economic depression we suffered in the early 1980s and which is just beginning to end is that perhaps the first time in Oklahoma history, education became the priority issue. Surprisingly perhaps, it has remained, I think, at the top of the public agenda for the last three or four or five years."

This sense of urgency was reflected throughout the Leadership Symposia. It is not an exaggeration to say that virtually every speaker and panelist at the four Centennial Leadership Symposia stressed the need for education reform as prerequisite to solving the other problems facing the nation. So often did the subject arise, and in so many different and varied contexts, that it will not be possible in this chapter to review everything that was said about it. Instead, we will survey main themes and issues arrayed under three broad topics: common education, higher education, and leadership in education.

The Education Symposium discussion of common schools was framed and dominated by the then recent passage of House Bill 1017, the $230 million education reform and funding bill passed by the state legislature only a few months before. Among the panelists who had been directly involved in the development and enactment of 1017 were George A. Singer, chairman of Task Force 2000, the citizens' panel charged to study the state's education system; Sandy Garrett, secretary of education in the Bellmon administration, later to be elected state superintendent of schools; and Carolyn Thompson, chair of the House Education Committee. The comprehensive legislation raised teachers' salaries, provided incentives for school consolidation, mandated curriculum reform, reformed the teacher tenure system, and set standards for student achievement, among many other things. It was enacted after a long and difficult struggle in the legislature (and in 1991 sustained by a popular referendum).

The issue of education reached these students in a very personal way. Their view of the debate was rooted in their own experience. Freshman communications major Lenny Rice's comment illustrates that for Oklahoma students, education is a gut issue:

I grew up in a small town in southeastern Oklahoma. I attended a small high school where education wasn't encouraged. I graduated in a class of 107, of which 45 are now pursuing a college education. That leaves 52 students not doing anything or some kind of unskilled job. I understand college isn't for some people. But I've heard some people say they can't afford it. I informed them that they could apply for financial aid. Most of them didn't even know anything about it. I don't feel we were encouraged to get an education. I probably wouldn't be here if my parents didn't realize how important an education is and didn't encourage me to go to college. That's why I believe students should be prepared and counseled for college. I wasn't prepared for college and I feel that I am way behind the class. I am struggling just to pass. Most of the courses I am taking are basics. I am very angry with my school and I feel I will always be behind everyone in my classes.

My high school is very outdated and that does seem to affect the students. When I hear what the other schools in the state got to do, I feel like I missed out on learning and a lot of fun and competition. I understand there are many other schools across the nation that are like my high school, but I don't feel it should be this way. We shouldn't be deprived because of where we are located. The only people being hurt are the students. They are the ones who are suffering.

Rice's comment demonstrates the importance of the issue to these students, an importance that was reflected in their papers. All of the panelists and students supported education reform; all of the panelists and most of the students supported 1017. Some students did not think that 1017 went far enough in the direction of offering choice to families. Whether they were in favor of 1017 or (in a few instances) against it, the students understood that their futures are at stake. A critic of 1017, Gail M. Puckett demonstrated as much concern as did Lenny Rice.

I was sorry to see the major portion of the Education Symposium turned into an epistle on the benefits of Task Force 2000 and its baby, House Bill 1017 . . . but the hard sell given in this forum seemed to imply that if you don't support House Bill 1017 then you are not a concerned citizen. This is a fallacy the students saw through. By appealing to the group's sympathy for education, some used it as a platform for their election instead of an educational forum with an open exchange of ideas.

As a concerned citizen and taxpayer I am interested in education in the state of Oklahoma. Having relatives who are teachers in this state, I am aware of the conditions that prevail in our classrooms. My son is in one of the so-called "better" school systems in the state. But the "behemoth of bureaucracies involved in education," as Ms. Smith called it, is much the same as the plant . . . in the movie *Little Shop of Horrors*. The behemoth needs constant feeding provided by increasing dollars from the taxpayers. Many taxpayers would like to look at ways to improve education across the state without feeding the monster. . . . Many believe the teachers settled for a tax package barely addressing the needs of education in this state.

This, of course, was not the view of the panelists who had participated in developing the reform bill. George Singer explained to the students the general philosophy underlying the bill.

There are really three philosophical underpinnings of the legislation that is now law in Oklahoma. First, we are changing the education system from one where we tell you that you need to have so many units of math, so many units of science, so many units of foreign language. Instead we are trying to switch to a system that focuses on *outcomes* or results. We are going to define what we want people to learn, and we are going to try to do it very carefully. The unit requirements are all good in the abstract, but in practice they tend to have people sitting in seats and spending time in the education process without focusing on what they are trying to learn. We saw many instances of kids who took the same math course three times and got credit, but by the third time started doing pretty poorly because they were bored.

Second, we want to change the system of instruction to one that is best geared to actually achieve the results that we have defined. In order to do that we must have a whole new system of *accountability* in education. We have got to have better tests to measure whether kids are really learning the things we have defined as outcomes, and we have also got to have standards to hold teachers accountable for whether they do their job properly. We have done that in the new law, and we have changed the rules for involving parents. We are trying to bring parents back into the system. We are trying to change the standards for the school boards, for their involvement in the process, for administrators' involvement. We want people to be able to look at a public institution like education and say, "Not only do we believe in it as an institution, but we can evaluate whether we are right or whether we are wrong along the way." The third thing we tried to do is establish *adequate and equitable funding*. We are trying to set standards at the state level, and then say to the local school districts and to the individual schools, "We are going to give you the maximum flexibility to achieve them." There has been a suggestion that we are trying to run the education system out of Oklahoma City, but in fact we are really trying to have the money come into Oklahoma City and flow back out to the local school districts, without the State Board of Education, the State Department of Education, and the legislature telling individual districts how to achieve what is best. I imagine you [students] cover a broad cross section of the State of Oklahoma, growing up in communities that have individual needs. We need to have a system that will recognize those individual needs . . . and give your individual communities the maximum flexibility to achieve consistent and meaningful standards.

Education Secretary Sandy Garrett stressed the need for local involvement in any significant educational reform package.

We need more flexibility and creativity at the local level, less regulation from the state, and more involvement from the parents and even the business community. We need to reach out to parents in a more creative way. During this last year what has made us shine as a state in comparison with other states in this nation . . . is the really special coalition of businesspeople, professionals, parents, and educators who have worked together to design the foundation for our future in this state.

Panelist Jeanne Hoffman Smith, who has a private clinical social work practice and is an active community volunteer, believes that the kind of increased flexibility that Garrett favors should carry with it a reduction in the scope of bureaucracy.

I see education as a bureaucracy that has a life of its own. The life cycle means that things can grow beyond human scale at times, and I think that that is the nature of bureaucracies. I am concerned about the bureaucracy of education, what has been called the "bloated beast of bureaucracy." If our goal is to make a difference, to make an impact on the future and improve the preparation of teachers, we must change the bureaucracy of which they are a part.

Singer, Garrett, and Smith reflect the "neo" approach to education reform, but are they "neoliberal" or "neoconservative"? Both neoliberals and neoconservatives favor decentralization of governmental control and harbor suspicion of centralized bureaucracy. Neoliberals, however, retain a traditional liberal commitment to public institutions whereas neoconservatives are more likely to look to private-sector alternatives. By this measure, 1017 was a neoliberal reform bill. Both Singer and Garrett stressed the importance of public institutions implementing state goals at the local level in a flexible system of administration. Smith appears to harbor neoconservative suspicions of government bureaucracy, but wants to improve it and not necessarily eliminate it.

In contrast, Business and Technology Symposium keynote speaker John Naisbitt endorsed privatization as an alternative to public education. He argued that only when families can choose among schools that are in open and free competition for their patronage will education improve. Public education systems are incapable of offering the freedom that markets require. The debate in Oklahoma centered on the concept of open choice among public schools. Republicans in the legislature generally favored this concept, Democrats opposed it. The Republicans believed that open choice combined with decentralized administration would foster competition, creativity, and higher quality. Democrats argued that a system of open choice presupposed equality of funding so that the schools could in fact compete on an equal basis. Absent equal funding, no truly free market could exist. Democrats likewise opposed proposals for education vouchers that could be "spent" at private schools, believing that this would lead to an exodus from public schools that would, in the end, undermine public education altogether. Many Republicans, backed by the editorial pages of the *Daily Oklahoman*, favored a voucher system.

John Naisbitt told symposia participants,

There is nothing on our economic or social agenda that is more important [than education]. Businesses are now getting more involved. They are not only interested in training, they are interested in education. Motorola has a wonderful education program on how to think globally. We must, in this society, either be vulnerable or be educated. The most important thing is education in the United States today.[3]

Naisbitt's solution to the nation's educational dilemma is privatization. He favors a greater involvement of private businesses in education, and would, in fact, turn education over to private business to the extent possible. His argument is as follows:

Education, I think, has to be a marketplace. I think governments ought to safeguard those things that we cannot know about. For example, most people overwhelmingly support the government making regulations about nuclear radiation because they cannot experience it. They cannot make judgments about it.

By contrast, there is a lot of resistance to regulating things like smoking because people feel they have all the information they need to make the decision and they do not want the government telling them what to do.

If you introduce a free market mechanism in education, the safeguards are that the parent takes a kid out of a school and puts him or her in another school. The schools compete to attract the children and parents by emphasizing not only quality but emphasizing subjects and so on. . . . The only people I trust to decide are the parents of the children who are involved, not bureaucrats and not other parents. Some parents are going to make bad judgments but that is what it is all about.

The education panelists disagreed with Naisbitt. Hans Brisch, chancellor of the Oklahoma State Regents for Higher Education and symposium panel moderator, is skeptical about privatization.

John Naisbitt mentioned the trend towards privatization and said he was very much a supporter. Let me make just one comment: our public institutions, elementary schools, and secondary schools are possibly the only umbrella that we as a society get under. In other words, people from all walks of life have an opportunity to be part and become part of society. I do not know if privatization would continue to facilitate that. We are becoming a more complex, heterogeneous society; in other words, diverse cultures are part of America. To become an even stronger America, our public schools have an especially critical role and perhaps will have to play an even stronger role in this particular arena.

George Singer agreed with Brisch:

If privatization is used in the traditional sense of the word, then I would have to agree with Chancellor Brisch: It is not really applicable in any wholesale way to public education. But I think we can look at ways to introduce competition and free enterprise

concepts into the school system. In the past we have had a system
of education based on all sorts of regulations through the State
Department [of Education], the State Board of Education, the
superintendent's office, the legislature, and the federal government. These regulations have been put in place as a kind of
safety net . . . to protect the broad number of people or specific
populations. We have told schools how to make sure that these
safety net provisions are respected.

With House Bill 1017, we have tried to change the safety net,
redefine the role of government in the process, define what we
consider an adequately educated populous, and then strip away
all of those kinds of rules and regulations that aren't absolutely
necessary to protect the health and safety of school kids. We
need to use the standards as the only safety net, turn around
and allow for competition. I am not convinced that parental
choice of schools is a panacea, but I am persuaded that it is a
concept that needs to be investigated. I am very much persuaded that deregulation can work. . . . If we remove the stric-
tures that say you have to do everything the same in every
school and community in Oklahoma, then you will begin to
privatize in some fashion by introducing competition, by introducing some incentive for creativity. There are financial incentives, too. If you can do things more efficiently by applying
technology and using innovative methods, then you have
money left over to do some other things that you wanted to do.
It really does create an incentive more like the free enterprise
system.[4]

Introducing flexibility, and perhaps competition, into public
systems is, of course, not the same thing as what John Naisbitt
means by privatization. Privatization means turning over the
schools to private vendors. The basic issue is one's commitment to the public character of education. Is it a public responsibility or not? If it is, then can it be returned to private hands
without sacrificing its essential character, and an essential
commitment of the American regime? Education Symposium
keynote speaker Ernest Boyer, president of the Carnegie En-

dowment for the Advancement of Teaching, came down squarely on the side of public education.

I believe in common schools for the common good. I really don't believe that [privatization] is the way I want America to go. If there is anything we share together, it is the notion that we want our children to have an even chance. And I have to say, with all due respect, I think privatization would lead to huge inequity. The people who are most advantaged, most skilled, and most affluent will find a way to make the system work for them. And the least empowered will be left behind. As a policy, it doesn't work.

If you want to know where I think privatization would leave education, look at the health care system. In fact, I think public education in America is the most effective system that we have. It is working better than the health care system. It is working better than the judicial system. I think it is working better than most governmental systems. What SAT score would you give to Congress?

The most commonly addressed issue in the student papers was privatization of education. Many students were for it, for much the same reasons as Naisbitt. Freshman Jana L. Gilbreath Cornelius put it this way:

Imagine a time in America when in late August the parents of school age children would be mailed a voucher worth $2,500 for each child in their family. All summer long the parents and their children would have been poring over the brightly colored brochures advertising the available schools in their community. Some schools would specialize in physics or computer science. Others would emphasize the study of Latin, romance languages, and the classics.

Some would stress religious teaching and Bible study. Some might advertise regulated dress codes and strict discipline. Some might stress a less structured environment and education based on field trips and laboratories. Some might claim a fast track for college entrance; others might emphasize vocational training. Each school would be accredited by a public or private agency and would be required to provide a basic core curriculum for each student.

Some schools would be in existing school buildings. Others might be located in newer facilities. All the schools would have transportation available to serve the citizens of their community.

There would be no more education monopoly where parents had one choice: the gray mediocrity of present-day public schools. If any of the schools in question did not deliver a product which satisfied their customers, these customers would take their vouchers and buy elsewhere.

Obviously if some schools wanted to offer a premium curriculum instead of the standard fare, they could charge more and apply the voucher toward the increased price. If parents could afford pricey extras, that would be their private decision.

All students would be guaranteed a basic quality education. Those who wanted more would not be forced to pay the full price of private education and the full tax burden of public education at the same time.

Another freshman, Daniel Dunlap, agreed:

If schools are not privatized, we will feel the impact, as other countries begin to surpass us in the decades to come. Privatizing schools will greatly increase the competition between the institutions. The better schools will bring in the better students. Each school will want to improve itself to make itself more attractive to the top students. The top schools will also employ the best teachers. Thus, as in higher education, schools will strive to maintain the best teachers along with the top students. This will create a much better education system for our youth.

Sophomore Keith Wiles saw economic advantages in privatization:

Many people are opposed to the privatization of government service. It is widely believed that costs of government services would go up following privatization, but the exact opposite is true. Privatization would result not only in better services, but also in less expensive ones. The reasons for this are twofold.

First, when an industry or service comes to be under government control, it tends to shift away from its original goal of providing a particular service . . . and it becomes occupied with maintaining its own bureaucracy.

Secondly, governments tend to "overspend" on anything they do. When a government begins to provide services normally provided by the private sector, it eliminates its own competition. Obviously the cost of the products or services increases, but this is not the only way in which the government drives up costs. These projects are supported by tax revenues in one form or another. Thus, government control of industry and services is bad business because it takes money out of the economy from two places: taxing the people, and the higher costs of services.

The necessity of privatization is nowhere more obvious than it is in the field of education.

The idea of privatization of education has an appeal in Oklahoma. The *Daily Oklahoman* has consistently pressed for a voucher system.[5] Most University of Oklahoma students are, by reputation, conservative. So it is somewhat surprising that many of the students who spoke to the issue spoke *against* privatization, sometimes in very strong terms. Here is a sampling of their statements:

I have doubts about how privatizing education would benefit the poor. I feel that some of the leaders would not stress the importance of making quality education equally accessible to all individuals. Privatizing education might allow a certain percentage of American students to receive a much higher quality education than they now receive; however, it might also prevent a number from receiving a quality education or any education at all. (Freshman journalism major Jamie Birdsong)

It is unrealistic to believe that private organizations could or would support or run schools in low-income areas or even rural areas that have small schools. Only in large middle- to upper-class areas would this process of competition eliminate poor quality schools and increase the quality of education for those students involved. (Senior letters major Marianne Dunlap)

Privatizing public school systems brings visions of doom and destruction to my mind. If the human race has a future, it is in the hands of our children. If we fail to properly educate these future leaders and entrepreneurs, what future do we have? The United States of America has lived through times when public education was not available. The citizens of this country then decided that it was necessary that each child receive an education. The poorly educated are not easily employable and will more readily end up on public assistance of some kind. Naisbitt suggested that a system be created that allowed each child a certain number of credits to attend the school of his/her choice. Each school would then be more competitive in trying to entice student enrollment, more like a university. This competitiveness would encourage the school to provide quality education. The problem that I have with this picture is that standards must be adhered to in school systems to ensure that our population is receiving at least a minimum education. Therefore, government intervention is necessary. There is also the immediate problem that quality schools would cost more than the credits allowed, or rich parents would buy their child a spot at the expense of the poor who can't compete in a price war. Many rich and valuable minds come from families of the poor. Can we as a nation afford to let those minds fall through the cracks because we played a money game with our educational system? I don't think so.

Therefore, in my limited and humble opinion, privatization is a good that can be stretched too far, and contains the potential for evil. It does not necessarily hold that if a little is good a lot is great. (Senior management information systems major Deborah L. Jernigen)

Vouchers are a kind of "educational food stamp." Consumers of educational services would be able to use these vouchers to pay private institutions for educational services. The question is, How much will these vouchers pay for? What will keep the more productive "elite" schools from raising their tuition rates so high that a voucher will not even come close to covering the educational expenses? Some argue that if this happens a new market for people who can't afford these high-priced schools will open and businesses will fulfill their needs in much the same way that McDonald's opened a restaurant to meet the needs of those who can't afford to eat at the more expensive restaurants. However, this still does not make McDonald's hamburgers taste better than the gourmet hamburgers served in the expensive restaurants. In the same way, the education in the cheaper schools will not be nearly as good as the services provided in the more expensive schools. I see very few ways that the poor could benefit from this private system of education. I still believe in the "American Dream" and that everyone should have an equal opportunity to achieve success. Education is the basis for success. What kind of chance for success does a child of an economically stressed family have under a system such as this? (Sophomore aerospace engineering major James R. Jones)

While I respect John Naisbitt's view, I feel that if education is privatized its main goal and purpose will be defeated. He said that parents would be able to place their students in the school they felt would be best for them (test scores would also play a part). Also, if the parents were not satisfied with the education that their child was receiving, then they could simply pull them out and put them in a different school. Many problems could arise from this policy. First, children get attached to their teacher and moving a child around a lot could be detrimental to his or her learning. Also, if a parent is allowed to move a child, then the curriculum would have to be identical in all schools, and this is not really practical. Last, unfortunately many parents just do not care what their children are doing in school. This is sad, but it is true. It is not realistic to think that all parents will be able to choose which school is best for their child. (Junior elementary education major Kelli Kinder)

I believe the privatization of education could do more harm than good especially if corrupt businesses were allowed to step in and take the role of the federal government.

I realize that it is safe to say that some minorities might benefit in such a system, but it should be obvious from the present situation under the control of the federal government that the majority of minorities would suffer. Privatization is not the answer to improving our educational system. Privatization would only prove to stifle what progress has already been made in trying to better educate minorities and in trying to establish equality in education. Dr. Ernest Boyer stated that privatization of education "would lead to huge inequity." . . . This inequity would only serve to widen the already large gap between the rich and the poor and between Caucasians and minorities. I would like to present to you my interpretation of the results that corrupt, prejudiced businesses would create for minorities if they were allowed to filter into public education.

Do you think that a business will be concerned with turning out competent leaders of all races to one day run this country? I don't. I think that businesses will be concerned with turning out competent young Caucasians to run their firms, to make money for their firms, and then to take over the country. I realize that I may be exaggerating, but this is a topic that I feel strongly about and because I am a minority I am even more alarmed at such an idea. I realize that there are businesses owned and operated by various minorities, but is the idea to create segregation? The instigator of such a plan may have had the idea of bettering and upgrading the educational system, but greed and prejudice would eventually become the motivator behind this type of a program. There would be more jobs, but who aside from people who are receiving a quality education would be capable of filling them?

Ethical or unethical—it does not matter. Entrepreneurs have no business in education. (Freshman Cassandra D. Smith)

Now let us consider John Naisbitt's argument for privatizing education. His main complaint is that public schools are not producing enough or the right kind of leaders we need. It is not for lack of funds he feels, but rather inefficiency. If schools have to compete for students they will be forced to be more efficient so as to give the student the most for their parents' money. Unfortunately, Naisbitt is overlooking a very important factor: a business would be in business to educate, but also to make a profit. As one article in the *Chronicle of Higher Education* noted, "Whenever a lot of money is involved, particularly where for-profit organizations are providing service, there is a natural tendency to do whatever is necessary to maximize profitability, including skimping on quality. This temptation and the incentive to cut corners become even greater when a firm gets into financial difficulties."[6] This "natural tendency" undermines Naisbitt's claim that competitiveness will solve any inefficiencies that schools have.

Another point that he makes is that the competition between schools would hopefully improve the caliber of education that would be offered. This might occur, but not in an entirely positive way. Schools, because they would be in the business of making money, would want to attract those students who could pay the most. The schools would offer curricula that catered to the economically elite. . . .

The schools charging higher rates would also have more money for equipment, resources, and most importantly teachers. The best teachers would then tend to gravitate toward the higher-paying jobs. . . . Of course the schools for the less fortunate could pay their teachers more than the higher-priced schools but this would greatly diminish the use of their funds for other areas. If a school has a tight budget they can hire either many inferior teachers or only a few quality teachers. Of course there would always be the possibility of hiring some excellent teachers who would work for less money. If there were a substantial number of these people, though, our country would not be in its present uproar demanding better salaries for teachers in order to attract more intelligent people to the field. . . .

In addition, this type of school system would eventually produce very few world leaders. If parents were given a choice of what type of school they want to send their children to, they would choose those schools that reflect their own special interests and philosophies. Thus all the students in a given school would be there because the school advocates and indoctrinates the ideals of the parents. Therefore the student would never be exposed to any other perspectives or cultures besides his own. This would lead to the homogenization of schools and "education apartheid." Schools would splinter into little shelters of conformity. They would be comprised of students with almost identical socioeconomic backgrounds. The schools would be divided on almost every possible level of society, i.e. race, religion, sex, class, economic level, and even special interests such as drama or medical preparatory schools. Students would only deal with people like themselves. This would widen the schism between every socioeconomic group in the U.S. because they would never have an opportunity to gain any respect, understanding, or sensitivity for people different than themselves. . . . As Dr. Boyer stated at the Centennial Leadership Symposia, "the purpose of education is not conformity" but, as Victor Bravo Ahuja states, "it is to improve on what the individual inherits at birth by adding to it the rights of citizenship." (Senior letters major Virginia C. Storm)

The debate among these students over privatization revealed several important things. The first is that these students, all of them, care deeply about education, their own and the system that provides it for all. The second is that they disagree over the direction that common education should take. While all want a strengthened system of common schools, some believe that this must be done through public education while others believe that privatization offers a more efficient alternative. The third is that those students who favored strengthening public institutions and opposed privatization were as much concerned by equity as with quality; those who favored privatization believed that quality must take precedence over equity, since education is in crisis.

We see, then, that among these students, as among the population at large, the subject of education has a single strong thrust but multiple and conflicting vectors. The students want a good system, with better and better-paid teachers, better facilities, more resources, higher standards, and as a result, better education. They recognize that the existing system of public education has not delivered the goods. While some see the solution in offering private-sector alternatives, others are skeptical that the private sector would offer equal educational opportunity to all. The debate over education in Oklahoma has changed. No longer is the debate between the "pro-education" and "anti-education" blocs, if that was ever indeed an accurate description of the forces at play. Now everyone is for education. But there are deep-seated differences about how to go about improving education, and these differences seem likely to continue in the next generation. They reflect a profound difference between the public purpose of American education and the private aims to which its students wish it to be put.

As the higher education community sought to present its case for better funding to the people of Oklahoma through their elected representatives in the late 1980s, the theme has been "economic development through excellence in higher education." State Representative Carolyn Thompson, in whose district the University of Oklahoma lies, made the connection between economic development and education clear.

A lot of people feel that those businesses that are looking to Oklahoma and those that are struggling to survive in Oklahoma know that education is the foundation from which either a business will remain in Oklahoma or on the basis of which we will attract new business. The first question on every economic development tour that I have taken is, What is going on in your school system? What can we expect for our employees, how will you help us educate our work force, and what investments are you making in education?

Thompson and other officials have stressed the direct and indirect benefits to the state in developing the research potential of its two comprehensive universities. There has occasionally been talk of developing the corridor from Norman to Tulsa, encompassing Oklahoma City and Stillwater, as a "research corridor" similar to the Research Triangle in North Carolina that includes Duke, the University of North Carolina, and North Carolina State University. One small step in that direction was taken when the state legislature created the Oklahoma School of Science and Mathematics and chose to locate it within sight of the state capitol building. This new school is modeled on a similar project in North Carolina. The legislature also created the Oklahoma Center for Science and Technology, a device that channels state funding into the University of Oklahoma, its Health Sciences Center in Oklahoma City, and to Oklahoma State University to support research. The legislature has created an endowed chairs program that largely benefits Oklahoma's two major universities and has for the most part sustained the request of the state's colleges for tuition increases.

These steps to strengthen the state's comprehensive universities are in marked contrast to the state's experience in the three decades following World War II, during which higher education was dominated by the many regional universities and small colleges. During that long period of time state funding was based almost exclusively on full-time equivalent enrollment, and state regents' policies aimed to ensure that a student could move from one institution to another without paying a penalty in time lost due to different or more stringent requirements. The effect of this "articulation" policy was to hold all institutions in the system to the same standards in admissions, curricula, and requirements. The result was a very egalitarian system in which the smaller institutions often carried more clout with the legislature than the larger institutions.

In spite of the difference in the rhetorical emphasis of higher education's officialdom, and a genuine change in public attitudes, the underlying circumstances that shaped the system from World War II until the oil crash of the early 1980s have not fundamentally changed. The education system is marked by three main characteristics. First, the entire system is underfunded relative to the expectations of political and business elites, and to the requirements of the kind of system they would like to develop. Second, the state has, and will continue to have, too many institutions to permit any to be funded at nationally competitive levels, given reasonable assumptions about the Oklahoma taxpayer's willingness to pay up. Third, the representatives of the smaller institutions have, and will continue to have, sufficient influence in the legislature to ensure that their institutions are not sacrificed to the larger universities. They still have numbers, and if they come to lack numbers they can succeed by playing off the Tulsa and Oklahoma City delegations against each other.

The enactment of H.B. 1017 was a major event in the history of Oklahoma's common schools, but it was purchased at two prices. The first price was paid in weakening some reforms in order to solace rural legislators who feared school consolidation and opposed tax increases. The second price was paid more directly, as the $230 million in new revenue was distributed across the state. Even were it proposed to rejuvenate Oklahoma's higher education system, reformers would face the necessity of paying off the rural interest in precisely the same ways. Oklahoma is still very much a rural state, and even if its farms and ranches are more a part of its past than its future, they and the towns they surround are a part of the larger Oklahoma community whose interests need to be served. In a state with few private institutions of higher education, the broad network of public institutions serves a legitimate public function.

So there are constraints on Oklahoma's ability to vault over its history and into the front ranks of America's top systems of higher education, and there are limits on the ability of the University of Oklahoma to earn the credentials that would win it membership in the prestigious American Association of Universities (the goal of one recent president) or a place on the Carnegie Endowment's list of America's leading federal grant-receiving institutions (the goal of the current president). It is in light of these barriers that the stress on economic development must be understood. The argument aims to provide the lift necessary to free the university from the constraints imposed upon it by its environment.

The Education Symposium was kicked off by remarks from two prominent Republicans: United States Senator Don J. Nickles from Oklahoma, and then White House Chief-of-Staff John H. Sununu, the former Republican governor of New Hampshire. Both leaders made strong statements in support of the importance of education, reflecting the current national consensus, and both emphasized the primary role of the state governments in funding it, reflecting the position of the administration and the Republican party. Said Sununu,

> I think Washington can give focus to a national agenda and can target resources from around the country. But in my opinion people should not expect that Washington is going to write out checks to solve this problem. With checks generally come mandates and controls. This is not a command and control situation where somebody ought to be telling you what to do and what not to do, and then trying to buy your response with a big check. As a former governor, I feel very strongly about this. The real key to quality education at the primary and secondary levels, and even in publicly supported university systems, is the involvement of the states and the private sector within those states. I think Washington can draw attention to the need for better quality, but education has to stop measuring its quality in terms of the price tag that is spent. I think there has to be a little bit more focus on the quality of the end product. Just as American industry has reestablished quality control as a very important part of its responsibilities, that kind of a focus is important at the higher education level. The real solution to that problem is in the hands of those who run the universities and those who are much more involved at the state and local levels.

The emphasis that Republican politicians give to state and local responsibility is frequently questioned by their critics, who argue that if President Bush really wants to be the education president he ought to recommend greater federal spending. Sununu's remarks reflect the views of the president he then served, although it might be noted that, when he was chairman of the National Governors Association, Sununu resisted the efforts of other governors to place education at the top of state agendas.[7] Still, any Oklahoman who thinks that the appeal to local control is a cop-out should compare Sununu's statement with that of George Singer quoted above. It was a main goal of Task Force 2000 to ensure flexibility for local control of common education. Statewide bureaucracy was to be resisted and dismantled where possible. Singer's rhetoric is not far removed from Sununu's, but there is a key difference. Singer wants *state* funding of education combined with *state* standards for outputs, with local control over how the money is spent; Sununu wants *federal* standards for the outputs, but wants the states to pay for it.

In only one area did Sununu support increased federal funding, that of research and development.

Support for research and development can and should come out of the federal budget. There has been a tremendous increase in that spending in recent years, accompanied of course by a tremendous increase in the demand for such spending. But I do think that NSF [National Science Foundation], the Department of Defense, Department of Energy, and other federal agencies ought to have a broadening of the funding in those areas. You have seen that in the last two budgets, and we are going to try and continue that thrust.

Senator Nickles shares this view:

On the federal level, I think we can help possibly through research grants, scholarships, and incentives to encourage scholarship recipients to stay in teaching for a while. They could earn their way through and achieve their doctorate degrees, and then some kind of a contract or incentive might keep them in teaching for a certain number of years. I think we can provide a lot of carrots to put our best and brightest people in the teaching professions.

One step toward getting the best and the brightest into the classrooms lies in greater involvement by business and professional leaders in teaching. It is interesting to compare the statements made by Sununu and Nickles with the view taken by Vartan Gregorian in the Arts and Humanities Symposium. Gregorian, concerned about the moral dimension of American life, favors a broad education in the humanities for America's future business leaders. Sununu and Nickles, worried about economic development, believe that the humanities need to be infused with technical training and that there need to be stronger links between private business and public universities. Sununu, an engineer by training, put it this way:

> The higher education system in this country has to accept some of the responsibilities that we ask the private sector to accept. Our universities have to become more competitive, both in terms of costs and the quality of education. They have to be a little bit more aggressive and more willing to get involved in cutting-edge technology, and in student participation in that research. I think there has to be a broadening of the commitment of cross-relationships between colleges of liberal arts and colleges of engineering and the sciences. There has to be a heavier component of the technical education for folks who in the past did not traditionally get a technical education. I think that our competitiveness is going to depend on the response of higher education to these challenges.

The observations of Sununu and Nickles tie the subject of higher education very closely to that of economic development. Underlying the discussion of higher education was the simple question, What is the purpose of Oklahoma's system of higher education? George Kaiser, the chairman of the Oklahoma State Regents for Higher Education, spoke eloquently to the question during an afternoon discussion. Kaiser made it clear that, while economic development is important, it is not the sole or main purpose of higher education. Taking note of the historical factors that have helped shape Oklahoma's system, Kaiser held that

We need to continually reiterate that the purpose of higher education is to focus the scarce resources that we have in Oklahoma to develop programs of academic quality to promote student success. The ultimate goal is the students' success through higher education. We will have to modify the populist attitude that has governed higher education in Oklahoma for many years, and may require a reduction in regional parochialism. We cannot see higher education as a series of competitive, public works projects, but instead we must see the system as serving a general greater good throughout the state. We will have to be able to demonstrate conclusively to the public that higher education has a value in its own right as well as for economic development purposes.

Kaiser, a leading Oklahoma businessman, is the product of his Harvard education. Like George Singer, who holds degrees from Harvard and Yale, George Kaiser believes in the principle of liberal education. When asked to elaborate on his vision of higher education in Oklahoma, he recurred to the liberal arts:

In the Bloom and Hirsch books, there is a justification for higher education that says an educated person should know certain things. To be cynical again, I could call this the cocktail party justification for higher education, knowing just those facts that will impress all of your peers. I think we ought to fall back on the tried and true liberal arts university justification, which is that

higher education is the appropriate training for anything you are
going to do in later life. As Carolyn Thompson said, students
gain broad-based understanding, analytical reasoning, critical
thinking skills, and the self-fulfillment gain from the styles of
training and methodologies used in higher education. I would
hope that is the end result. In addition, there have been
studies which demonstrate that people with a broad-based,
nontechnical higher education achieve more in their business
careers relative to comparably prepared students in technical
specialties. But let me pose the question, Does higher education
have any value? The unacknowledged premise of this whole
forum this afternoon is that higher education is a greater good.
Maybe each of you ought to think about what your life would be
like, would you be a different person without higher education?

There is implicit in Kaiser's vision the Oxbridge concept of
the "educated" person, one who is prepared to deal with
anything that life presents. This conception is the corner-
stone, as Kaiser rightly noted, of liberal education in the
United States. In an earlier day, the conception of an
educated person carried with it a certain moral overtone. In
the nineteenth century, curricula were structured to produce
morally well-rounded graduates. The keystone course was
typically in civics and morals, and often it was taught by
the president of the college. This vision is evidently at
odds with the technocratic emphasis of a graduate of the
Massachusetts Institute of Technology, such as John Sununu, or the practical orientation of Senator Nickles, graduate of a land-grant institution. There is, under the umbrella
of the modern multi-university, room for all of these competing visions, but which ones speak most urgently to the
students for whom they exist?

The student representative on the higher education panel
was senior economics major Craig Adkins, the president of
the University of Oklahoma Student Association in 1990.
In response to the question about the purpose of higher
education, Adkins had this to say:

It is very difficult to put one student on the spot and ask that question. I think every student probably attends college or university for a different reason, or probably a variety of reasons. In the past, a main motivation has been to become proficient in a skill that they wish to use for the rest of their lives. Maybe students nowadays come to college to learn how to learn, so that for the rest of their lives, they can be proficient in some avenue. A lot of students come for the experience, for the background, for the opportunity to meet people and interact in an environment that will allow them to compete in the future. There are a variety of reasons students come to college, but I think the basic reason is to garner the skills that will make them marketable when they want to go out and pursue their career choice.

Adkins hit the nail on the head. The students do not care about economic development so much as about *their* economic development. They recognize that their own prospects depend upon the health of the economy; they understand emphatically that their future depends upon their marketability. This, they believe, depends in turn on choosing a major that will prepare them for a specific career. It is a very striking fact that when the student participants came to address the issue of higher education, their primary concern was with their own careers, and with the education that they expect to pave the way for them. In considering the quality of that education, many felt that the University of Oklahoma was not serving their needs as well as it might. Their main grievance—the university's emphasis upon research—put them squarely at odds with the economic development argument and the main thrust of the university administration's policies. The students' appetite for this issue was no doubt whetted by the remarks of Business and Technology Symposium speaker John Foster the night before. Foster decried the sacrifice of teaching to research, and cited California Institute of Technology (Caltech) as an example of a leading research university that still values teaching and requires its research professors to teach undergraduate courses. This image was congenial to a group of University of Oklahoma students who saw many graduate teaching assistants in the classroom. The specific objects of the students' grievances were several: inattention by faculty under the "publish or perish" gun, lack of course offerings, and required courses taught by "foreign" graduate students were among the main complaints. But the general object of their concern was their own educational experience.

The counterarguments were well put. George Singer made an emphatic statement to which many OU faculty members would subscribe:

A disservice has been done by trying to divide the question of teaching versus research. In my opinion, there cannot be any good teaching if you don't have good research. If you cannot scratch the horizons of new knowledge, what will you have to teach? I think what we need to work on is how we fashion it in an educational environment. To what extent will research find fulfillment in an undergraduate program? To what extent will that new knowledge find an expression in your courses, in chemistry, the fine arts, or whatever field? How will you be exposed to that new knowledge? How will that individual who has become a leading force in his particular field nationally and internationally be able to share with you that love for learning? How can that individual entice you to think and to raise questions just as he or she has done to come up with new knowledge? I personally do not accept the proposition that there is a conflict between teaching and research.

The issue concerns OU President Richard Van Horn in particular. Van Horn came to the University of Oklahoma in 1989 preaching the gospel of funded research. He wants more faculty, he wants better faculty, and he wants undergraduate students to receive a quality education. In order to get from here to there, he stresses the importance of dramatically increasing funded research at the university. In his remarks he made the case for his vision of the university's future, pointing out the problem with Foster's Caltech comparison in the process. The colloquy between the president and the students went as follows.

Van Horn: Let me talk about the challenges for universities. One of the things that is always interesting and fun is to find yourself a part of an ongoing national discussion. I sometimes think when you go to a university, you have left the world. People talk about being in the "ivory tower" and no longer in the real world. But most of the debates going on right now in our country relate in one way or another to education. If you look at the papers and at the television, education is really very much in the center of things.

Do we have to somehow change education dramatically? The president of Stanford, Don Kennedy, has said that we have to really rethink education and whether we need any more research universities. It is a little bit like Saddam Hussein saying that we should renounce the use of force now that he has finished his particular activities. Stanford, being one of the major research universities in the United States, finds it very easy to say we don't need any more at this point.

We are in this great debate, and let me just suggest a few things that maybe help the debate. I think we should ask the question, Should universities strive for excellence in undergraduate education? I don't think anybody here today would have any trouble answering that. The answer clearly is, "Yes, we should strive for excellence in undergraduate education." It appears in all of our policy and strategy documents at this university. I think we can only agree with the Ernie Boyers and the Don Kennedys and people all over the United States who are saying, "Don't we want to look again at undergraduate education and decide how to make it better?"

Yes, we want all faculty members to teach. We want them all to teach undergraduate courses. We want all faculty members to be prepared. We want them to perform well. We want them to be available outside of class. That is not an argument of teaching versus research; that is an argument about good teaching versus bad teaching.

But then a second kind of issue is, what else? Is there something special about education at some universities which is above and beyond what you might get at, let me say, an average university? Is there something special? Many of us believe there is, and that the debate going on right now on education should not lose sight of the fact that there are some special things. If faculty members are leaders, they are special kinds of role models. If faculty members are really at the frontier of their field, they can—maybe they don't always do it—but they can teach better. If faculty members are people who are generating new knowledge, then they can communicate something about the process of how you move into new areas and you can be productive.

Let me note a couple observations. Good researchers generally, but not always, are good teachers. One of our faculty members, Art Johnson, in chemistry, has just won the so-called CASE Award, from the Council for the Advancement and Support of Education. It's a national award recognizing him as the best teacher in Oklahoma. He also is one of the best researchers on our faculty. He is also one of the most vocal critics of the administration.

There is every reason to believe that people who are good at one thing are probably good at other things. One might also note that the great majority of leaders in the United States come from the major research universities. If you look at any list or index of leaders, the leaders come out of the major research universities. All these things must make a difference, and those differences somehow have to get into this debate.

Now we get down to a lot of other questions which are interesting and relevant. The one that comes up the most is, Why is a graduate student teaching my course? The corollary to that is, Why doesn't he speak Oklahoman so I can understand him? We do have graduate students teaching. Most universities have graduate students teaching. They are not there because faculty members are doing research. Graduate students are there for two reasons, one noble and one not so noble. The noble one is that in any profession, it is important to train people to go into the profession. Graduate students have to be trained as faculty members and you want to train them in an environment where you can supervise them and work with them. So graduate students are teaching classes as an important part of the process of generating faculty members for tomorrow. Many of them are excellent teachers; some of them are not as good as all of us would like.

The much less noble reason is that we simply don't have enough money to teach all courses with tenure-track or with tenured faculty members. Dr. Foster mentioned Caltech. Caltech has three students per faculty member. We have 19,000 students here and 800 faculty members. If you do that division, you will find out we do not have three students per faculty member. We have significantly more. The only way open to us to provide quality education and to meet the educational needs is to use graduate students. Now you may say that's not a terribly noble reason maybe. We are doing it because we don't have enough money.

But think of the alternative. We could play the Caltech game. Caltech has perhaps 1,000 undergraduates. We could cut our undergraduate student body to 1,000, I suppose, and we would have plenty of faculty members to teach every course. I don't think that Representative Thompson and the other members of the legislature would think that that's a very constructive approach to higher education in the state of Oklahoma. So we do what we have to do in order to provide the very best education that we can. And we're increasingly going to face those kinds of challenges in the future.

Question: You indicated that our tuition and our state monies are not going toward research. If our researchers are having to get their own money for their research, isn't that putting more pressure on them? If we did spend more money toward that research, wouldn't that take some of the pressure off and put them back into the classroom?

Van Horn: I think the answer is probably not. Recruiting faculty members is like anything else. You have to provide an attractive environment for faculty members. If we want to recruit outstanding faculty members, if we want faculty members who are going to be leaders in their fields (whether an accomplished pianist or a distinguished physicist with a lot of articles), if you want to recruit really first-rate people, then there is a limit to the amount of teaching that they are willing to do. At community colleges, people teach five courses per semester. At the University of Oklahoma, or any of the other major universities, faculty members are willing to teach two courses, some teach three, some teach less than two. That is part of the competitive hiring process. We do provide faculty members with a significant amount of time in order to carry out their research. And so that is one of the things the university does provide, and that is one of the ways that you can hire good people. If faculty members want to hire graduate students to help them or if they need travel funds, it is quite reasonable to suggest that they go out in the competitive grant process in peer review, which is a quality control process. If the university hands out the money, you always worry a little about whether you are handing out the money to the people you happen to like, or to the best people. The external funding system is good because it is peer reviewed, and it really puts a high emphasis on quality. I think the current system works pretty well. I don't think it is unreasonable, and I think it has operated for some time and seems to produce pretty good results.

Question: Doesn't research take faculty time away from teaching and advisement?

Van Horn: Research faculty members should be able to meet with students during office hours. Our faculty members work a lot harder than faculty members at some other universities simply because we have a lot fewer faculty per student. But we do try to design the system so the faculty member has enough time to do research, and the research time should not take away from good teaching. Faculty members should have enough time to do an excellent job teaching and still be able to do their research. It is not easy. Faculty members work very hard, but the system is designed to be reasonable.

Question: President Van Horn, I don't think that the issue of debate today is teaching versus research. I think that we will all agree that they are both important. Instead, I think the issue is the issue of teaching and research. They both should exist. They go hand in hand. The only way for either one of them to exist is together. Even though there may not be university funding for research, the fact that our faculty are performing research seems to me to be an opportunity cost, and as long as research and teaching do not exist together, then that opportunity cost is borne by the students. I would just like to ask you a question, President Van Horn. Wouldn't it be dynamic if tenure-track professors could share their research ideas and knowledge with some of the young bright minds here at the university?

Van Horn: Your suggestion is an excellent idea. There is an increasing attempt to involve undergraduate students in research. Some faculty members do that very well. All faculty members should share the special expertise that they have in the classroom. It doesn't have to be subject related. Faculty members frequently have insight about how you solve problems. But if you are referring to using undergraduates in the research process, that is a great idea. We are working very hard on that. We do some of it. It is high on the list of priorities to do a lot more of it.

I have also suggested a middle ground, an extension of the seminar process. Five or ten students could have a once-a-week hourly session with a faculty member or a teaching assistant, who is in the process of developing a research project, and they could see the project as it is developing.

Regent Kaiser's idea is a very good idea. If you look carefully at the bulletin boards in departments, there are going to be a large number of research seminars going on every day of the week. Many of them are very interesting.

As this exchange indicates, the students put hard questions to their president and he answered forthrightly. A number of students felt strongly enough about this issue to address it in their papers. Here is a sampling of what they had to say.

This argument really can be debated on two different levels. First, do the time and resources necessary for research take time away from the students and the professor's preparation for class? Second, do you punish an excellent teacher just because he or she is not interested in or cannot do research? John Foster pointed out that a combination of the two would enhance both, but that research must not be emphasized to the detriment of teaching.

I feel that while the two are theoretically compatible normally you do not find an individual who is good at both research and teaching. . . . Both of them take time. I feel that if a person concentrated more on doing one area well instead of trying to do two areas adequately that students would benefit more. I think we need to have both teachers and researchers, but I do not think that these are always the same person.

I believe one of the greatest problems with the educational system today is that the student is no longer important. People have looked so much at the bigger picture that the individual has been lost. . . . Students need to feel that someone actually cares about them and that they are not just another student or, at the college level, just a number. (Senior letters major Marianne Dunlap)

I do not think research should take precedence over the actual teaching of students. As Dr. John Foster, chairman of the National Defense Science Board, said, "Teaching, over research, must become the prime purpose of education." But in our quest for technological superiority, I think everyone tries to ease research into the educational basics with a "separate but (silent) equal" theme. President Van Horn claims that "good researchers are generally good teachers." While I can think of one teacher who did use the class in an effective research experiment, I have had five others who employed their students in research endeavors that were not curricula related and were, therefore, totally self-serving. If a teacher is spending an equal amount of time doing research and class preparation, then he or she is not a good educator in my book. There are a dime a dozen full-time researchers out there, but really excellent teachers are hard to find.

Dr. Van Horn wants to reap the benefits of hosting important research projects—as he said, "leaders in the U.S. generally come from major research universities"—but the university must provide a catalyst for these endeavors to take place. Alleviating a lot of the pressures involved in research, I feel, is the only way in which research and teaching can coexist. (Senior language arts major Shane A. Hainzinger)

Another problem in education at the college level . . . is the lack of American professors at the university. The science departments of this school in particular are overrun with foreign exchange students that do not speak fluent or articulate English. This is most upsetting to young American students who feel that their education is being compromised in order that a foreign student can obtain a better education and then return home with it. If we as American students cannot understand our foreign teachers, then we cannot expect our educations to improve. (Junior zoology major Rebecca LeAnn Harmon)

Many of my classes are directed by graduate assistants [GAs]. What is the professor doing during this time? After all, he is getting paid. Or is this the time he tries desperately to seek funding for his research? In most cases the GA is uncomfortable with the situation or does not feel he has the control to teach the class as he feels best. The students are thrown into a catch-22. They are not able to turn to the GA with problems and the professor is unavailable a great deal of the time. (Sophomore zoology major William D. Huff)

As so many campuses have been transformed into mammoth research centers, a disturbing proportion of the faculty have come to look upon classroom teaching the way their secretaries look at filing: an unrewarding job that somebody has to do. More than ever, a professor's pay, prestige and perquisites depend not on classroom skills but on frequency of scholarly publications and on how many research dollars he or she can attract. In reality the venerable dictum "publish or perish" has become the virtual rule of law on many campuses, where research, not performance in the classroom, is the overwhelming factor in determining a professor's status and salary. Fortunately, however, some of the most prestigious of the universities are concerned that in carrying out their research and scholarly missions they may have short-changed undergraduates.

Students will receive a tremendous advantage in the value of their education if the research and teaching can be successfully balanced. One major advantage is that students will be better educated. As a result our educational system will produce many more well-educated undergraduates who will be able to find valuable and meaningful work experience. . . . The professors will have a better opportunity to mingle with the students, who will give a professor an interesting insight about how students feel about a professor's specific area of interest. Not only will the professor gain from the experience of teaching and the student gain from the experience of being taught by a scholarly instructor, but the university will also gain from a balance of teaching and research.

After revaluating the concerns of teaching versus research at the University of Oklahoma, I feel that a couple of changes would promote a much higher quality education to an undergraduate. First of all I feel that the university should raise tuition. This will not be appealing to many students, but you can't get something for nothing; and a student must realize that if he is to receive a higher-quality education, he must pay for it. Tuition increases will allow the university to increase its faculty-to-student ratio. This increase in the ratio will give the student a better chance to communicate on a one-to-one basis with faculty concerning his or her area of interest. It is important for students to receive personal support and instruction from faculty and with such an increase in the faculty-to-student ratio a student will receive a much more valuable education.

Finally, the University of Oklahoma will be able to promote its educational courses if it requires tenured professors to teach the introductory-level courses. This doesn't sound like it will promote education, but indeed it will because students will receive a much more valuable experience in the classroom early in their studies to inspire them to continue.

I propose that the federal and state governments restructure their fund allocation systems to the universities so that a balance can occur that rewards both teaching and research. I would also recommend that the federal and state governments start a bonus system that would reward institutions for successful implementation of such a balance of duties. (Senior accounting major Rebecca Johnson)

. . . Anyone teaching a college course [should be] required to take at least one education course. The professors are so good but many times they have a difficult time communicating all of their knowledge to the students. They are on a level that is so much higher than many of the students and they are unable to express what they are really thinking. They get so bogged down with all of their knowledge and being the best in their field that they are unable to communicate what they really know. Many times they are attracted to the limelight and the incentives are such that if one does do research the professor forgets his real job, as a professor. . . . Many students would agree that research is important and it is nice for some professors to do it, as well as beneficial for the department. But they [the students] just feel like they have been put on the back burner while the professor tries to bring in a little extra money. (Senior mathematics major Jill McKenzie)

The talents necessary to be a good researcher are often totally different than those necessary to be a good teacher. Researchers are good at figuring out solutions, analyzing situations, or drawing conclusions, but do not have the necessary human relation skills to relate themselves and the information to their students.

I do not disagree that professors should be up on the latest information in their respective fields, but because one is informed or knowledgeable does not mean that they can effectively communicate it to others. Research skills are often those of inquiring, where the skills needed to communicate that information are those of sharing. Teachers can be up on the latest information in ways other than conducting all of their own research. The research conducted makes up only a fraction of the total knowledge that an instructor possesses, so an effective instructor can be on the forefront of his or her field without conducting intensive research.

2

58   THE NEXT GENERATION

President Van Horn also stated that the great leaders of the
United States have come from the great research universities. It
is true that the great research institutions have produced a large
number of leaders, but there are many leaders in our country
who have less than a high school diploma or a small college
degree. Attendance at a research intensive institution is not necessary to become a great business, community, national, or world
leader.

An important point is that professors concentrating on their
research must share their time between their study, their preparation of lectures and their time for students. There must be a
compromise somewhere. . . . The University of Oklahoma must
do the best job of educating its students, given the funds allocated
to it. In this process it must balance research with the transferring
of knowledge to others. (Senior economics major David C. Wise)

The disparity between the opinions of these students and
that of OU's president reflects the difference in their perspectives. President Van Horn sees the whole from the perspective of one whose obligation it is to steer the university to
serve the needs of this and future generations of Oklahomans. He believes that the state will be best served if the
University of Oklahoma becomes a leading national research
institution. The students are not taken with this vision because it does not speak to the reality with which they daily
deal. They know that the university will not become the kind
of institution that Van Horn envisions during their time
there, even if it is so fortunate to become such an institution
at some time in the future. They believe that their prospects
will be fundamentally determined by what happens now,
not later. Even granting the possibility that the university
may become a major research institution, many students
doubt that this is in the best interest of its student body,
which will remain the kind of diversified population that
comprehensive public universities are built to serve. When
the subject of research is brought up, university administra-

tors such as President Van Horn and university supporters such as George Singer typically invoke the image of the great scientist or scholar. If such persons are available on the campus, the student leaders who participated in the symposia appear not to know it. Instead, they say that they deal with underprepared graduate students, harassed junior faculty who are expected to meet the publication standards of "peer" institutions, and sometimes indifferent senior faculty who are preoccupied with their funded research. Sometimes they do; but as President Von Horn noted, the strength of the university overall is directly related to the quality of the research it produces.

The symposium discussion on this topic, as on so many others, did more to clarify the issues than resolve them. What is clear is that there is a genuine tension between two visions of the University of Oklahoma. The university is now and has always been the leading institution in a small state whose citizens want state institutions to serve them. The combination of parochial attitudes and a limited funding base sets limits upon the ability of the university to compete with better-funded institutions in larger and wealthier states. In order for the University of Oklahoma to prosper it is as important that it be warmly received by the people of Oklahoma and their children as by grant review panels.[8] Yet if the university is ever to offer more to its students and to the state than a middling education, it must "go national" by hiring excellent faculty from other places. Excellent faculty from other places will have only a derivative attachment to the state and people of Oklahoma. They are, as the president notes, more strongly oriented toward their academic discipline and its national organizations. Finding the correct balance between the two poles of the university's universe is not an easy task. Explaining the necessity of it to the university's various constituencies is no easier.

Whether in common or higher education, the challenges facing leaders are significant. If the common subject of the

Centennial Leadership Symposia was education, their central
theme was leadership. We conclude, then, by considering
the challenges facing leaders in education, the subject of the
keynote address by Ernest Boyer, president of the Carnegie
Foundation for the Advancement of Teaching.

Not on Competence, but on Conviction

Ernest L. Boyer

For one hundred years, the University of Oklahoma has contributed to the sciences, to the arts, to the education of the coming
generation, to the highest intellectual searches, and to the deepest
yearnings of the human spirit. I salute all of the leaders, past
and present, who have made the University of Oklahoma an
institution of national and international reputation. In joining the
celebration of the university's centennial, I want to focus on
leadership, using education as the vehicle that carries my remarks. Leadership is, of course, an elusive term and it comes
in many shapes and sizes. Consider, for example, the cigar-
chomping Winston Churchill, or the statuesque Charles de
Gaulle, or the stocky Teddy Roosevelt charging up San Juan Hill.
Or consider Dwight David Eisenhower, a military hero who,
when he became president, seemed more like a kindly grandfa-
ther than a soldier. Who among this list was the most effective
leader, or can they even be compared?

Or consider education. When we speak of leaders here, who
comes to mind, past and present? If you were nominating your
education hero, who would it be, beside perhaps your first-grade
teacher—who, incidentally, is one of the greatest heroes of my
life? About a hundred years ago, when I marched off to school,
I entered the class room and there she stood, half human, half
divine. And I was sure that every afternoon she ascended into
heaven and the next morning came down to teach the class. I sat
with twenty-eight awestruck, frightened, anticipating children,
and the first words I ever heard in school were Miss Rice's an-
nouncement, "Good morning, class. Today we learn to read."
And not one child said, "No, not today. Let's string beads." If

Miss Rice said you learn to read, you learned to read. We spent all day on four words: I go to school. Wasn't that inspired? We traced them, we sang them, and God forgive her, we even prayed them. I had a little prayer, "Well, thank you, God, I go to school." Incidentally, on that delicate subject, I heard recently that the one prayer in school that is acceptable to all faiths is "Dear God, don't let her call on me today!"

But I ran home that night, ten feet tall, and said proudly to my mother, "Today I learned to read." I hadn't learned to decode, to be candid; I had instead learned to memorize. But Miss Rice taught me that language is a centerpiece of learning, and fifty years later, when I tried to write a book on high school and another one on college, I had a chapter right up front entitled "The Centrality of Language," the inspiration of a long-remembered first-grade teacher at Fairview Avenue Elementary School in Dayton, Ohio.

It was Miss Rice who inspired me to this day to understand that language is the key to learning. Great teachers live forever, so perhaps in our inquiry into the leadership of education, we should move first into the classrooms, where unnoticed heroes everyday shape minds and direct the destiny of the nation. And I am absolutely convinced that if this nation wishes to reestablish excellence in education, we have to affirm the essentialness of teaching.

Moving beyond those private heroes, often unnoticed in the larger scene, who would you name as being heroic in the world of learning? Do we mean the brilliant, almost arrogantly self-conscious Robert Maynard Hutchins, thirtyish president of the University of Chicago who challenged the traditions of higher learning? Do we mean the reflective philosopher, John Dewey, who caused us to rethink the nature of learning and the centrality of students as learners? Do we conjure up the memories of President James Conant, a Harvard professor who left the ivory tower to crusade for better schools? Some might even nominate Jaime Escalante, that California teacher who is brilliantly successful in helping Hispanic kids pass the advanced placement calculus examination. Or taking perhaps a longer view, who could ignore Horace Mann, who was America's crusading evangelist for public

education? At a still more elevated level, surely we should salute
the brilliant Thomas Jefferson, who elegantly affirmed that education and a free society are inextricably interlocked.

What is absolutely clear in this reverie of mine is that the quality
and characteristics of a successful leader differ surely from person
to person and from one era to another. And it is also clear that in
education, we need leadership at many different levels. We need
education leadership from the classroom to the think tank to the
presidential office. Still, diversity notwithstanding, I am absolutely convinced that just below the surface there are several
fundamental characteristics of effective leadership of education
that are both essential and enduring, regardless of the time or
place. And this evening, at this moment of special celebration, I
should like to focus briefly on five principles of leadership that
will be absolutely crucial for those who seek to guide the destiny
of education in the United States in the year 2000 and beyond.

First, in the days ahead, education leaders, in my opinion,
must have a clear sense of where they wish to get. They must not
only define clearly their own objectives, but inspire others, too.
They must believe deeply in the mission of their institution. They
are inspired by the tasks to be accomplished, and must find ways
to inspire others, too. The loyalty that people feel toward a school
or college, for example, and their willingness to help make it
work, depend on the clarity of the goals and the vision that is
shared.

Thirty years ago, I became dean of what was, I suspect, the
world's smallest higher learning institution. Upland College, at
its peak, had about 150 students, and while this struggling school
closed its doors many years ago, I still remember those days
with considerable satisfaction. At Upland College, a young and
committed faculty was recruited. The college came together late
at night to talk about purposes and goals. All members of the
staff worked together enthusiastically to implement the slogan of
the institution: "A small college with a vision for service." We
had brown bag seminars, we introduced a 4–1–4 calendar, and
convocations were held midday for the entire student body to
meet and talk about important issues. Looking back, I recall the
place with pleasure not because the ideas were particularly novel,

but because we had a shared vision of what the institution was seeking to accomplish. Leadership has the capacity to give focus and vision to an institution.

Contrast that story of tiny Upland College with the mighty Office of Education in Washington, D.C. Contrary to conventional wisdom, there are dedicated, hard-working people in the federal bureaucracy. And yet when I worked there, I found deep frustration among the workers. The signals were always changing as new administrations came in, and the sense of purpose was endlessly confused. During my first week on the job, the head of the civil service union in the Office of Education came in and asked if she could meet with me. In anticipation of what I thought would be a confrontation over wages and working conditions, I boned up on the salary schedule in the Office of Education. I studied the employee benefits, and I concluded that our case of worker satisfaction was airtight.

When I marched in Monday morning, I greeted the head of the employees' union, and after a few casual and pleasant comments, we sat down to the informal bargaining table. I have to tell you that I was totally unprepared for the first question, which almost bowled me over. The head of the employees' union in the United State Office of Education looked me in the eye and said, "Mr. Commissioner, can you tell us why we're here?" Here were workers in government who had a good payroll and eternal security, but who lacked a larger sense of purpose. And I am convinced that the institutions we call colleges and schools stand or fall on the extent to which there is a shared and inspired vision that has only marginally to do with earthly benefits. It has everything to do with the satisfactions of the human spirit.

The lesson I encountered in the Office of Education never left me. We all want to be well paid and feel secure, but in the end, we want meaning in our lives. Men and women, as the Scriptures put it, cannot live by bread alone. And to make a difference in educational leadership, I am convinced we must provide a vision and creatively define the spirit of the institution and clarify the purposes of education. At every college and university, forums are needed to address common educational questions and to consider campuswide matters that cannot be handled in any other way. Without such arrangements, the college drifts. Students, faculty, and administration will carry on their work in isolated pockets. Larger purposes are blurred, and the potential for unity of the enterprise is lost.

Looking down the road, defining transcendent goals for the nation's colleges and schools, I believe, will become at once both more difficult and more urgent. I worry that America is becoming a fragmented, deeply divided nation. Increasingly, we are separating ourselves along racial and ethnic lines. There is a growing and terrible gap between the privileged and the poor. And in the public schools in this country, there is great inequity between the affluent and the disadvantaged. More than that, there is an increasing intergenerational gap, where the old are separated increasingly from the young. Margaret Mead said on one occasion that a healthy culture is one in which three generations vitally interact. And yet now we are organizing ourselves so that three-year-olds are in day care centers, children are in schools, adults are in the workplace, and retirees are off in villages living and dying all alone. We have, in effect, organized a horizontal, not a vertical, dimension to our culture.

My parents lived in a retirement village for several years where the average age was eighty, which is about as unhealthy as a day care center where the average age is three. A person can now go from birth to death and talk only to his peers. When he was in his mid-eighties, my father had a birthday, and he said, "No big deal being eighty around this place; you have to be ninety just to get a cake." An interesting feature of the place where he lived, though, was that they had a day care center there. Every morning they had four- and five-year-olds coming in, and every little child had an adopted grandparent. When I would call my father, he wouldn't talk about his aches and pains, he would talk about his little friend. There is something remarkably appealing about seeing a four-year-old inspired by the agonies and dignity of aging, and doubly inspiring about seeing an eighty-year-old who is stimulated and overjoyed by the energy and innocence of youth.

This discussion of intergenerational relations in America today may serve to preface the main point of my discussion. I believe it is the central obligation of the nation's colleges and schools to find ways to build community and bring us all together at a time when fragmentation and tribalism tend to dominate the cultural scene in the United States today. If we do not find transcendent purposes that somehow can define the nature of community amidst diversity, I do not think that this great nation with quality will survive. So I look to education leadership in the 1990s and beyond to begin to ask careful questions about the degree to which we extend fragmentation or somehow reinforce the sense of togetherness while celebrating diversity as well.

The Carnegie Foundation's report, *Campus Life: In Search of Community*, has, since its release in April 1990, been the fastest-selling document ever published by the foundation. It was out of print three times in six months. This suggests to me a deep, abiding yearning in the United States today to find those purposes that can somehow transcend the divisions in our midst. The report, based on a survey of college presidents conducted by the foundation in cooperation with the American Council on Education, explored the character and quality of life on our college campuses. As its title suggests, a common theme among the presidents who were surveyed was the need to recover a sense of community among the various groups of which their campus communities are comprised. All too commonly today, college campuses have become fragmented, not only due to the kind of cultural pluralism from which racial and ethnic divisions are spawned, but also because of the nature of the institutions themselves. Campuses are divided into educational cohorts, with graduate and undergraduate students sharing little in the way of a common life. Students are directed by their academic program into colleges and departments that are like islands in the sea. In their private lives, they are divided between Greek-letter organizations and dorm life, or are further scattered among apartment complexes in which they become isolated from even their immediate neighbors. In the face of these natural and deepening divisions, the challenge of campus leaders is to draw the disparate elements together into what the report calls a "compact for community."[9] If colleges and schools cannot find the points of common interest, if we can't find those commonalities that bring us all together, how in the world do we expect to have a sense of community and even civility on the city streets where tribalism, not community, is the growing pattern?

Lewis Thomas—educator, physician, and distinguished Sloan Kettering Cancer Center administrator—said on one occasion that "if this century does not slip forever through our fingers, it will be because learning will have directed us away from our splintered dumbness and will have helped us focus on our common goals." If leadership does nothing else, it challenges colleges and schools to break down the points of fragmentation and isolation and to urge academics occasionally to come out of their isolated boxes and engage in discourse around the core of common learning. It encourages college forums, even, if I might say, the kind of elegant centennial celebration that marks the beauty of this great institution.

I was fascinated to read Allan Bloom's remembrance of the 1960s.[10] Bloom recalls the Vietnam War period as a time when, at many colleges and universities, the pursuit of knowledge was sacrificed on the altar of political expediency. Cornell University, at which he then taught, was indeed witness to a degree of political turmoil unusual even in those troubled times. But while that was the decade when my hair turned from black to white, I also have to say that there were occasional moments when I thought the university was at its very best. There were many moments when I thought it was at its worst. But rather than remembering the 1960s as a time when we administrators simply capitulated to the demands of thoughtless and arrogant students, I would rather remember it as a time when the university provided a forum where we intensely debated common concerns. I believe if we did not have discourse within the academy during that decade, we would have had more blood on the city streets. Most especially, I remember the times in the 1960s when we had something that we called teach-ins. It was a time when university presidents were so harassed and were usually so driven by confusion and even, if I might say so, by fear that they turned to the final and ultimate weapon that they had and said, "Let's all get together and let's start to talk to one another." It was a fairly reasonable suggestion, now that I reflect on it.

The teach-ins would bring people in a forum like this. They would be crowded on the floor in front of me and jammed against the wall, and it seemed like everyone had come. There was a lot of angry talk and not much listening, but there were occasionally moments of powerful inspiration when speeches would be given. Suddenly, all of us were caught up in a sense of common inquiry. What was the nature of the university? What was the nature of this war? What are the values in this country? I remember those days, if I might say so, as a time when the university was at its best because we stopped preening ourselves as psychologists and administrators and deans, and we somehow were human beings, intellectually engaged.

I don't think the universities nor surely the schools can do that every day, but I would hope that in the midst of a fragmented and increasingly divided culture, we could use the university as a forum in which we affirm not just the greatness of differences, in which I rejoice, but also the fact that in the end we are powerfully dependent on each other. Finding leadership that can understand the essentialness of common goals, it seems to me, will become increasingly important in the decades just ahead.

This leads me to a second main priority. I believe that leadership in education in the 1990s and beyond means more than just pursuing common goals. It means lending perspective too. It means leaders who see their jobs as being driven not just by pedantry but by wisdom, and who have the capacity to put their institution in larger scale. The nation's colleges and schools, I am convinced, will increasingly be influenced by social, economic, and even perhaps ecological forces far beyond the campus. I believe that being a successful leader in education requires people who stay well informed and who have the capacity to put the work of colleges and schools in national and even global context.

To put it as simply as I can, education does not exist in isolation, and contextual planning will become increasingly imperative as we move to the new millennium and beyond. John Gardner put it this way. He said today's leaders must look beyond the systems that they lead and grasp their relationship to the larger realities that surround them. So leaders are not micro-managers; they are contextual. Understanding must be key. What are the larger realities that will affect the nation's colleges and schools in the days ahead? I could list a dozen, but let me simply cite briefly three or four.

I would like to consider first the essentialness of preschool education. The disturbing fact is that the learning potential of children is profoundly shaped long before they march off to school. If this nation wants excellence in its colleges and schools, we had better start looking at the problems and pathologies of little children, even before they are born.

My wife is a certified nurse midwife. She works with pregnant adolescent girls. She comes home night after night with anguish in her heart because she has worked with a little child who was having another little child. She tells me that she tries to tell young girls in their early teens what is happening to their bodies in between the labor pains. They don't even know what the birth process is all about. For nine months, they fed another human life on soft drinks and potato chips. All the evidence shows that at the time of birth, that young, innocent life will have already been educationally diminished. This nation's special education program is growing at an exponential rate. Our schools, and ultimately our colleges, are going to be diminished by the incapacity of students who, before they ever came to school, had some of their potential tragically destroyed.

Educational leaders must not just study budgets. They must become familiar with prenatal care; with the problems of children and nutrition; with the significance of Head Start, as it gives our children a better prospect for future learning; and also with the relationship of parents as partners in the process. It may startle college presidents and school superintendents to hear that they had better understand the importance of little babies, but if they do not become engaged in the tragedy that is happening to many little children in the early years of life, I can only assure you that the future of this great system of learning will increasingly be eroded.

Leadership in education also means knowing something about the technology revolution in our culture and the impact that it too is having on the nation's colleges and schools. More than thirty years ago, the great essayist E. B. White (the author of *Charlotte's Web*), after he had seen television for the very first time, wrote as follows: "What I have just seen will either be a great new radiance in the sky or an unspeakable disturbance." He was right, and I am afraid it is more of a disturbance than a radiance at this point in our history. When college presidents report, as they did in *Campus Life*, that students today are not prepared to undertake college-level work, that they lack the necessary study skills and discipline, who can doubt that this is in part due to the pervasive influence of television in their upbringing?

It is my deep belief that education leadership in the year 2000 and beyond must think more creatively about both the negative impact and the potential that the technology revolution is having on our children. I would like to see education leaders begin to ask questions about how technology can become a more effective partner in the process rather than a problem. How can computers and television and videocassettes be seen as the solution, not the problem? It really does bewilder me that the great technology revolution has made a pervasive and positive impact on almost every system in our culture except our colleges and schools, where perhaps the impact could be of the most benefit.

Now I understand that at the college level, certainly, the computer has become ubiquitous. It helps us administratively and in research. It helps us in the great libraries in our information searches. But most of the schools in this country are, at present, very inadequately supplied with advanced technology equipment. Many have only a broken overhead projector. The children spend more time with television at home than they do with teachers in school. Somehow we must find a way to join the power of visual images with the wisdom and inspiration of teachers in the classroom.

The educators who are leaders in the twenty-first century are going to have to confront some of the powerful, contextual problems, and these include the full spectrum—running from the pathologies that surround the poverty of children to the influences of the technological revolution that have hardly begun to penetrate the nation's classrooms and certainly the schools.

I am convinced that in looking at the context, we need to understand the relationship of our educational system to global events. I believe leaders in education must increasingly have a perspective that is not only national but global so that they can begin to shape a curriculum that will help to introduce global studies. When we surveyed five thousand undergraduates several years ago, 30 percent of them said they had nothing in common with people in Third World countries. Nothing in common. It is another planet.

William Bennett, when he served as Secretary of Education in the Reagan administration, urged that students study Western culture in order to understand our past, and I agree; but I think that students also need to study non-Western cultures in order to understand our future. Let us understand that this world is becoming increasingly interdependent, and that we must begin to shape the experiences and the curriculum for future students so they can have a better perspective on the nature of the world they will inherit.

And what about the ecology of our planet? Are leaders in education sufficiently mindful of the fact that we are, as Lewis Thomas put it, embedded in the rest of nature as working parts, and that what happens to our ecology is, in the end, what happens to all of us? When I was commissioner of education, Joan Cooney—that wonderful inventor-developer of Sesame Street—came to me one day and said that Children's Television Workshop wanted to start a new program on science called "3–2–1 Contact." In doing research for that program, she surveyed some junior high school students in New York City and asked such questions as, "Where does water come from?" A sizable percentage said, "From the faucet." She asked, "Where does light come from?" and they said, "From the switch." "And where does garbage go?" "Down the chute."

I believe that educational leadership means being in touch with national and global developments—politically, economically, and ecologically, as well. And if we are not mindful of these trends, and if we do not argue for more enlightenment in the curriculum in schools, how do we expect the next generation to be well informed? Increasingly, we will have to have a curriculum that somehow breaks out of the academic boxes and begins occasionally to help students see connections.

We now have curriculum requirements called "distributions." Every transcript analysis that has ever been done shows that this is, frankly, another name for electives in which there are no patterns or integrations. To put it simply, we are in the thick of thin things, and larger understandings frequently are lost.

The inexorable trend must be not only toward the greater integration of knowledge across the disciplines, but eventually toward a search for the issues that are transcendent, that relate to human survival, too. Victor Weisskopf, the internationally known physicist, was asked on one occasion what gave him hope in troubled times. He said, "Mozart and quantum mechanics." What he was suggesting was that very often our divisions within the academy—in which we see scientists and artists as living in separate worlds—tend to mask the fact that, at bottom, there are perhaps some commonalities around the search for beauty and the understanding that is gleaned as a product of our investigations. Those connections are too rarely discovered.

In the days ahead, education leadership means far more than managing the budgets or organizing the structures. It means, I think, looking for larger patterns and discovering the context of our work, and understanding just how much education will be shaped by the social, economic, and political forces in the nation and the world.

This brings me to priority number three. In the days ahead, effective leadership in education will mean focusing more on people than procedures. I am convinced that the American public education system is today making a historic transition. For years, we have believed passionately in local school control. But now the citizens of the nation are more concerned about national results, and there is a major push to impose excellence by rules and regulations.

Incidentally, for the first time in our history, we have had a president who has announced that he is the "education president." What does that mean? Is he the head of the national school board? The president called together all fifty governors, and they signed an agreement to work together. And then in his 1990 State of the Union address, Mr. Bush, in what was really a startling break of precedent, announced six goals for the nation's schools.

To my knowledge, he didn't survey the local school boards. He declared that these goals should be adopted by all the nation's schools.

What we have happening in the United States in our education system is a movement toward convergence, and we are, for the first time in our history, more concerned about national control than we are about governance at the local level. I should remind you that Gallup, in its latest poll last fall, found that over 60 percent of all Americans said that they would support national standards, national testing, and a national curriculum for the nation's schools. There is, now, a National Assessment for Educational Progress that is beginning to measure the results. So something is happening that will somehow establish a kind of standardization throughout the public education system.

At the same time, there is a recognition that somehow we need to give more support to principals and more empowerment to teachers. I believe that the real test for educators in the *public* sector of education below the college level will be to find a way to balance national goals while still maintaining vitality at the local level and focusing on the creativity of the people.

Let me draw an analogy to higher education. We build, in this country, large, multi-universities that are administratively complex. At the same time, faculty and students often feel left out. Several years ago, again when we surveyed five thousand undergraduates, over 40 percent of them said that they feel like a number in a book. And 60 percent said they have no faculty member who is interested in their personal lives. One student put it directly. She said, "I don't want the university to be involved *in* my life, but I would like for the university occasionally to be concerned *about* my life." And I don't think this student was just playing with prepositions.

There is a yearning, a search, for a human dimension to education. The question is, How do we *govern* the system of education? What is the proper role for leadership? I suggest that the leaders in the days ahead will understand that managing the system must still, in some powerful way, draw on the talents and the humaneness of individuals, and be more concerned about people than procedures.

I remember very well twenty years ago when Sam Gould, who was the chancellor of the State University of New York, asked me if I would join the system. I knew very little about that university, so I went to *Time* Magazine in the library and found a story. I was startled to discover that the State University of New York had seventy-two separate campuses enrolling 350,000 students. I was being asked to join the bureaucracy in the central office. I concluded that this Rube Goldberg structure would, like the dinosaur, soon become extinct, because it was obvious that the body surely had outgrown the brain. My suspicions were reinforced the first time in the fall when I went to a meeting in which all seventy-two presidents were in attendance. Have you ever seen seventy-two presidents in a room?

They were sitting like blackbirds on a telephone line, solemnly writing notes—I do not kid you on this matter—while bureaucrats from the central office gave them the rules and regulations. I have never seen a more depressing scene in which procedures seemed to suffocate the people. Soon after that meeting, I met with Gould, and I said, "I can't believe what I've just seen. Is this what it means to have a university that's big and complex? Have we built such a horror story as this?" And we asked together whether it would be possible for the university to become a more collegial place. Could the presidents be viewed as human beings instead of as branch managers in the bureaucratic system?

So as an experiment, we decided to run a seminar that summer to which we invited them in small groups and asked them to bring their spouses. We sat around, not only talking about the university, but about intellectual renewal. The next fall, when those seventy-two presidents came together, it was like colleagues at a class reunion. There was a vitality and a humaneness, and people were asking about each other's families.

I mention that little exercise not to be heroic or self-serving, but to raise a question. To what degree does the energy of education focus on the processes and the paper clips and the procedures, and to what degree does it try to tap the talent of the human spirit and say to the individuals in the system, "You're the center of it all"? That, to me, is the central question that educators must ask themselves in the days and years ahead.

I do not suggest that the regulatory aspects of administration will go away. Indeed, the financial, political, and legal barriers will increase. Students must understand the enormous pressure that those administering our institutions are under as they try to negotiate the pressures from outside, the limits of their resources, and the multiple demands that come from departmental expectations. They must bring it all together and give it a human face. This is an excruciatingly difficult task, and it will not get easier in the years ahead. We have built huge and complex systems, and it will be up to their leaders to determine whether we will succumb to them or rather invigorate and keep humane the institutions that we have created.

The more I have thought about it in the last few years, the more I have concluded that we do not have things called institutions. We only have people who carry ideas about institutions in their heads. The nature of leadership is to plant the right idea. You can't find the University of Oklahoma. You can find some bricks and mortar. But the University of Oklahoma is not the physical facility; it is really the people who occupy the buildings and their conception of what the University of Oklahoma is. Everything, then, depends upon what those people believe. The task of leadership is to plant those ideas in the heads and in the hearts of the people around them.

Excellence cannot be externally imposed; it must be internally inspired by good leaders. Leaders must, it seems to me, trust more in people than procedures and must find ways to tap creative talent up and down the line. It was John Gardner who said that in the end, the quality of leadership ultimately must be measured by the dedication of those who follow.

If leaders in education are to perform this function they must be good communicators. Those responsible for educational institutions must not only manage; they must also listen. During my days as chancellor at the State University of New York, the nation was in crisis. Protests were intense, and at every press conference there was only one question: How are you going to control the bomb throwers on your campuses? I was often

confronted by frustrated students, and my talks were interrupted with nonnegotiable demands. And time and time again,
I found myself talking *at*, not *with*, the students.

But there was one occasion when real communication was
achieved. I was speaking to university faculty and the Board
of Trustees at Binghamton when 350 students moved in with
placards, chanting slogans, demanding that I free a group of
students who had been arrested on the Buffalo campus the night
before. The microphone was grabbed and, once again, we kept
talking past each other. Finally, after almost an hour, I concluded
that I was talking not to people, but to a faceless mob. More out
of desperation than inspiration, I left the platform and walked
into the crowd. I began talking with a single student. I asked her
name. I asked about her family, and I asked why she was so
angry. Soon several others joined us. I described how I truly felt
and what I could and could not do with integrity at the moment.
When the session ended, a compromise was reached, and in the
process, I became acquainted with some most attractive students.

Wayne Booth, Pullman Professor of English at the University
of Chicago, wrote on one occasion that "all too often our efforts
to speak and listen seem to be a vicious spiral moving downward.
But we have all experienced moments when the spiral moved
upward, when one party's efforts to listen and speak just a little
bit better produced a similar response, making it possible to move
on up the spiral to moments of genuine understanding." I am
convinced that almost any struggle can be negotiated successfully—almost any difficulty can be overcome—if there is a sense
of openness and trust. But leadership will surely erode when
communication stops, or when a leader tries to tell each separate
audience what he or she thinks it wants to hear.

I have a fourth priority to propose. Educational leaders in the
coming century must have ideas of their own and be the source
of intellectual leadership and not just administrative efficiency in
the educational process. Some years ago, I discovered that in
every administrative job I had, every waking hour could be ab-
sorbed by doing what other people wanted me to do. The "in"
basket was never empty, no matter how late I worked or how
much paper I brought home at night. There seems to be some

kind of a reproduction factory going on in the bureaucracies that always produces more paper than can be read. Photocopying has simply made the bureaucracy more efficient in burying leaders in paper.

I discovered that while I responded to all the memos and I returned all the calls, I became increasingly fatigued and creativity was lost. It slowly began to dawn on me that leadership means walking away occasionally from the sewers of Paris and devoting at least 5 percent to 10 percent of one's time to something interesting, to an exciting idea that was mine and mine alone. I, as a leader, needed something to get me out of bed each day. I decided that the only way to survive was to somehow determine inevitably that I couldn't manage all the paper, and the only way to stay renewed was to be driven by some ideas that I could claim as my own.

To put it as simply as I can, educational leadership does not mean just efficient management. It also means having creativity in one's head. It was at about this time when the Board of Trustees at the State University of New York started, at my suggestion, a new college called Empire State College. It was a noncampus institution that had students studying on their own with mentors. Empire State was a novel notion. At the press conferences that were held then, I suddenly discovered that the reporters wanted to talk about education and about how students learn. They were asking, "What is this new crazy thing called Empire State College?" And for one brief moment, they weren't pestering me about budget cuts or riots on the campus.

I discovered that it is possible for administrators to claim their own turf and to take the initiative instead of always being on the defensive, but that can only be done with the integrity of an idea that is yours and yours alone. This was a lesson I never forgot, and I am convinced that in the days ahead, we will need bold new strategies and creative new ideas to educate an increasingly diverse group of students and to prepare our students for an interdependent world. Schools, colleges and universities grant educational leaders something precious: a forum for their ideas. Those ideas may not always be approved, and they probably should not always be approved in precisely the form that they are proposed. But I would expect leadership to be at least the origin of creative debate about the nature and future of the institution.

We need leaders in education who are creative, not reactive. Take the example of Empire State College. I am convinced that one of the greatest challenges educational leaders will confront in the days ahead will be lifelong learning. We have created institutions that serve students from eighteen to twenty-one years of age. Surely, in the years ahead, we must have institutions that are more flexible and more open so that students of all ages can move comfortably in and out. At Empire State, we created a strange new college that was built on the assumption that students could study independently, that they could work closely with the mentor, and that they could, through contracts, lay out their own educational goals and complete their credits without going to class every morning from 9:00 to 9:50, three times a week, slicing out education like the hunks of a salami as it moved along the assembly line.

As a matter of fact, my wife, who was then—how should I say it—over thirty-nine, is a good example. She had picked up college credits as she followed in the trail of a peripatetic husband. She kept trying to trade them in for credits toward a degree, and admissions officers would always say, "Mrs. Boyer, this is wonderful, but you're going to have to start coming back to class three times a week—Monday, Wednesday, and Friday." She said, "You don't understand. I'm married to a very strange man, I've four children, and I just can't slice up my life that way. I'm very busy." So she gave up. But finally, in desperation, she enrolled in this strange new college. She had a wonderful mentor, a woman with a degree from Yale, and they worked together on a major that she defined. She finished the degree, went on to Georgetown Medical School, and became a certified midwife. There you have it. Empire State College was started to get my wife through college! Actually, that is both true and untrue. It was not started just for her, but it was started just for people *like* her.

This brings me then to one final observation. I believe that finally, when all is said and done, educational leadership, if it is to be effective, must ultimately be driven not just by competence, but also by conviction. In concluding, I want to move away from the system, from the goals, from the strategies, and say just a word or two about the quality of the person.

It is often said that leadership is the art of compromise, and often that is the case. I do believe that good leaders should see both sides of the equation. They should have the skill to bring issues and protagonists together. They should have the capacity to find ways to make the whole greater than the sum of the separate parts, and every good education leader that I know is really skilled in the art of compromise. He or she must be one who listens with great care, grants credibility to all positions, and then seeks to mediate and find the point of common cause.

But occasionally there are times when principle transcends compromise, when a leader has to say, "It is here that I stand." There is one side that must be affirmed, and another that therefore must be rejected. One does this only rarely; one does it only when fundamental principles are at stake, but one does it. Alexander Miller, in his provocative book, *Faith and Learning*, observed that a decent tentativeness is an appropriate expression of scholarly humility. But he went on to say that in education we have a kind of dogmatic tentativeness in which it is intellectually indecent to make up your mind.[11]

There are situations in which compromise masks conviction. Again, let me stress that mediation is essential. It is perhaps the most essential tool that educational leaders have at hand. But I also believe that educational leaders occasionally must stand alone, not out of petulance or pride, but out of purpose and conviction. And so, in the days ahead, we need leaders in our colleges and schools who speak out eloquently on issues of great moment. Let me, then, conclude by speaking out on some issues that are important to me.

I think we need leaders who speak powerfully for the least advantaged people and give voice and conviction to the poor who cannot often be heard themselves. We need leaders who plead the case for America's neglected children. Winston Churchill said on one occasion that there is no greater work for any nation than putting milk into little babies.

Is it unthinkable that college presidents might argue that we need to provide nutrition for little children, even if it means that the university budget will be cut? We need leaders who vigorously denounce racism and sexism on the campus, who vigorously defend free speech, and who denounce censorship in every form. But we also need education leaders who call for larger loyalties on the campus, who have the courage to condemn alcohol and drug abuse and decadent behavior, and who urge students not to be just self-centered, but to engage in service.

It is my own feeling that one of the real tragedies in our society is the sense of disconnectedness among the youth and teenagers who do not feel that they belong. Go into large schools and there is a sense of anonymity. Many drop out because no one noticed that they had dropped in. Our educational institutions must somehow reconnect with the nation's youth. Many college students are ready to be engaged. Martin Luther King, Jr., said on one occasion that everybody can be great because everyone can serve. And I believe the young people of this nation are ready to be inspired by a larger vision.

If education is to exercise a moral force in society, it must take place in a moral context. In our deeply divided nation, I believe educators must somehow morally and ethically help lead the way. Reinhold Niebuhr once wrote that man cannot behold except he be committed. He cannot find himself without finding a center beyond himself. It seems to me that education leadership, at its best, means moving from competence to conviction. I am convinced that the quality of education and the future of the nation are inextricably interlocked. But for colleges and schools in the United States to be effective, we need leaders with clear goals. We need leaders who can put their work in large perspective. We need leaders who focus more on people than on procedures. We need leaders who are courageous and creative. And above all, we need leaders who are driven not just by competence, but by conviction.

There is an old Chinese proverb that puts it this way: It is not the cry but the flight of the wild duck that leads the flock to follow. Effective leadership in education will be accomplished not by the formality or efficiency of the structure but by the

integrity of the process and by the willingness of educators at
all levels to bond together and be inspired by a larger vision—
by a vision that means educating all people, and not just the
most advantaged. James Agee wrote on one occasion that with
every child who is born, under no matter what circumstance,
the potentiality of the human race is born again. And it is this
audacious conviction that, in my judgment, is the source of
inspiration for those who aspire to be leaders in this wonderful
world of education.

Boyer presented five principles for leadership in education.
First, leaders must have a clear vision of what they want their
institutions to become. Second, they must lend perspective
and explain the context within which their institutions must
function. Third, they should focus on the people, who are
the institutions, and not on the procedures by which the
institutions may come to be defined. Fourth, leaders must be
creative, they must have ideas of their own. They cannot
merely manage, they must lead by the force of their ideas.
Fifth, leaders must stand for something, must stake out positions on important issues, and must on those issues transcend
the compromising that university governance otherwise often
requires.

Underlying these generally applicable principles is a set of
personal beliefs that permeate Boyer's remarks. In the debate
over the nature of higher education, Boyer stands for the
university's role in bringing society together in a shared understanding and appreciation of our diverse, yet common,
cultural heritage. He believes that the university must call
together the people of whom it is composed and draw them
into a sense of shared community. He believes that those
who participate in the life of the mind must recognize their
obligation to put the education they receive at the disposal of
their society and its least advantaged members. He believes
that the university has a special role to play in guiding society
into the future, by preparing the minds that will be at the

helm. This requires broad vision, creative ideas, and firm convictions. Leaders must stand as role models for society, articulating a vision of its future, standing for principles to which society can and should be drawn. They cannot merely manage; they must lead.

This address provided a fitting culmination to the four Centennial Leadership Symposia. As the people of Oklahoma celebrate the centennial of the Oklahoma Territory and the founding of its education system, they must consider the role that they want their educational institutions to play in shaping their future. In the year 2007 the State of Oklahoma will celebrate its centennial. By then, key decisions will have been made, decisions that will largely determine the direction the state's second century will take. The University of Oklahoma and its sister institutions will figure large in that future, that is certain. But what kind of institutions will they become?

Ernest Boyer reminds us that, in charting a path for the university, its leaders must not only define specific institutional objectives suitable to the context of the twenty-first century; they must also shape the university's self-conception and the conception that the people of Oklahoma have of it. The university is more than the sum of its objectives, just as it is more than the bricks and mortar of which its buildings are made. It is, indeed, even more than the people it comprises, for they will come and go. The University of Oklahoma is and must continue to be a *community*, situated within and reflecting the culture of the people of Oklahoma. It can and must reflect that culture, but it can play an important role in shaping it. Above all other institutions, the university is a place that beckons people to share in the richness of culture. It is a place that offers to each the common heritage of all. It is a place in which learning takes place, minds develop, and values are formed.

It is also a place where people are trained to work, where knowledge is advanced, and where students are brought into contact with the larger universe of business and society. It must serve the needs of the people of Oklahoma, and of the United States, by pushing back the horizons of knowledge. It must be a place to which people who are not native Oklahomans want to come to teach and engage in research. It must be a place to which corporations look for knowledge and talent. It must be a modern institution of higher learning, responding to the various communities that make up higher education nationally.

Those who are called to lead the university face the challenge of reconciling these two fundamental roles that it must play. To do so will require the vision, creativity, conviction, and indeed the compassion of which Ernest Boyer spoke. In order for leaders to succeed, followers must be prepared to follow. Alumni, members of the faculty, students, and members of the staff must come to appreciate the complex nature of the University of Oklahoma and how they can relate to it. To instill in all of these component parts of the university an appreciation for the others, and for the whole, is the task that lies ahead. It is preeminently a task of leadership.

NOTES

Chapter 1: **The Next Generation**

1. U.S. Department of Education, Office of Educational Research and Development, National Center for Education Statistics, *Digest of Education Statistics, 1990* (Washington, D.C., 1991), 167.

2. Tom Biracree and Nancy Biracree, *The Almanac of the American People* (New York: Macmillan Publishing, 1988), 37.

3. Charles Anderson, Deborah Carter, and Andrew Malizio, American Council on Education, *1989–90 Fact Book on Higher Education* (New York: Macmillan Publishing, 1989), 273.

4. Tom Wolfe, "The Me Decade and the Third Great Awakening," *New York Magazine*, 23 August 1976, 34.

5. Oklahoma State Regents for Higher Education, *Biennial Reports* (Oklahoma City, 1990), 8–13.

6. Oklahoma State Regents for Higher Education, unpublished report (Oklahoma City, August 1991).

7. John Naisbitt, *Megatrends* (New York: Warner Books, 1982).

8. John Naisbitt and Patricia Aburdene, *Megatrends 2000* (New York: William Morrow and Co., 1990). Mr. Naisbitt's presentation was derived from this book and contractual arrangements prevent his remarks from being presented in full. The following summary of the main themes of the book will provide a basis for understanding the response to his remarks by panelists and students. All parenthetical citations to Naisbitt are from this book.

9. Garry Wills, *Reagan's America: Innocents at Home* (Garden City, N.Y.: Doubleday, 1989).

10. Sandra Postel, "Toward a New Eco-Nomics," *World Watch*, 10 September 1990, 20–28.

11. Oscar Ameringer, *If You Don't Weaken: The Autobiography of Oscar Ameringer*, foreword by Carl Sandburg (New York: H. Holt & Co., 1940; Norman: University of Oklahoma Press, 1983).

12. The Carnegie Foundation for the Advancement of Teaching, *Campus Life: In Search of Community* (Princeton, N.J.: Carnegie Foundation, 1990), p. 27 and appendix A–1.

13. Since the survey reports the perceptions of presidents rather than the attitudes of students, some allowance should be given for report bias. Nevertheless, the reported result is striking. Presumably, most research universities have smaller percentages of minority students than do comprehensive, four-year, and community colleges. Yet racial tension appears as a problem to over two-thirds of the presidents of the research universities and only 15 percent of the presidents of the two-year colleges. Why?

Chapter 2: The Call to Public Service

1. Paul Kennedy, *The Rise and Fall of the Great Powers* (New York: Random House, Vintage, 1989).

2. *Congressional Quarterly Weekly Report*, 9 March 1991, 596. Undissuaded, Senator Boren won Senate approval for an amendment to the 1992 foreign aid authorization bill that increased the percentage of American aid to be given in the form of credits. *Congressional Quarterly Weekly Report*, 27 July 1991, 2097.

3. Godfrey Hodgson, *America in Our Time* (New York: Random House, Vintage, 1976), 114–15.

4. Francis Fukuyama, "The End of History?" *The National Interest* (Summer 1989): 3–18; Charles Krauthammer, "Democracy Has Won," *Washington Post*, 24 March 1989, A23.

5. Dave McCurdy, "Change in the Soviet Bloc: A Call for New Directions in U.S. Foreign and Defense Policy" (Remarks before the George C. Marshall Foundation, 29 January 1990), 3.

6. Allen Ehrenhalt, *The United States of Ambition* (New York: Random House, Times Books, 1991).

7. McCurdy, "Change in the Soviet Bloc," 3.

8. James MacGregor Burns, *Leadership* (New York: Harper & Row, 1978)

9. Ibid., 4.

10. J. Irwin Miller, "The Importance of Humanities in Business," *National Humanities Center Newsletter* 2, 1 (Fall 1989): 1–7.

Chapter 3: **The Matter of Culture**

1. Carl J. Friedrich, ed., *The Philosophy of Kant* (New York: Modern Library, 1949), 116–31.

2. *The Compact Edition of the Oxford English Dictionary* (New York: Oxford University Press, 1971), 1247.

3. Loren Eisley, *The Immense Journey* (New York: Random House, 1946).

4. Jean-Claude Lamberti, *De Tocqueville and the Two Democracies* (Cambridge, Mass.: Harvard University Press, 1989).

5. Harriet Martineau, *Society in America* (London: Saunders & Otley, 1837).

6. Nien Cheng, *Life and Death in Shanghai* (New York: Grove Press, 1987).

7. Naisbitt and Aburdene, *Megatrends 2000*, chap. 2.

8. I am indebted to Ellen Jonsson for this insight. One might note that the relationship of art and artists to society is one of the most enduring motifs in twentieth-century Western literature. See for example Marcel Proust, *Remembrance of Things Past*, 3 vols. (New York: Random House, Vintage, 1982), 1:572, 3:917, and elsewhere; Thomas Mann, *Dr. Faustus* (New York: Random House, Vintage, 1948) at p. 373 and elsewhere. The reader who is interested in this subject might begin with Frederick Nietzsche, *The Birth of Tragedy*.

9. "Report of the Task Force for University-wide General Education," 1 May 1989.

10. *Spotlight on Teaching* 12, 3 (May 1991).

11. Balkanization of the states that composed the former Soviet Union is creating a number of problems. Some are simply practical, such as the question of whether there will be a common currency and the question of whether there will be more than one nuclear power. Others are more fundamental. It turns out that the nationality groups of which the Soviet Union was composed are not geographically isolated but instead overlap, just as is the case with the Serbs and Croatians in Yugoslavia. Russia may claim to be a nation entitled to self-determination, but what about the cultural minorities within it? The distinction between nations and nationality groups is a fuzzy one indeed. At what point do nationality groups have the right to

declare themselves nations? Among the languages spoken in the republics that made up the Soviet Union one finds the Baltic languages, Armenian, Kazakh, Karakalpak, Kirghiz Uighur, Uzbek, Turkmen, Persian, Tadzhik, and of course, Russian. It appears that there is no way to draw national boundaries that will not cause one nationality group or another to be in the political minority. The problem is salient not only in the Commonwealth of Independent States but also in such places as Palestine, Quebec, and South Africa. The fault lines do not need to be along national or ethnic lines, as witness the case of Northern Ireland. Within a generation, a third of the population of the United States may have Spanish as a first language. How will we, in the United States, continue to assimilate diverse peoples to a common constitutional order if that constitutional order is regarded as a mere cultural artifact of Western civilization? Somehow the ideals upon which our constitutional order rests must transcend the cultures it comprises.

Chapter 4: The Economic Challenge

1. Godfrey Hodgson, *America in Our Time: From World War II to Nixon—What Happened and Why* (New York: Random House, Vintage, 1976), chap. 3.

2. James Q. Wilson, *Bureaucracy: What Government Agencies Do and Why They Do It* (New York: Basic Books, 1989).

3. The plight of the honest savings and loan dealer is not without pathos. The Resolution Trust Corporation seeks to hold the industry accountable for its losses, while the industry wants to be trusted to salvage what it can from the ruins. See Tim W. Ferguson, "An Arizona Banking Official's Broadside," *Wall Street Journal*, 2 July 1991, A11.

4. George Gilder, *Wealth and Poverty* (New York: Basic Books, 1981).

5. Johnson et al., "Shameful Bequests to the Next Generation," *Time*, 8 October 1990, 42–46.

6. J. Irwin Miller, "The Importance of Humanities to Business," *National Humanities Center Newsletter* 2, 1 (Fall 1989): 1–7.

Chapter 5: The Education Crisis

1. Bureau of the Census, *1989 Higher Education Directory* (Washington, D.C., 1989), press release CB49–87; National Center for Educaton

Statistics, *Supplement to the Education Directory, Colleges and Universities* (Washington, D.C., 1988).

2. National Education Association, *Rankings of the States* (Washington, D.C., 1990).

3. Given the rhetorical emphasis placed upon education by Naisbitt, it seems worth noting that the subject does not earn an index reference in *Megatrends 2000*. Perhaps, in a book that stresses the good things that are happening, this is what we should expect.

4. In considering the "choice" model of public education implicit in Singer's remarks, the example of the Richmond, California, school system should be carefully studied. Charged to revitalize a declining inner-city school system, Superintendent Walter L. Marks did all the right things. He hired four hundred new teachers, bought new equipment, and implemented a system for choice in which each school could choose a different curricular emphasis and parents could choose among the schools. The results were dramatic improvement in test scores in the first three years. By the fourth year it materialized that Marks had purchased this miracle by spending $60 million in excess of the district's income, leading to a crisis in which the school board proposed closing the schools six weeks early in 1991. By then, Marks was off to Kansas City, where he reportedly holds a $140,000-a-year job as the superintendent of schools. The Richmond case seems to demonstrate a simple principle: choice works only when there is enough money to provide for meaningful choices. See Robert J. Wagman, "Why Did 'Model' School Fail?" *Norman Transcript*, 8 June 1991.

5. See, for example, its lead editorial on 7 June 1991.

6. Angus Paul, "Privatization Sparks Vigorous but Inconclusive Debate," *Chronicle of Higher Education*, 16 September 1987, A4.

7. "From 1984 through 1987, the National Governors Association focused on welfare and education reforms. In 1988, when Sununu was chairman, he ordered instead that the governors debate an academic study of ways in which states might attempt to regain some of the sovereignty he said Washington had usurped." David Broder, "Bush's Eminence Grise," *Washington Post National Weekly Edition*, 13–19 May 1991, 4.

8. Recognizing this, President Van Horn has sought to enhance the university's recruitment efforts throughout the state, has placed substantial new funding into tuition and fee waivers, and has ques-

tioned the desirability of raising admissions standards. These policies aim at stabilizing enrollment.

9. The Carnegie Foundation for the Advancement of Teaching, *Campus Life: In Search of Community*, 63.

10. Allan Bloom, *The Closing of the American Mind* (New York: Simon & Schuster, 1987).

11. Alexander Miller, *Faith and Learning* (New York: Association Press, 1960).

Index

paring leaders, 115–16; teaching
versus research at, 247–59
University of Central Oklahoma, 7
University of Oklahoma, 7–8, 172;
curriculum at, 157–59, 165–67;
quality of education at, 247; racism at, 37, 38–39; as shaper of
culture, 281–82; student demographics at, 36
Upland College, 262–63

Values: importance of, 155–56
Van Horn, Richard, 34–35, 38, 40,
287–88n.8; on importance of research, 248–51, 254–55, 258; students' dialogue with, 251–53
Volcker, Paul, 44–45

Walesa, Lech, 61
Warsaw Pact countries. *See* Eastern
Europe
Wealth and Poverty (Gilder), 195
Weisskopf, Victor, 271
White, E. B., 268–69
Wiles, Keith, 232–33
Will, George, 136
Williams, Christopher, 15
Williams, Joseph H., 192, 194, 218;
on leadership, 207–10
Wise, David C., 258
Wolfe, Tom, 170
Women: in leadership roles, 196–
206

Yohannan, Bincy, 19, 136–37